HIJACK FOR FREEDOM

D1604311

HIJACK FOR FREEDOM

The Memoirs of Mark Dymshits:
Soviet Pilot, Jew, Breacher of the Iron Curtain

ההסתדרות הציונית העולמית
World Zionist Organization

gefen גפן
publishing house בית חרושה לאור
JERUSALEM ◆ NEW YORK Est. 1981

THE הסוכנות היהודית
JEWISH AGENCY לארץ
FOR ISRAEL ישראל

Cover Design: Jaki Levy
Cover illustration: Jaki Levy
Typesetting: Optume Technologies
All paintings by Mark Dymshits

ISBN: 978-965-7023-25-9

1 3 5 7 9 8 6 4 2

Gefen Publishing House Ltd.
6 Hatzvi Street
Jerusalem 9438614,
Israel
972-2-538-0247
orders@gefenpublishing.com

Gefen Books
c/o Baker & Taylor Publisher Services
30 Amberwood Parkway
Ashland, Ohio 44805
516-593-1234
orders@gefenpublishing.com

www.gefenpublishing.com

Printed in Israel
Library of Congress Control Number: 2020914725

Contents

Foreword by Isaac Herzog

David Ben-Gurion's eldest daughter, Geula, walked into our primary school classroom back in 1970, and as my beloved teacher, she held up the front page of the newspaper and introduced us to our new childhood heroes.

I instantaneously memorized the names of the sixteen refuseniks, fourteen of them Soviet Jews who challenged the USSR in order to make aliyah to Israel. Who knew Jews were capable of such a daring endeavor? Why were they so desperate to make aliyah, and who was stopping them? What would be their fate?

Fifty years since have afforded us historic perspective. The daring operation and subsequent Leningrad Trials were an indisputable turning point in the struggle for Soviet Jewry's freedom. This failed attempt to get to Israel ended, after a painful, long struggle, in a historic victory.

As it turns out, Mark Dymshits knew he was being followed. The entire group, led by Edward Kuznetsov and Dymshits, a humble, retired Red Army pilot, were painfully aware of the stakes and anticipated their arrest or being shot down in the air. And yet, they made an active decision to go ahead with an audacious, ludicrous plan. In this book, we learn why. They made history and finally opened the gates of the USSR for Jews to return to their ancient homeland.

A year ago, I sat down with Mark Dymshits's daughter and son in law, Elizaveta and Yaakov Rivkin. They told me about his personal diary, which has been concealed all these years. As we discussed the deep significance of her father's legacy, I understood from Elizaveta that this book, which reads like a Hollywood thriller, is not a gesture honoring the memory of a hero of the past; rather, this is a gift to us. This inspirational tale proves how a single act can set a historic process in motion and literally change the world.

Operation Wedding triggered a burst in the previously suppressed evolution, and at once focused the public eye on the plight of the Jews to make aliyah to Israel. The results were staggering: 1970 saw 12 Russian Jews immigrating to Israel, in 1971 there were 193 olim, while in 1972 the numbers jumped to 21,000, and the 1970s saw a total of over 123,000 Russian olim. The Jewish Agency, which I now chair, was with them from the beginning and continues to support and facilitate aliyah, which has enabled millions of Jews from all over the world to restart their lives in their historic homeland.

Mark Dymshits made a conscious decision to put his life on the line to come to Israel, linking him to generations upon generations of Jews who dreamed and changed history. In 2015, he passed away, in Israel, and was buried alongside his wife Alevtina, one of the sixteen heroes who envisioned a better life for their people and paved the way to Jerusalem. Half a century since their courageous sacrifice, we look around our beloved State of Israel and know the dream has become reality.

Isaac Herzog
Chairman of the Executive, the Jewish Agency for Israel
Jerusalem, July 2020

Foreword by Liza Rivkin (Dymshits)

Fifty years ago, on June 15, 1970, my family together with other twelve people were brutally arrested at Smolny Airport, the small airport near Leningrad (now St. Petersburg) on our way to board the plane that would have taken us to freedom. I was eighteen years old and remember very well watching as KGB agents jumped on my father, floored him, and began to beat him with their boots.

After that, I heard someone yell, "Fire." I saw the blood.

Following our arrest for attempted hijacking, I was detained and interrogated day and night and deprived of sleep. They put me in a small room with stone walls, a steel bed connected with two chains to the wall (the first night without any mattress), and an open lavatory without any curtain – opposite the door of the cell with its peep hole. The guard could look inside the cell any time he wanted.

The prison food was terrible, so I would eat only a quarter of a loaf of bread with a teaspoon of sugar and would drink a cup of tea in the evening. That was all I ate in a day.

The KGB interrogator threatened me with imprisonment for ten years in a concentration camp with women criminals.

Finally, a month and a half after the arrest, I was released from the KGB prison along with my fifteen-year-old sister and my mother. I suppose that they did not need us for the show trials.

After my release, I worked at a factory that produced leather bags. I began to work day and evening shifts back to back (sixteen hours every day, without days off).

The family needed money and my mother's salary was not enough for the lawyer and everyday needs. We needed money for visits to my father (two or three times a year) and for sending parcels to the prison. Afterwards, I started to study engineering and worked only one shift (still without any days off). We did not have any help from anybody except my mother's sister Kate, but she had her own family and it was very hard for her, too. I am very sorry to note that from the beginning of the legal procedures at the Leningrad City Court, many families of the prisoners kept away from us. This was perhaps because they regarded my Russian mother as a traitor. We were lepers. By the way, at the age of sixteen I chose to list Jewish nationality on my official papers, like my father's.

The days before the escape attempt, I remember well.

My father had asked my mother, my sister, and me if we wanted to take part in the attempt. It was a very hard question, because there was a very small chance for success. I knew that if his attempt succeeded, and we remained behind in the Soviet Union, we would be imprisoned as hostages, and our lives would become an extended tragedy. We discussed the problem and decided that we would stay together with my father.

The end of this odyssey is well known. After nine years of imprisonment, my father and Eduard Kuznetzov were exchanged for Russian spies and came to Israel. With his arrival in Israel, my father received a very special present – his first grandson, Israel, who was already one month old.

I am very glad that my father's book will be printed in the United States in English. First of all, because of the help of President Nixon to cancel my father's and Eduard Kuznetzov's death sentences – he called Leonid Breznev and requested it personally. Later, the support of many Senate and Congress members helped achieve their preterm release from prison.

The autobiography of Mark Dymshits will teach the reader about a Jewish man without any connection to Judaism, a Soviet air force pilot officer who became an ardent Zionist and was ready to strike for his Zionist dream. He was ready to sacrifice his freedom and even his life for the right of Russian Jews to make aliyah to Israel.

I find it interesting that it was one hundred years ago on June 15 that the Haganah was founded, and fifty years after that our attempt to escape to freedom, to Israel, took place. This heroic attempt of the Jewish and Russian people failed, but it opened mass aliyah from Russia, and the Soviet Empire fell.

I want to thank Isaac Herzog, the Jewish Agency chairman, for his great help in publishing this book. Without his help, it would have been impossible to publish the book this year. Our thanks to Ilan Greenfeld, the publisher at

Gefen Publishing House, for his tremendous efforts to publish this book at the fifty-year anniversary of the hijacking attempt. Last but not least, I would like to thank my dear husband, Yakov Rivkin, for his tremendous help editing this book.

With blessing and love,

Liza Rivkin (Dymshits)
June 19, 2020

Letter from the Publisher

It is not every day that we at Gefen Publishing House receive a manuscript of such historical significance.

Over the past forty years, we have been fortunate to publish many unique and important books on Jewish history, Jewish heroes, and the history of the Land of Israel.

When my friend Isaac (Bougie) Herzog approached me and told me about the manuscript in Russian found by the daughter of Mark Dymshits, it right away struck a chord in my heart. When I was a child, my parents, Murray and Hana Greenfield, had people come over to our house and make telephone calls to their relatives in the Soviet Union, an expensive proposition in those days before cell phones, when many people didn't even have phones in their homes.

My father started his Zionist activity in 1947, bringing survivors to what was then British Mandate Palestine on the *Hatikva* ship of the resistance movement Aliyah Bet. Aliyah to Israel has always been a top priority for us as Israelis and as publishers.

So when I received the Russian manuscript of this book, although I couldn't read it until it was translated, it felt like a historic opportunity had fallen into my hands. We immediately began our efforts to get this important book published.

Isaac Herzog introduced me to Marcia Riklis, who met us in Tel Aviv and became enthusiastic about the project as well and right away agreed to support its publication. I would like to thank Marcia, an active American-Israeli Jewish leader, for her generous support in memory of her late father, the renowned entrepreneur and philanthropist Meshulam Riklis.

We are proud to publish this unique episode in the history of the Jews of the Former Soviet Union and to shed light on the courage and persistence of these heroes, whose goal was to come to their homeland, Israel.

For years they used to say, "*L'shanah haba'ah bi'Yerushalayim*" (Next year in Jerusalem)! At long last, after a courageous struggle, they and many other

Jews were able to fulfil their dream and come live in Eretz Yisrael, the Land of Israel.

May their determination shine as a beacon for all people struggling for human rights around the world.

Ilan Greenfield
September 2020

Acknowledgments

We wish to thank the Jewish Agency for Israel and the World Zionist Organization for facilitating the publication of this important book.

Our special thanks are extended to Mr. Isaac Herzog, Chairman of the Jewish Agency for Israel, and to Ms. Marcia Riklis, for actively supporting this project, which would have been almost impossible without their aid.

We deeply thank Mr. Ilan Greenfield, owner and publisher of Gefen Publishing House, for his extremely personal contribution to the project.

Finally, many thanks to our good friend, Mr. Irmi Kfir, for his help in beginning the project.

Liza Rivkin (Dymshits) and Yakov Rivkin

Preface

Today is September 29, 1989. According to the Jewish calendar, tomorrow marks the beginning of a new year, 5850. On June 15, 1990, it will be twenty years from the day we attempted to hijack an Aeroflot An-2 plane, with the aim of the leaving the Russian Empire behind – its totalitarian regime, its lawlessness, its antisemitism. We hoped to make it to Israel and become citizens of our homeland; and by homeland, I do not mean the country where we were born. I mean the country that needed us, and that we needed.

Not long before our time, thousands of Jews who had dreamed of Israel were shot to death, or thrown into prisons and Stalinist death camps. Their bones lie scattered over the boundless expanses of the Russian Empire, which to this day has retained the name of USSR. Many who fought for the ideals of Zionism did not live to see the formation of the State of Israel, let alone the aliyah of the 1970s.

It has now been ten and a half years since I emigrated to Israel, and many people have suggested I write a book about Operation Wedding. I have been offered assistance with editing, proofreading, and even translating the book from Russian. In the meantime, Hillel Butman's *Leningrad to Jerusalem with a Long Layover* (1981) and *A Time to Be Silent and a Time to Speak* (1984) have been released. Yosef Mendelevich's *Operation Wedding* (1987) has been published. Articles by V. Boguslavsky, H. Butman, and D. Mahon (Chernoglaz) have appeared in the journal *22*.

Each of the above-listed authors participated in the operation and is hardly in any position to claim objectivity. I claim no objectivity for myself. There is a saying that goes, "Two Jews, three opinions." Well, each of us has at least one opinion. It goes without saying that my recollection of events, both serious and trivial, differs from that of my comrades.

Time, like subjectivity, leaves its mark. However, I have spent a lot of time reflecting on my actions and their consequences, and I anticipate the omissions here will be minimal. I cannot say the same for all the dates or names of the people I met over my nine years in prisons and camps.

Additionally, there are important details of the operation that are known to only a few individuals and organizations. The books mentioned above contain inaccuracies, some of which are significant, others of which are not.

I doubt if I will ever finish these recollections, let alone publish them. It is difficult to rub salt in the wounds of friends and relatives. Although all of us who participated in Operation Wedding came out alive, we were left wounded and traumatized, bearing grudges and nursing complaints.

Though the experience was new to us, and many of us made mistakes, this did not prevent us from gaining the final victory in the struggle for aliyah.

I will try not to be overly repetitive in my descriptions of prison life. It has been amply illustrated in literature published in the West, as well as, in recent years, the Soviet Union.

Rather than giving a detailed account of my life, I will describe only part of my life's journey: if only to help the reader understand my progression from a Young Octobrist, Pioneer, Komsomolets, and communist to critic of an antisemitic regime, highly dangerous state criminal, and citizen of the State of Israel.

While remaining an internationalist, I nonetheless support an undivided Israel. This is, in my belief, a necessary condition for the country's safety, due to the proximity of hostile Arab neighbors who are bent on gradually dismantling the Jewish state.

Regardless of all that has happened, I remain a proponent of socialism. Though put to shame in the USSR, it has been meaningfully implemented in Sweden and Switzerland – where instead of class struggle, revolution, or dictatorship of the proletariat, its core principles are labor, social equity, democracy, and justice. Even the USA shows more signs of true socialism than the world's first "socialist" country.

1 Childhood before the War

1927–1941

I have rarely dwelt on the events of my childhood and rarely dwell on them now. Even during my years of imprisonment and forced labor, I often recalled my time in the air force but never my childhood.

Back then there was a popular slogan: "Thank you, Comrade Stalin, for our happy childhood!" My childhood was not especially happy, but it wasn't tragic either, or even difficult. In short, I have no reason to accuse the dictator of ruining my childhood. To this day, I remember from portraits and newsreels the image of Stalin with a little girl in his arms. That he was responsible for making that little girl an orphan, we would discover much later. By the way, all twentieth-century dictators loved being photographed with children.

I thank God that up to age fourteen, when I was evacuated from Leningrad during the war, I lived with my parents. True, I saw them rarely, as they left for work early in the morning and returned home late in the evening. But by then, millions of children had already been left without parents, and many would themselves become victims of Stalin's purges.

And so, a little about my family. My parents were Elizaveta Markovna Baevskaya and Yuliy Izrailovich Dymshits. I was not their first child, but rather inherited the title from my elder brother, who died either during or immediately after birth. My younger brother died from hunger and sickness during the siege of Leningrad.

I was quite keen to "slip away" myself, but it was not to be. What did happen was this: at an age when children move about on all fours, I crawled off on my first hunting expedition. Either I was a cunning baby, or the cockroach was a wimp; but whatever the reason, I cornered my prey and lost no time in swallowing it. In the days that followed, I might have joined my older brother, had it not been for the intercession of one Professor Dikly. At this point, I can hear my readers saying, "What an amazing memory he [that is, I] must have!" But of course, I don't remember that particular event. My mother told me about it much later.

1

Here in Israel, a few religious people have assured me in the course of conversation that it wasn't I who tried to hijack the airplane, but God acting through me. I am not a religious person, but if that was God's idea, then it was definitely he who saved me from death in the form of Professor Dikiy, and he who planned the aliyah of the 1970s, probably far in advance of the actual event:

> At that point, the Lord, your God will reverse your exile and show you mercy; he will return and gather you from all the peoples to which the Lord, your God scattered you. If one of yours was scattered to the far end of the *sky* [emphasis mine], your God will gather you even from there; he will go there and get you. (Deuteronomy 30:3–4)

This is the 263rd line of Deuteronomy, 263 being also the number of the first cell I was placed in after my arrest. We had hoped that by rising up into the *sky*, we would make our exodus from Russia and escape to Israel. But I will get to that later.

Back to my childhood. My family lived in the town of Lozovaya, in the province of Kharkov. Lozovaya was a large railroad hub and a regional center which had fallen within the Pale of Settlement during the tsarist era. As a result, it was mostly settled by members of minority ethnic groups – at a time when belonging to an ethnic minority was not yet a matter of life and death.

According to my mother's stories, the people of Lozovaya were proud of their regional committee secretary. At that time, regional committees didn't have palatial headquarters; there were no black Chaikas or Volgas prowling the streets. Our Secretary, an idealist who dreamed of equality and a bright future for all people, walked the streets of the regional center barefoot in warm weather like many other townspeople. That's what it was like in the years immediately following the Revolution.

One of Lozovaya's main attractions was our housemate, a well-built young man of about thirty who paraded about town in his birthday suit. It was a kind of one-man show, but with tragedy at its heart. Far from being inspired by high-minded ideals, our housemate went naked as a result of psychological disturbance following a pogrom. Though the police periodically arrested him, they never sent him to the madhouse. It was a confusing time, even for harmless lunatics (though the low point of Brezhnev-era psych wards had yet to be reached).

That is what I remember of my mother's stories. Now for what I remember myself.

On warm summer nights, we used to sleep between the wall of the house and the vegetable patch. I remember the black starry night and the chirping of cicadas. I also remember that not long before our move to Leningrad, my parents gave me two rabbits to keep as pets. I had scarcely let them out of their cage into the vegetable patch when our neighbor's cat throttled them to death, one after the other. After crying a bit over their carcasses, I dug a little hole and, with my father's help, buried them behind the house. That was the first time I saw death with my own eyes – in this case, animal death. I would witness human death much later, during my air force service, without tears.

I don't remember my father's parents. My grandfather had a small book-binding company, and my father, together with his brother Iosef (my father had two brothers and three sisters), worked in the family business. Later, my father worked as a photographer.

Both my father and my uncle Iosef fought in the First World War. Both were wounded. My father was even disabled – when a shard of shrapnel tore off the fingers of his right hand. I will write in more detail about Uncle Iosef later. His story is interesting.

Father's older brother, Zakhar, tried to get to Palestine in the 1920s but fell ill with typhus near the Turkish border and returned home scarcely alive. This was the first attempt by a member of our family to reach the Promised Land.

In the autumn of 1931, my father, mother, and I set off for Leningrad, the most beautiful city in the USSR. True, they say that lately it has been looking dirty and unkempt. Back then, the city greeted us with the usual autumn drizzle and slush – "gloomy, wet Leningrad," as the song goes. Years later, when I would come home on leave, I loved to walk from Moscow Railway Station to the Admiralty along Nevsky Prospect in exactly the same kind of weather.

So, here we were in Leningrad. We loaded our belongings into an open-top cab and set off for our new place of residence, 25 Plekhanov Street, apartment 1. The kitchen, seventy square feet, was divided down the middle. Our room was thirty square feet. Similar solutions to the housing problem were common at that time. Rooms and kitchens were divided with screens. Single-family apartments (relics of the past) were transformed into communal apartments for three or four families. I have even seen apartments that housed up to eight families (prototypes of the "Communist future").

Under such circumstances, it is very important to have good neighbors. Indeed the saying "Good neighbors are better than good relatives" must have been invented around that time. We were lucky in that regard.

Thirty square feet for three people is pretty cramped, and that was before my mother's mother, Mina Grigoryevna, moved in with us. After that you could barely squeeze between the table and the sofa. I had an easier time of it, as my movements took place mostly under the table.

As a rule, I wasn't aware of any problems, let alone the housing problem. All I remember about my grandmother is that on Fridays she would light a candle and pray.

Besides us in the apartment there were two other families. We got on well with them. One woman, Natasha, who kept house for an elderly couple, looked after me whenever my parents were at work and I happened to be at home. I spent most of my free time in the courtyard.

Soon, I was sent to a kindergarten which was a fifteen-minute walk away from home. It was then that I began to familiarize myself with the streets and courtyards of Leningrad. As the years went by, I expanded the borders of my familiarity. I made friends in my building and at kindergarten.

I spent my afternoons playing in the courtyard until my parents got home. The only window in our room had a view of the courtyard and stood one-and-a-half feet above the ground. It only took two seconds to slide through the window hatch and out into the courtyard, or to climb back into the room if I heard my parents coming. I always managed to get home first.

My parents spent the whole day at work. Father worked as a photographer and Mother as an accountant. It could be said that the courtyard brought me up, in those afternoons after kindergarten and, later, school.

Our building contained about eighty apartments. Its inner courtyard was shaped like a well. In the center of the courtyard stood a two-story house, with a communal laundry on the first floor and a few residential apartments on the second. The building was home to many children of various ages, and as the courtyard provided only limited space for our games, we made the basements, attics, and even the roof our domain. Fights were common within the various age groups, though when it came to conflict with the neighboring courtyard, our principle allegiance was to our own. For fights and games we made slingshots, wooden swords, and daggers. There was an unwritten law that fights would end at first bloodshed. Most likely for this reason, I don't remember any serious injuries.

Many buildings in our area were home to workers' collectives, storage rooms, workshops, and utility rooms. All of these were objects of industry for us local kids. We took everything that wasn't bolted in place: colored metal, glass dishes, and other knickknacks. We were constantly looking for ways to amuse ourselves.

In 1935, I started going to school. Back then, children started school at age eight. The First Model School of Oktyabrsky District resembled a palace. It remains the most extravagant school building I have ever seen. The school was a stone's throw from home, and its notable features were a huge assembly hall with crystal chandeliers and broad wooden bannisters on the central staircase. These bannisters were a favorite form of amusement during the breaks between lessons. To slide from the third floor to the first without touching the floor was considered a particularly impressive feat. However, this carnival ride was shut down after some hooligans started sticking broken razor blades into the wood.

Until fifth grade, I was a good student. I never got a single 3 in quarterly or yearly exams.[1] In fifth grade, however, I started getting 3s, and in the second quarter of sixth grade I managed to earn four 2s. A "band of four" sprang up in our class, of which yours truly was a member. Beginning in fifth grade, we started skipping classes and wandering the city, sneaking into movie theaters through the back door, riding between train carriages or on the back of trams, jumping out of moving vehicles. Once I jumped off the back of a tram at high speed, slipped on the ice, and escaped the wheels of an advancing car within a hair's breadth.

When the purges of 1937 began, several "enemies of the people" were removed from our building and their families exiled. We ten-year-old patriotic idiots would respond to the stories of nighttime arrests with cheers. I even managed, once, to make my father fear for his life. It happened like this. There was a garbage disposal unit in the middle of our courtyard, adjacent

---

[1]   In the Soviet Union, schools awarded marks based on a five-point grading system (from 1 to 5).

to the two-story house. Its hatches, three feet above the ground, could be opened, and its contents removed. Among the garbage lived hundreds of rats so big that even the cats were afraid of them. So it was that the garbage heap became a prime location for hunting. We made sharp hooks out of thick wire, and while two boys speedily opened the hatches, a third used his hook to catch a rat. Our booty then went to feed the local cats.

Once, however, instead of a rat, my hook landed on a box, which I dusted off, wiped down, and took home. There, I discovered that the box contained rifle cartridges – shiny, lubricated with axle grease – thirty of them. When my father came home from work I showed him my find. In the spirit of 1937 or '38, his reaction was instantaneous. He grabbed the cartridges and had me at the police station in a matter of minutes. There I told my story, point by point. A report was taken and we were released. Only once we got home did my father give me a slap in the face, followed by a good talking-to. After that, he returned to his normal self.

Of course, they could have made things much worse for us. But I would only realize this later, as a result of personal experience. If my father had occupied an important position, or someone had been eyeing his job… My father, by the way, was not only unable to fire a rifle, but any amount of physical labor in the camps would have killed him.

Every new day brought news or rumors of new arrests, and we Young Octobrists and Pioneers, brought up in the mold of Pavlik Morozov and Pavka Korchagin, slashed up our textbooks, gouged out the eyes of "enemies of the people," and drew fangs and horns on their portraits. Basically, we were put through the school of hatred.

I was, of course, gratified when the people of Lithuania, Latvia, Estonia, and Bessarabia "decided" to "put an end to the troubles of the past" and join forces with the USSR. The invasion of Karelia wasn't even up for discussion. After all, the Soviet Union could hardly permit the Finnish "aggressor" to threaten my beloved city, Leningrad.

Let it not be said that I spent all my time skipping classes and messing around. I made my own movie projector. I built model ships and boats, despite the fact that I had no intention of becoming a sailor and was afraid of swimming more than fifty yards out to sea. I also liked to draw and took after-school art classes at the Pioneer Palace in Leningrad. My mother even said that I wouldn't make a bad artist.

I kept myself busy at home by coming up with diversionary tactics. Right before my parents got home from work – on days when I had a teacher's note or low marks in my class diary (this was in fifth and sixth grade) – I would take a table lamp, slide the plug partway out of the socket, and touch the pins with a knife to create a short circuit. While my parents were searching for the faulty appliance and replacing the burnt fuse, they would forget to check my diary! After that, they wouldn't dare distract their "diligent" son from his homework, although often I was actually hiding a novel inside my textbook. I loved fantasy writers, especially Jules Verne.

On New Year's Eve 1939, I brought my parents a "gift" of four 2s for the second quarter and a warning that if I didn't improve my marks next quarter for the subjects in question, I would be expelled from school.

Around the same time, two events occurred which pushed my grades far into the background. The first was the appearance of my little brother, Misha. I'll skip ahead a little to say that Misha had a tragic fate. His kindergarten fell under quarantine during the war and was unable to evacuate Leningrad. As a result, Misha remained in the besieged city and died in 1943.

The second was that my parents decided to exchange our small room for a larger one, and I was consequently transferred to another school, No. 316 in the Frunzensky District. We moved to a fifty-square-foot room in a fifth-floor communal apartment with four doorbells – that is, four families. Fifty square feet came out to about twelve square feet per person. By which I mean, there was some breathing space. You could get from one side of the room to the other without crawling under the table. The only window in our room overlooked San Galli Park instead of the dark courtyard, which was a boon – except that I lost my shortcut through the window hatch.

At my new school, far from the "band of four," I improved my grades and finished the year with a few 3s, but mostly 4s and even two or three 5s.

Our building, 64 Ligovsky Prospect, was also large and home to many children. In fact, the kids from Ligovsky Prospect were famous throughout the city for their exploits. However, I had to focus on my studies and help Mother with the household chores. In the end, I never had a chance to make friends in that building. The war got in the way.

Before we get to the war, however, I would like to describe how my family spent summer vacations. For a few years running, my mother and I went out of town together. We would rent a room and stay there all summer long.

Father would visit on the weekends with provisions from Leningrad. I spent the summers of 1938–39 at Pioneer camp or in the city. In 1940, we went to Strelna, on the Gulf of Finland. Every morning I either went fishing or to the tankodrome. There, during hours spent watching tank crews in training, I first became conscious of the wish to become a tankman, a wish I would carry with me for the next ten years. I would often accompany the soldiers to their field exercises, and I clearly remember how their commander highly praised my topographical map of the area and even showed it to his soldiers as an example to be followed. Of course, I couldn't wait to boast about this to my parents.

In Strelna, I usually spent my days helping my mother with chores, spending time with my brother, running errands, and playing *lapta* and *gorodki* (traditional Russian ball games played with a bat) with other kids from the area.

After I finished eighth grade, my parents sent me to a children's sanatorium in Teriyoki on the Karelian isthmus (former Finnish territory). The sanatorium was surrounded by a pine forest, and we children were completely cut off from the outside world. There wasn't even a public address system, and the only radio belonged to the administration. On June 24, 1941, one of the kids overheard something on the radio and told us that a war had just begun. Rumors spread that German paratroopers had landed only six miles away from us. We began to get unruly and demand information. In two or three hours' time, as if an alarm had sounded, we were gathered up and taken to the railway station.

It took us five or six hours to get back to Leningrad, stopping occasionally to make way for convoys of troops and supplies. Only once I got home did I learn the details of Germany's attack on the Soviet Union. From that day forward, I became a regular radio listener and newspaper reader.

However, it never once occurred to me that the Germans could win the war, even in the darkest days of 1941–42. Most likely this confidence was a result of exposure to prewar films such as *If War Comes Tomorrow* and *Deep Raid*, which I watched multiple times and which left a deep mark on my childish imagination.

2 Evacuation, Boarding School, and Air Force Special School

1941–1946

In the first weeks of the war, there were no aerial bombardments. The army was mobilizing. German spies, both real and spurious, were being apprehended. Only individual reconnaissance aircraft appeared in the skies over Leningrad.

We children helped the grown-ups clear the inner courtyards of easily flammable materials. We got rid of junk in the attics and prepared barrels of sand and water.

The city's schools and kindergartens opened evacuation registers for children, and the first convoys of children left for the East only a few days after the war began.

Many parents, assuming the war wouldn't outlast the summer (as the songs, films, and radio programs assured us), packed off their children as if we were going to Pioneer camp. Many thought we would be home again in time for the new school year.

At School No. 316, where I had been for only half a year, the last day of registration was already imminent, but my parents couldn't make up their minds. My opinion counted little with them. I can clearly remember my mother's words: "We've got to send him [me] with the school. Then at least one member of the family can survive." My mother's conclusion (or rather, prediction) was incomprehensible to me, and I'm not sure my father was convinced by it either. For a long time before the Leningrad siege, my mother had a premonition of the tragic events to come.

Ultimately, my father entrusted her with the decision, and she signed me up. Together, they gathered the necessary clothing, underwear, and shoes, and, at the appointed time, took me to the railway station.

Our school was lucky to escape. Almost immediately after our departure, the Germans started bombing transports of children and Leningrad itself. Evacuating children became too dangerous.

9

Our first destination was the village of Bogorodskoye in Yaroslavl province. At first, it really was like Pioneer camp. Though we would occasionally help the local farm workers with weeding or gathering flax from the field, most of our time was spent wandering about the village.

When autumn came, our food was rationed. Temperatures dropped, and the rains set in. Hoping that the Germans would be defeated and we would be home before the end of summer, we hadn't brought any warm clothes with us. Our shoes were wearing out. The situation was far much more serious than we had anticipated. When the night frosts began, we ran to the canteen barefoot, in an effort to save our shoes for winter.

Our age, and the constant activity which accompanied it, required a full ration of food. But there wasn't enough to go around. On one occasion, two friends and I climbed through the window of the village bakery when the bakers had gone to lunch. Arming ourselves with three loaves, we dashed to the nearby cemetery and hid our plunder in the basement window of the chapel. Our plan was to come back that evening and feast. However, when we did return in the evening, we found that the birds had reduced our loaves to crusts. At that point, we set eyes on a chicken, pecking about near the cemetery. And though "a chicken is not a bird…," it was precisely this chicken who had to answer for the crimes of ravens or jackdaws. After catching the chicken with difficulty, we set it to boil in a rusty tin can, on a fire made of wood chips. In fact, we didn't so much boil the chicken as warm it up. But we essentially made up for our loss: leaving only a pile of bones and feathers behind.

Meanwhile, the Germans were racing toward Moscow. When they took the city of Kalinin, we could hear the artillery fire. Then followed the units of exhausted men, sent back for reorganization. They looked terrible, and there really was little cause for cheer. The situation at the front was precarious. The enemy was nearing the capital.

A hurried decision was made to send us children deeper into the country. Smaller children and luggage were loaded onto carts, while older children went on foot. Hungry and shivering in our summer clothes and worn-out shoes, we must have made a sorry sight. The drizzling rain soaked us through, while providing us with puddles to drink from. We journeyed for twenty miles on foot in this state before making it to the town of Myshkin.

In Myshkin we were dried off, fed on rabbit meat, and allowed to rest for a week, before being taken to the *debarcator*. The *debarcator* was a riverboat station on a floating platform, both floors of which were occupied by waiting areas, a café and various utility rooms. The waiting areas were fitted out with several rows of bunks, allowing this "dreadnought" to house two thousand children, along with their teachers, doctors, nurses, and cooks. The density was so great that we had to sleep in our clothes, pressed up against one another, and turn in our sleep synchronously. As it was cold, we were able to keep one another warm in this way, and later, we were able to exchange fleas in this way, too. The smallest children were accommodated in the utility rooms, where conditions were much better.

We stayed in port for a day, until a tugboat was attached to our *debarcator* and we set out on what was, for many of us, the first water journey of our lives. After resting in Myshkin, our mood was much improved. An exciting journey lay before us. We didn't know where we were going, but that hardly worried us.

For the first week we were fed decently, on bread, sugar, a few boiled potatoes, butter, and tea. As the journey drew on for longer than expected, our rations began to decrease. After a week, the butter had finished, and as we drew closer to our destination all other supplies dwindled.

Our tugboat was regularly stopped for checks, and we often had to spend more time waiting in port than on the water. In the town of Kuybyshev, we were able to go ashore for the first time, and some kids even got to see the American color film *The Jungle Book*. As we approached the town of Gorky, we managed to collide with a low-hanging bridge, which took off part of the *debarcator's* roof. Now, in addition to the cold, hunger, and fleas, we had raindrops to contend with.

In Gorky, our *debarcator* was made to anchor in the middle of the Volga, where we stood for several days. On the seventh and eighth of November, during celebrations for October Revolution Day, the city was bombed. We could see the glow from the fires. German dive bombers flew only 2,000–3,000 feet above the ground. The whole sky was peppered with exploding shells and tracer bullets from anti-aircraft cannon.

We boys sat on what remained of our mangled roof and watched the duel of aircraft and anti-aircraft, rooting for our team like fans at a stadium. Not a single Nazi plane went down. Somehow, it didn't occur to us that one little bomb would be enough to send our *debarcator* to the cold bottom of the Volga, and us with it. But somebody must have realized that, moored in the middle of the river, we presented an attractive target. Consequently, we were towed out of the city and after a few days resumed our journey.

Soon, ice began to close its grip on the Volga and our *debarcator* began, slowly but surely, to sink. Working the pumps day and night in shifts, we learned the rule: "It takes the hands of a drowning man to save a drowning man."

In the last days of the journey, many children became sick from cold, hunger, and the unsanitary and crowded conditions. Though there were doctors and nurses aboard the "dreadnought," they had almost no medicines at their disposal.

We barely made it to Cheboksary, the endpoint of our river journey – although I think the original plan had been to float us as far as the Urals. However, the people of Cheboksary, capital of the Chuvash Republic, gave us Leningrad children a warm welcome. Small children were lifted up and embraced, while older ones were wrapped in blankets. Complete strangers gave us the coats off their backs and took us frozen, sick, flea-infested young travelers into their hearts.

They accommodated us in the Red Army Commander's House – where, finding that it was both clean and warm, we spread out on the floor, over chairs and benches, even in the auditorium. It was heaven compared to the sinking barge.

While our clothing, full of lice and fleas, was being disinfected, we were taken to the bathhouse. In the evening we went to the local restaurant and filled ourselves with hot food before returning to our new residence. We were shown newsreels from the first difficult months of war, which were nonetheless very upbeat – for example, farm workers taking on German paratroopers armed only with pitchforks and scythes. Warmed and fed, we willingly applauded the heroic farm workers.

For the last two weeks of November 1941, we had dinner every night at the town restaurant. Pearl barley (sometimes called "shrapnel") with vegetable oil and sweet tea with bread became our regular ration. It all seemed luxurious after the scraps we had been eating on the river. Every dinner was accompanied by a local vocalist and a quartet of musicians. Their repertoire (and the singer herself) was always the same. Each concert began with the song "Little

Blue Scarf." To this day I remember the Cheboksary period of evacuation with fondness.

But now that we were warm and full of food, it was time to get back on the road. Toddlers and school-age children alike were sent by railroad to various parts of Perm province in the Urals. This marked the beginning of my acquaintance with that part of the country. Then, it was called Molotov province, and my first encounter with it dates from 1941. In 1967, my best friend died in a plane crash there. Later, from 1972 to 1979, I was imprisoned there in camps No. 36 and No. 35. As you can see, the Urals occupy a significant place in my life and memory.

Our school was assigned to the village of Troytskoe in the Kungur district, which was fifteen miles from the nearest railway station. The weather was frosty. Snow lay in drifts three feet high. We would have frozen in our summer clothes before even arriving at the village had we not been wrapped in sheepskins and driven there on sledges. For two weeks, we lived with farming families in groups of four. I and the two friends I was placed with spent most of our time sitting on our hosts' Russian stove, in order to keep out of their way. They were fairly prosperous peasants, but in the two weeks we spent with them, they gave us only a few onions to eat. In contrast to the townspeople of Cheboksary, these villagers treated us almost as enemies.

After two weeks, we were moved into the village school. By then, any trace of the school year had long since disappeared. We wouldn't attend a single lesson until September 1, 1942. Books from the school library were all we had to help us while away the short winter days. In the evenings we sang irreverent songs. As there was no electric lighting, we lay on our cots in the dark and howled. The teachers tried to quiet us down, but if the kids in one room stopped singing, the kids in another room would begin straight away. The singers were boys and girls from the seventh and eighth grades.

Food was scarce, and if anyone had any clothes left, these would be promptly exchanged for extra rations. We once discovered a box of soap under the piles of junk in the school storage room, and in a few evenings were able to swap all of the soap for bread. It was with the help of strategies like this that we kept ourselves from starving.

In late December 1941, I became a member of the Communist youth league, or Komsomol. All the children who had turned fourteen that year were taken to the regional Komsomol headquarters and we were solemnly handed our Komsomol identity cards and badges.

In the spring we began to do menial tasks for the local farmers. We cleared the paddocks of manure and prepared bundles of cut wood in the forest. For a day's work, each of us would receive half a loaf of bread and a quart of milk, and we were given lunch during the day (albeit without meat).

In summer, when greens began to appear in the kitchen gardens and pea shoots on the fields, we took additional measures to ensure our sufficient nourishment – in the form of raids. Our relationship with the locals soon deteriorated. We made knives out of handsaws with aluminum-spoon handles to scare off the local kids. But although there were fights, we never had to draw blood. Our advantage in numbers, as well as quality and organization, was too obvious.

The new school year was about to start, and the village of Troytskoe had no secondary school of its own. Children who had finished the fourth, fifth, and sixth grades were sent to other villages. Those of us who had finished sixth grade ended up in the village of Nevolino, about five miles from Kungur, the district center. I studied quite hard in Nevolino and finished seventh grade with straight 5s. Such a result was only possible in the absence of a German teacher at the school. If German had been one of my subjects, I would definitely have earned at least one 3. I couldn't bear rote learning and in general have little aptitude for foreign languages.

It was time to decide what to do next. I could continue through to tenth grade at the same school, or transfer to a special military school which accepted pupils of my age. An announcement appeared in the local newspaper that two such schools, specializing respectively in artillery and aviation, were accepting applications. But my inclination was still towards tanks, especially after I learned that a tank academy, recently evacuated from Kiev, was currently based in Kungur. Not wasting any time, I set out for town.

On my way to the academy I met a group of tank officers, smoking and talking animatedly among themselves. As the academy entrance was guarded by a sentry denying access to anyone without a pass, I decided to try my luck with them. I approached, apologized for the disturbance, and inquired whether the academy was taking on pupils. It was only after I had asked the question that I realized they were drunk. Their answer came before I had time to walk away: "You should go to Tashkent. That's where you'll find your academy and your front." Then all four of them burst out laughing. This was my first serious experience of antisemitism, and I will remember it to the end of my days.

In the future, I would encounter worse antisemitic abuse, and even institutionalized antisemitism perpetrated by the government, but until 1967 I practiced self-deceit. I reasoned that antisemitism was a holdover from the past, a result of low cultural literacy, a mistake as yet unredressed by the Party and the administration.

The officers' reply had offended me to tears. I took a moment to collect myself, then went over to a captain by the academy entrance and asked him the same question. The captain sized me up at a glance and asked how old I was. I answered, "Sixteen." He then explained that the sergeants were sent to the academy straight from the front. After three months of study, they would attain the rank of first lieutenant and be sent right back again. Even the draft board did not send new conscripts to the academy. "Slow down, kid," the captain concluded. "Your time will come. Make the most of the time you have and go to school."

My dream was dashed. Now it was a choice between artillery and aviation. While I had seen tanks up close and watched them at the tankodrome, my knowledge of artillery and aviation was limited to what I had seen in movies. But I knew that if I wanted to serve in the army, a decision had to be made.

To a certain extent, I was aided in my decision by a prewar anecdote: "During an air parade, two men are standing next to each other in a crowd of onlookers. Their names are Ivan and Abram. As a plane soars overhead, Abram looks up and cries: 'Our falcons are flying!' To which Ivan replies: 'No, our falcons are flying. Your falcons are sitting in pawn shops.'" I may risk sounding trivial, but since I had no preference one way or the other, this anecdote may have tipped the balance in favor of aviation.

I do not know what proportion of the air force has historically been made up of Jews. Before the war, I doubt that there were quotas or statistics on "pollution" of the ranks. I only know that the air force commander before the war, General Smushkevich, twice-decorated Hero of the Soviet Union, was shot in 1941 as an "enemy of the people" as the Germans were advancing on Moscow. The political significance of Jewishness would change later, during my air force service, together with a general change in the party line. But I will get to that later. For now, my decision was made. I sent my papers to the town of Okhansk in Perm province, where the Seventh Stalingrad Army Special School had been relocated after evacuating from Stalingrad in 1942.

In a week's time, I was summoned to Perm. They were putting together groups of about two hundred boys. Every day for a week, group after group went through medical examinations at the military aerodrome. The medical requirements for candidates were the same as those for the air force itself. To my surprise, many boys of titanic build and rosy complexion were eliminated on the basis of internal defects. Skinny kids like me passed the commission with greater success. All in all, of the thousand boys who attempted to jump the medical hurdle, only two hundred were successful. Then, all that was left was the mandate commission, where they got the lowdown on our families (starting with our grandparents) and our own political convictions. Here, being Jewish didn't seem to matter. All of my details were in order. After the mandate commission, only 180 of us were left.

Still in our civilian clothes, without any sense of what we would be study-ing, what rules we would be following, or what our living conditions would be, we were packed off to the town of Okhansk in Perm province. This, my first step in the air force, was made in the summer of 1943. The town of Okhansk was a regional center on the banks of the Kama River, a tributary of the Volga. Our school was housed in a large brick building, the largest in town. Its internal courtyard served as a parade and drill ground. Surrounding the courtyard on four sides were the dining room, sick bay, woodpile, and a stable for five horses.

The purpose of such special schools was to prepare young men for admis-sion to military colleges. This meant that in addition to the normal secondary school program, we studied the Red Army code of conduct, tactics, aero-dynamics, and basic navigation. These military subjects were taught on a relatively superficial level. Many hours were devoted to sport and marching practice. We also learned to shoot from a rifle.

In a military context, the whole school made up one battalion. Our battal-ion commander was Lieutenant Colonel Bashkirov, a former cavalry officer. Stocky and bow-legged with an enormous mustache, he never parted with his saber, and whether in town or on the school grounds, he could almost always be found on horseback or driving a horse and cart. In short, Bashkirov loved horses, and had more sympathy for them than for us. When there was a heavy load to haul, he usually gave us the job and spared the horses.

Our battalion consisted of three companies: the third company was made up of eighth-grade students, the second company of ninth-grade students, and the first company of tenth-grade students. Each company was divided into four platoons, corresponding to each class: 8a, 8b, 8c, and 8d. The platoon and company commanders were also our class teachers. All other subject teachers were civilians.

The platoon I was assigned to was commanded by First Lieutenant Yudin. Short, fat, and clumsy, he immediately received the nickname "Roly-poly." Yudin's life story was fairly interesting. In the 1930s, he had been at flight school with Chkalov, and was so successful as a pilot-in-training that he was written about in the papers – articles which Roly-poly had kept. Then the NKVD caught on to him and found a "dark spot" in his record. As he explained it himself: "I wanted to know what white bread tasted like, so I went to work as a chauffeur for Kolchak." All this he recounted quietly, pausing after each word. How Yudin managed to avoid repression he never told us, but we did learn that he had been immediately removed from the air force. And now here he was, a first lieutenant at forty-five, commanding our platoon, raising boys in wartime. Just as the battalion commander never parted with his saber, our Roly-poly never parted with his flight tablet.

Our company commander was Captain Telin. Tan and well-built, with an attractive spring in his step, he was the polar opposite of our platoon commander. In the first place, Telin would often order us to strip to the waist, and then review the company, prodding our clavicles, ribs, and stomachs for excess fat – ironic, considering our meager diet. A former cavalry officer like Bashkirov, he would often check our teeth, as if we were horses on sale. The gallant commander loved marching exercises and always drove us to a blind sweat.

Before classes began on September 1, our teachers were concerned with organizational questions. They dressed us in second hand uniforms, taught us to march, issued us textbooks and workbooks. We also did some housekeeping: tidying the school building, working in the kitchen, gathering firewood. As winters in the Ural region are long and bitterly cold, and fuel rations were minimal, Captain Telin found a way to gather firewood in excess of official quotas. That is, by organized robbery. In the evening, just as dusk was falling, our company would make its way to the bank of the river where felled timber was floated downstream. We would hear the command: "The enemy is trying to land on our side of the river. Take all the prisoners you can!"

In a matter of five minutes, we would manage to undress, pull twenty logs out of the river, get dressed again, load the logs onto our shoulders, and run to a safe distance (the river was under surveillance). Such raids continued until the first frosts. They enabled Captain Telin to kill not two but three birds with one stone: develop our stealth tactics, gather all the firewood we needed, and mortify our flesh. When the temperature in our barracks got down to 5°C and our folded uniforms froze overnight, I don't remember even once catching cold.

Our academic life was fairly intensive: six hours of classes, followed by two hours of homework in the evening. Aside from that, we had one hour of marching practice every day and one hour of physical education. We were always a bit lackluster in physical education classes. Systematic underfeeding left us with less than the requisite amount of energy. For most of the lesson, we would sit on benches watching one of our fellows do pull-ups on the bar and another on the rings.

Around that time, the wearing of shoulder boards became standard army protocol, and our commanders already had theirs. There were no cadet shoulder boards for us, however, and the school couldn't get hold of the necessary blue fabric. So as not to shame ourselves before the local residents, Lieutenant Colonel Bashkirov ordered us to tear the blue bindings off our USSR History textbooks, dye some white trimming material with quinine, and make the shoulder boards ourselves. On November 7, 1943 (October Revolution Day), our battalion, adorned with historical blue shoulder boards, paraded before a horse-drawn open carriage to inspire the local population with confidence in a fast-approaching victory. In the open carriage were Colonel Bashkirov, who received the parade, and his one-time mistress, a local beauty.

Aside from our school, there were no other military divisions based in Okhansk. For this reason, the first company, i.e., boys in the tenth grade, had an important mission to carry out among the local ladies. The energy they expended was compensated by the girls in the form of extra food (in the town, many residents had hidden stashes), and everyone was kept happy. So we warriors of the third company sat at our desks learning lessons, reading novels, or engaging in harmless chitchat.

In the spring, rumors spread that the school would be relocated. Our suspicions were justified when at the end of the academic year, it was announced that we would be moving to Stalingrad province. A week later, the process of packing all of the school's property into a riverboat began. The cadets of the first company finished classes, took their exams, and were distributed among the country's aviation colleges. At that time, pilots were being trained in six months before being transferred to a military base and, from there, straight through to the front. If a "fast-streamer" was still alive after ten missions, his chances of future success were greatly increased.

The remaining two companies and some of the new third-company recruits were loaded onto a boat and sent downstream on the Kama River to the Volga. Our destination was the city of Stalingrad.

We boarded the boat in pretty bad shape, but during our two weeks on the river, with intermittent excursions on shore, we were given decent meals and issued with new uniforms. The supply division had managed to obtain food for the whole journey before our departure, and took on fresh supplies – American ones – a further two times. This meant that we spent our time admiring the scenery and munching on provisions. In the evenings, we read books and played chess, dominoes, or checkers. It seemed more like a holiday than anything else. We arrived in Stalingrad invigorated, cheerful, and well-fed. Amid the ruins of the city (it had been practically razed to the ground), we held a parade and a short rally together with the local residents and authorities. Then we set off by train for our new destination, the village of Nizhniy Chir.

At Chir railway station, all the school's property was unloaded onto the platform. As there were no cars, our battalion set off along the dusty road, marching in formation, with our band and banner taking the lead. The village itself was about fifteen miles from the station on the banks of the Chir, a tributary of the Don River.

At the first sound of our marching band, the whole village spilled out onto the street. Little boys ran beside and behind our column. We moved into the school building and spent that first night on the floor. After breakfast the next morning, we went back to the station for our things. This routine was repeated every day for over a week: early-morning fifteen-mile marches, two boys carrying a bed, one boy carrying a nightstand, and so on. Moving slowly, and with pit stops, it took us until evening to get back. Eventually, we were given captured German trucks, and although their diesel engines took an hour to start, it was still better than hauling everything on our backs.

It was only once we were settled in our new home and had a chance to look around that we noticed an absence of adult males, and an abundance of fruit, vegetables, and dairy products. While the first company took upon themselves the function of husbands and lovers, we younger cadets fell upon the milk and fruit, the likes of which we hadn't tasted for three years. This had sad consequences: whether from diarrhea or dysentery, half the cadets fell ill.

Around that time, we were given a month's leave and told we could go home. Only Leningrad was off-limits. But those of us whose families lived in the city didn't let that get in our way. We simply added an extra line to our leave tickets: "Leningrad, via Stalingrad and Moscow." The school issued us with dry rations for the journey, and we were off. There was scarcely room to breathe on the train. During the day, we climbed out on the roof, or sat on the carriage steps. A world away from the cigarette smoke and noise of the carriages, we breathed the fresh air and admired the view as the train went clickety-clack.

And so, after three years of evacuation, I arrived back in Leningrad. I had missed my mother, my city, my friends from before the war. Were any of them still alive? I was flying homeward along Ligovsky Prospect when, one hundred feet from my front door, I "fell into the arms" of a patrol. They say that the strictest, most fault-finding officer of them all is a second lieutenant. "Fortunately" for me, the patrol leader turned out to be just one such.

"Where's your salute?" he asked, wasting little time.

"I didn't notice…" came my standard reply.

There was no use explaining. It was all part of a larger plan to get free labor. From the city commandant's office, fifty of us rank-breakers were marched in convoy to the depot at Moskovsky Railway Station – as luck would have it, the very depot where my mother worked as an accountant. For four hours we sorted scrap metal and bound it up in rolls. After working my share and receiving my documents from the officer on duty, I managed to find Mother, and we went home together.

Our conversation lasted late into the night. Mother spoke in detail of the siege, of the deaths of my father and brother. She described how she had gone to exchange clothes for potatoes and fallen in the street on her way home – how the car behind her had stopped and the driver had helped her up. He drove her home, escorted her to the fifth floor, gave her half a loaf of bread, and wouldn't even accept the ring she offered him in payment. There were people like that, Mother said, but there were also people who would rob you of your last crust, if you let them. There's no need to retell the whole story here. Many books have been written about this dark time in Leningrad's history. Nine hundred thousand dead. The number alone speaks volumes. In reality, it was closer to two million, if you count those who fled to the city from other parts of the province.

My holiday flew by, and it was time to return to school. I met up with my comrades (there were three of us from Leningrad) and together we set out for the distant village of Nizhniy Chir.

In tenth grade, we were no longer the rookies. They made us do fewer drills and menial tasks – that was what the new recruits were for. Now they were in the third company, and we were in the second.

I was earning 5s and 4s. Our mandatory foreign language was German, which was also my academic weak point, as it meant learning vocabulary by heart. However, before the end of the year, an unexpected development occurred that put an end to this problem for good. Somehow, during one of our German lessons, our teacher began to speak his mind. A middle-aged man of German heritage, he had either been drinking, or found himself unable to control his emotions – but whatever the case, he began, in the middle of the lesson, praising Hitler for his talents as an organizer and orator. After that, we wouldn't give him any peace. Before every lesson, he was met at the door by our class monitor and two assistants: the former, pointing an anti-tank gun in his face, the latter holding their hands outstretched in the Nazi salute. Each time, he would jump with fright, stumble out of the room, and take a few minutes to calm down before entering once more.

Our teacher carried a large pocket watch on a chain, which he would glance at constantly in the final minutes of class. During this period, a group of boys developed a practice of ambushing him in dark corridors, with a cry of, "Give me your watch!" This frightened our teacher so much that he eventually stopped wearing the watch, and generally began to avoid dark places. After two weeks of conflict, an agreement was made that though none of us knew a word of German, we would all receive 4s.

The food in Nizhny Chir was better than it had been in the Urals: tolerable in both quantity and quality. Almost every day we had a starter of millet soup, followed by a main course of millet porridge. Even our bread was made of millet, which meant that it disintegrated when it got too dry. After the vacation, many boys had brought various things from home to barter for food. And with such a diet, we were able to give the requisite amount of energy to physical education, as well as to our regular classes. Almost every day, my friend Boris and I would spend two hours training on the gymnastics equipment. Without any particular aim or skill, we built up our muscles and developed our coordination. In the future, during my air force service, this would truly come in handy.

As 1944 came to a close, we were given ten days' leave. The school's administration saw this as a way to economize on food. Once again, the three of us Leningraders doctored our leave tickets and set off on our journey. Because it was winter, we couldn't ride on the roof of the train, and inside there was barely room to stand up. We were forced to make room for ourselves on the narrow baggage racks, attaching one end of our belts to the hot water pipe – so we wouldn't fall off. On the evening of December 31, 1944, we arrived in Moscow. Leningradsky Station was teeming with people. Even senior officers were unable to get tickets. But because we didn't require the comfort of the coupé, or even of an ordinary sleeper, it was easier for us to find a solution.

As if by magic, we ran into a cadet from the artillery school who had got his hands on a key to the carriage doors. Together, the four of us went through to a platform where a suburban train was about to depart. We took that same train to Klin station. After waiting for ten minutes, we saw the Leningrad train approaching. When it arrived, we lowered ourselves onto the tracks in order to climb in from the back, unlocked two different carriages, and entered in pairs. In the vestibules, we noticed there were compartments in the ceiling, what they call "entresols." We hoisted ourselves up, closed the hatches, and – exhausted after freezing on the platform – soon fell asleep. Either one of us began to snore or shifted noisily in his sleep, because the train conductors soon discovered us and threw us out. We greeted the new year riding between two carriages in -23°C weather, wearing only short boots and woolen overcoats, whipped by a cold current of air.

During a ten-minute stop at Kalinin, we managed to buy tickets through to Leningrad. It so happened that the only free bunks were in a coupé carriage. It was warm and bright in the coupé. Music was playing. Officers and their lady friends were ringing in the new year, or rather, ringing out the old, with champagne and toasts to Stalin, to victory, and so on. We blue-nosed cadets, having found our bunks, immediately fell asleep.

We arrived in Leningrad the next morning. The week went by quickly. Meetings with friends, conversations with Mother, two or three trips to the theater or the cinema, and then back, back to the school which had become my second home.

May 1945. On Victory Day, when the war with Nazi Germany ended, I drank a shot of vodka for the first time in my life. I was already eighteen, and in June I finished tenth grade. Like many other cadets, I had begun to smoke, although smoking was officially forbidden. Our platoon commander Roly-poly detested smoking so much that he would not even allow us to sing the marching song "Tobacco." Whenever we did marching practice in the village and Roly-poly gave the command to sing, we would immediately start sing-ing "Tobacco." He would then stop the marching line and command us to jog the rest of the way, at which point we would break into a sprint, as if we were running a hundred-meter dash. The commander couldn't sprint like that, so we would disappear behind the nearest corner and return to the school with-out him, as if nothing had happened. In the end, this strategy led to a removal of the ban on "Tobacco," after which we stopped singing it.

Our former company commander, Captain Telin, newly promoted to bat-talion commander, was busy burning fat off the new recruits. The gallant commander made one company carry stones up a hill, and another company carry them back down. Such "useful" exercises were repeated almost every day. Some new recruits couldn't bear it and ran away from school, while oth-ers who were too weak or clumsy were expelled.

At the beginning of July we were allowed to go home. This time, we didn't have to alter our leave tickets. Leningrad was no longer off limits. The journey passed without any adventures.

Peace. The city was healing its wounds. Even the center was full of ruined buildings and boarded up windows. At the station, crowds of people had come out with banners and flowers to meet the Leningrad Rifle Corps.

After a week of vacation, my temperature rose to forty degrees, and I was stricken with fevers and chills. My mother called an ambulance, and I was taken to hospital. The diagnosis was abdominal typhus. All the wards, and even corridors, were overflowing with sick people. I stayed in hospital for a day or two. They gave me some medicine, but my condition did not improve. It was a miserable way to spend the vacation.

To make my temperature appear lower, I started shaking the thermom-eter. After that, they concluded that I had malaria rather than typhus, and discharged me.

I was feverish for two more days before I started to feel better. The vacation passed, and as I was pulling into Stalingrad on the train, my temperature began to rise once more. In those days, there was a medical carriage on the sidetracks by the ruined station. The nurse immediately diagnosed me with malaria, which was widespread in that part of the country, and gave me three pills – quinine or quinacrine. Without much of a thought, I gulped down all three pills, and was almost immediately staggered by a blinding headache and ringing in my ears. On the other hand, I never came down with malaria again.

With only two weeks left until the beginning of classes, we cadets of the first company, i.e., of the twelfth, graduating class, were allowed to move into our own accommodations. The school itself paid our rent, as we were not given any money for room and board. The three of us from Leningrad found a room near the school and carried our cots and nightstands over from the barracks. In the morning, we would go to class the same way adults went to work, and in the evening we came home to our apartment. Our landlady, a widow of about fifty-five, slept in the same room as us, behind a screen. Before bed, she would tell us various stories from her life, of which she had an inexhaustible supply.

Soon her daughter-in-law returned from evacuation. She, the daughter-in-law, had married two months before war was declared, and only a few months into the fighting had received notice of her husband's death. She was only twenty-five years old when we first met her, and would be the first woman I ever slept with. True, we boys had to move out of the apartment and find a new one. But my relationship with Katya (the daughter-in-law's name) would continue until I finished school. So it was that in addition to smoking and drinking, I acquired a third vice in that victory year of 1945.

My final exam results contained no mark below a 4. Delegates from Armavir Flight College arrived and began to seduce us with tales of life in the air force. The delegates obviously knew what they were doing, as many of us were leaning in the direction of technical college or civilian universities. The statistics speak for themselves. Of the thousand boys who applied to the Stalingrad Special School, 180 were accepted. That number had got down to 160 by the time of our graduation in 1946. Of these, only forty continued to the flight college, and only twenty-five – 2.5 percent of the initial thousand – would continue into air force service.

3 Armavir Flight College
1946–1949

Armavir is a fairly large town on the banks of the Kuban River. During the war, it was occupied by the Germans. After the liberation of Armavir, the flight college was returned to its former location. Although a year had passed since the end of the war, ragtag groups of bandits were still in operation. We were warned from the beginning to avoid going into town alone. We were also warned to be careful in our relations with women. During the occupation, the Germans had announced an open call for young ladies willing to staff their newly opened brothel. Over three thousand girls competed for only thirty vacancies. Venereal disease ran wild.

Armavir Flight College had roughly the following organizational structure:

1. Theory Battalion, which provided a foundation for further training.
2. Introductory Regiment, trained at that time on UT-2 planes, and later on Yak-18s.
3. Intermediate Regiment, which also trained on UT-2s, and later on Yak-11s.
4. Fighter Regiment, then trained on Yak-9s.
5. Fight Operations Regiment, trained on Yak-3s (back then).
6. And of course, commanders, staff, and auxiliary personnel.

Theory Battalion was based in the center of town and was made up of boys from Stalingrad Special School and elsewhere. Classes began immediately after our arrival. Before three months were up, we had taken the military oath, received our own firearms, and been assigned twice-weekly watches. Then, the watch company was mostly employed on maintenance work.

Once again, our platoon commander was a forty-year-old first lieutenant. Like Roly-poly, he had obviously also managed to get himself into trouble, and was also intent on apprehending smokers. For example, one rainy evening, a cadet decided to light a cigarette in our barracks. When the platoon commander came in, the place still smelled of cigarette smoke.

"Who has been smoking?"

Silence, followed by further interrogations. No one would confess.

"Fall in outside!"

I couldn't restrain myself. "What is the point of this system of collective punishment?" I asked, testily.

"You want the truth?" the commander shot back. "The truth is buried underground."

Back then, I had no idea how right he was. I would reach the same conclusion myself only many years later. Back then I found it surprising and unsettling. For a whole hour, the platoon commander made us run to and fro in the rain. A similar incident took place a year later, when we were already a regiment. A power outage in the area meant that we had lost electricity in our barracks. I was on orderly duty at the time and lit a kerosene lamp, which I placed on a small table near the door. Of course, one of the cadets used the lamp to light up – but when the commander came in, it was too dark for him to see who the culprit was.

"Who lit a cigarette?" he demanded.

"I didn't see."

"Twenty-four hours in the guardhouse!"

I spent the night on a straw pallet in the basement and the next day riding between headquarters and the aerodrome on a bicycle, delivering messages. But I didn't mind. In my whole time at military college, and even in the air force, I never spent another night in the guardhouse. On the whole, I responded well to discipline.

Our classes progressed successfully. I spent most of my free time playing sports. By the spring of 1947, we had fulfilled the course requirements for Theory Battalion, but that didn't mean the end of theory. Rather, in the years that followed, classroom learning would be interspersed with pilot training.

Now, it was time for us to learn to fly. Introductory Regiment was quartered in the village of Korenovskaya, in the Krasnodar region, which was very difficult to get to. If even the head of the college – who was also the town's garrison commander – couldn't manage to get us train tickets, you can imagine what the situation was like on the railways. Accordingly, we were given the order to climb onto the carriage roofs while the train was in the station, and stay there, no matter what anyone said. That is what we did. The train was stalled while the commandant staff executive (who was in on the scheme) was called to do something about us. He strode up and down the carriages, shouting, gesticulating, giving orders; in short, he played his part well. The train was dispatched forty minutes late, but we ultimately made it to our destination.

The village of Korenovskaya was a district center. Our barracks were just over a mile away from the aerodrome. We were divided into squadrons, flights, groups. Each instruction group was made up of five to six cadets. There were six in ours. One was later expelled for failing to meet proficiency standards. Another became ill during aerobatics training and dropped out. Four of us graduated from flight school, after which two would be killed in crashes, the third – I have lost track of him – and the fourth is writing these lines. Later, I will describe in greater detail the deaths of my two group mates, one of whom was my best friend.

On the first day after our arrival, we began to study the flight zones and the plane itself – its motor and other features. We practiced on aviation simulators and learned the basics of parachuting. We took our first training flights on the UT-2, a two-seat monoplane. It was from this plane that we made our first parachute jumps.

I was a little scared to trust a parachute with my life, but parachutes are an essential lifeline for pilots, and what's more, I had to. I had to jump, because if we didn't jump, we wouldn't be allowed to fly.

Imagine an early summer morning. The silence is broken only by the singing of larks. The aerodrome is waking up: the rumble of motors, the murmur of voices, commands being issued. The first plane rises into the air. I am the second in our group to fly. When my turn comes, I climb into the front seat. My instructor sits behind me. Takeoff. We ascend to a height of five thousand feet. I hear the first command: "Ready!" The instructor decreases our speed to sixty miles per hour. Obeying his order, I climb out on the wing, clinging to the side of the plane. I move toward the back seat of the plane, holding on to the ring with one hand. A current of air tries to knock me off before I'm ready. My instructor nods his head. I can only see his lips move: "Go!" I step to the back edge of the wing and dive into the blue-green abyss. The air whistles in my ears. I count to five, pull hard on the ring, and feel an abrupt change in speed. I check the dome of my parachute. Everything is in order. A pleasant quiet surrounds me. In the first few seconds, a feeling of suspension, then the ground begins to get closer. Now my goal is to land correctly on both feet, taking into account the direction of the wind. Here is the ground. I land

and gather up my parachute. A pleasant feeling of satisfaction. I am ready to jump again and again.

In a few weeks' time, this feeling would disappear. It didn't help that a cadet from one of the other squadrons was killed right in front of us, while parachuting out of a plane.

It happened like this. The guy was afraid to jump and couldn't overcome his fear. They took him up into the air twice, but he wouldn't even climb out of his seat. The instructors and cadets on the ground tried to encourage him, persuade him, make him feel ashamed, even threatened to expel him. He was taken up a third time. He climbed out on the wing, grabbed the side of the plane with both hands, and wouldn't budge. The instructor circled a second time, but the cadet still wouldn't jump. The instructor sharply tilted the plane and pushed the cadet off the wing. Back then, they didn't issue us with automatic activation devices. The guy lost consciousness and dropped like a stone (two hundred feet per second) almost all the way down. When he regained consciousness and saw the fast-approaching ground, he tugged at his ring, but it was too late. The parachute was released, but had no time to fill with air. The rest is self-explanatory, "bag of bones" and all. He was just nineteen years old.

We moved on to training flights with an instructor. The first cadet to fly solo dropped too low during his preparation for landing and got his wheels stuck in a fortification ditch. It was the first accident in our squadron. As a result, each of us was given ten additional flights with an instructor, and in a week, everyone was flying solo. To preserve the aircraft's balance during the first two flights, they put a sandbag in the back seat. In the flights that followed, we flew in pairs.

Then, an unexpected tragedy occurred. An instructor was conducting a training flight on a Yak-9 fighter plane. As he was performing the third turn in preparation for landing, his plane tilted sharply to one side, and plummeted to the ground from a height of over one thousand feet. Some wise guys decided to bring back fragments of the plane and motor for our general perusal. Some fragments still bore traces of bloody flesh. Larger body parts were gathered and placed in a coffin. You get used to that with time, especially when the people dying are strangers.

Accidents and tragedies became a part of our lives as pilots. We were told that before the war, they had been included in the annual plan for each regiment and each division.

There was no flying for three days, while the administration tried to determine the cause of the crash. The watch fired a salute from their rifles. A line of planes made one farewell circle over the cemetery, before everyone went back to business as usual. Life goes on.

At that time, there was no transitional aircraft between the training and fighter planes. The Yak-11 wasn't introduced until later. Our transition phase was carried out on the UT-2, but with more complicated exercises. As our planes were not equipped with radio technology, we navigated using only a compass and dead reckoning. The regimental navigator gave us meticulous ground training. Every week we drew a map of the flight zone within a hundred-mile radius, from memory, including all the major landmarks. Such solid preparation meant that not one of us ever got lost.

Our navigator's weak point was his fondness for vodka. He often asked the cadets to lend him money, and just as often came to class in a state of intoxication. He began our first lesson with the following exclamation: "If only I could get back all the money I've drunk away, comrades!–" we waited with trepidation to hear what he would spend the money on "–I'd drink it away all over again!" This was the major's dream.

One of the flight instructors in our regiment was a great original. When he was "merry with drink," he would give the local boys a ruble each to spend on candy. In return, they would run ahead of the lieutenant down the village streets shouting, "Make way for the best pilot in the USSR!"

As a rule, alcoholism was widespread in aviation. For drunkenness, pilots were banned from flying and could be discharged from the army. It led to the death of many a good man.

One former major and squadron commander who had since become an alcoholic could be found every day outside the cadets' mess hall in Armavir. Dirty, in torn military-issue clothes, he stood with a soldier's mess tin in his trembling hands, and asked each passerby to bring him something from the canteen.

Nor were we cadets exempt from the general tendency, especially on our one day off. The only thing that held us back was our small allowance. Some found a way around this by exchanging firewood for moonshine. (There was always a shortage of firewood in the Kuban region.) Local proprietresses would usually add pepper or tobacco to their brews for added strength. It was nasty stuff. But it was our poison of choice, and perhaps even helped to steel our bodies for greater trials. There is an old army joke that goes: "A Russian soldier drinks acid without even noticing, but when goes to take a piss later, his boots catch fire."

In autumn of 1947, we were allowed home on leave. In Leningrad I met up with a girl I had known in evacuation, Zina N. We went to the theater together, and to the movies. When I saw her again a year later, she told me that her mother had categorically forbidden her to marry a Jew, as all Jews would soon be sent to Siberia. I hadn't proposed to Zina, or even hinted at the possibility of marriage. And though I actually was sent to Siberia in 1949, they didn't manage to send all the Jews. They came close: cooking up the Doctors' Plot, making a plan of action, drawing up lists of names. But by then it was too late. Stalin, the "friend and teacher of all nations," had kicked the bucket.

After our return from leave, we studied various modifications of the Yak-9 plane before learning to fly it. After the UT-2, it seemed like the control speed had increased threefold.

In May 1948, the world learned of the establishment of the State of Israel. My reaction to this news was unemotional, calm. Absorbed in my own affairs, I was barely paying attention to the events of the day (my attitude would change in 1956, not to mention 1967 and 1973).

In 1948, ties between the former Allies were weakening and tensions were mounting. The college administration decided to retrain us on the Yak-17 fighter jet and accelerate our course so that we could graduate that summer – a year earlier than planned. When the planes arrived, the administration changed its mind and began training us on the Yak-3 plane, while the Yak-17s were redistributed.

Around that time, I had an experience which could have put an end to my aviation career. Late one evening, a friend and I were returning to the aerodrome from town. I walked ahead of him on the path, and he followed behind. It was dark. Suddenly we could see six people striding toward us. They came level with me, and suddenly I felt a belt hit my face. My friend managed to jump fifty feet to one side, while my eye was throbbing with pain. I was seeing fire rather than the proverbial sparks. The thugs gave me another few kicks with their boots, but by then I didn't care. The fortunate thing was that I had been hit with the flat part of the belt buckle. My eye puffed up, and was surrounded by a rainbow bruise, but I was in one piece and my eyesight didn't suffer.

An MVD[1] regiment was based in Armavir, and an enmity sprang up between the soldiers of this regiment of torturers and us air force cadets, which soon led to blows. On one of our days off, some fellow cadets and I armed ourselves with Bowden cables (in metallic casing) and went to town in search of revenge. On the one hand, it is pleasant to feel comradely solidarity, but on the other hand, the memory of how the three of us ganged up on a single MVD soldier makes me cringe. I comfort myself with the thought that he was a well-built young man, and we only used our fists.

In March 1949, I received a telegram informing me that my mother had died. She had survived the siege, and a few months before her death had sung at an amateurs' concert in Moscow. But it only took a few complications after a bout of flu, and she was dead. I was given ten days' leave. I arrived in Leningrad and went immediately from the station to the funeral. Everything had been arranged by her colleagues from work. Mother was buried at Preobrazhensky Jewish Cemetery. The weather was well suited to the occasion: rain, melting snow, chill, leaden clouds overhead.

For a few days, I could not come to terms with the fact that I was now entirely alone. First my father, then my younger brother, and now my mother was dead. Such is life.

As I was in the army, mother's room was immediately requisitioned. I had to sell or give away all of her possessions and get back to Armavir as quickly as possible. Now my only home was in barracks.

I returned to Armavir and made up for the classes I had missed. Each of us made another uneventful parachute jump before beginning our study of the Yak-3 plane, the lightest fighter plane in the world at that time. The Yak-3 was well equipped with either three 20mm cannons or one cannon and two 12.7 mm machine guns. On this plane, we learned military operations by participating in training skirmishes and shooting at airborne and land targets.

By the end of the summer, we had completed the whole program and began preparation for the state pilot exams. We also took our third parachute jump.

When the examination commission arrived from Moscow, our exams began. I received straight 5s in all areas of practical pilot training, with a few 4s in theory, but mostly 5s. For two months following the exams, we

---

[1]   The Ministry of Internal Affairs, formerly the NKVD.

waited for word from the Defense Ministry that we had earned the rank of lieutenant.

During that period, we were accommodated in the gym and given almost complete freedom to spend our time as we wished. Some of my classmates preferred to spend their nights with girlfriends in town. Those who came back late at night were usually met with a nasty trick of some kind: weight plates in their pillows, condoms full of water under their sheets, and so on. One of the guys, every time he came back from town, liked to wash his penis in a jar of potassium permanganate that stood on his nightstand. It was his personal hygiene ritual. Of course, someone came up with the bright idea of replacing the permanganate with purple ink. The guy came back late, as always, went through his usual motions in the dark, and got into bed. In the bathroom the next morning, everyone waited for his reaction. He turned white as a sheet and couldn't say a word. Only our raucous laughter brought him back to his old self. That was how we got our thrills back then.

The Defense Minister's order came. And we, yesterday's cadets, sporting new uniforms with lieutenants' shoulder boards, stood in line as the order was read aloud to us. A banquet was organized several days later, at which each guest was allocated five ounces of vodka – although we brought an additional bottle each. The seating plan was drawn up so that the newly minted lieutenants would alternate with instructors and commanders. There were no women present. The director of the flight college, Colonel Shubin, gave a speech half an hour long in which he expressed a desire to exchange his colonel's shoulder boards for a lieutenant's, as long as he got a little something else in the bargain. The colonel wished us luck, and so on. After that followed unnumbered toasts to Stalin, to the Party as the governing force of society, and so forth.

To my right sat the weapons instructor, who told me how in the 1920s, members of the Communist youth league had been sent to Palestine to agitate against the English colonizers. To my left sat the squadron commander. He spent the whole evening advising us not to envy each other once we had embarked on our military service: "Someone will live long enough to be made a general; someone will die a lieutenant –" only four months later, the first sacrifice from our graduating class would be claimed by the waters of the Baltic – "someone will end up covered in medals; someone will end up with his head in a bush. Everyone has their own fate." There was a feeling of complete equality, as if everyone had put aside his rank and position. The only other place that happens is at the bathhouse.

At the entrance to the banquet hall stood a crowd of girls, waiting impatiently for the solemn part to end. Two of them got married and left Armavir with their husbands. The others had to hang their hopes on the next lot of graduates, or catch one of the local boys. Toward the end of the banquet, many of them had to be taken home in cars which had been specially parked nearby.

The banquet concluded peacefully, and without incident. In several days' time, we learned what our new postings would be.

This is when I first experienced the government's antisemitic politics. Of about sixty graduates, twelve were sent to the Transbaikal Military District (or ZabVO, from *Zabaykalsky voennyi okrug* – the locals nicknamed it *Zabud vernutsya obratno*, no way out). Of the twelve, four of us were Jewish – all the Jews in our graduating class. All twelve of us were assigned to the same division. Before setting off for base, we had a month of leave remaining, and I decided to return to Leningrad. As our old room had been confiscated after mother's death, I had to stay with my uncle Iosef, whom I promised to speak about before.

Before the First World War, Uncle Iosef was an active-duty soldier in the tsar's army. He was posted near Warsaw. When the war began, Iosef's regiment began its march toward the front. But before it could get there, the regiment fell under heavy artillery fire. From my uncle's company, only a few men survived. My uncle himself was wounded and, together with some other wounded men, was taken prisoner by the Germans. The wounded were placed in hospital before being transferred to a prisoner-of-war camp.

It was not long before they gathered together all the Jews for political reeducation. The Germans described to them the lamentable position of Russia's Jews. They talked about discrimination and antisemitism, about pogroms, and so on. They also told them how different things were in Germany: complete equality, Jewish officers and generals in the German army. The question was, who and what were the Jews fighting for here in Russia? Mightn't it be time for them to go back home and tell their fellows how things really stood?

My uncle was a Russian patriot and hated Germans, considering them to be the root of all evil. He made a plan with one of his fellow prisoners to "accept" the Germans' mission. They were sent over the front line, but the front at that time was unstable. They lost one another. My uncle found his way to a small town near the front and took refuge in a synagogue.

Then, a Cossack unit came to town, and when my uncle went out on the street, he was arrested and taken to staff headquarters. The interrogations began, and all his attempts to explain how and why he had escaped from German captivity were fruitless. He was accused of espionage and condemned to execution by firing squad. In the morning, he and another soldier were taken to the outskirts of town to be shot. He was saved by a miracle. His former company commander, who had also survived the artillery barrage, saw and recognized him. In fact, the commander not only rescued Iosef from the Cossacks but had his name put forward for a St George's Cross, as the first soldier to escape German captivity. After that, it was back to the front: more wounds, hospital, reserves, reorganization.

Imagine – the eve of the February Revolution. Iosef opposes the monarchy and supports a democratic republic. To this end, he makes a speech before the soldiers in this regiment. The regiment is sent to the front. After the February Revolution, Iosef is elected chairman of his division's Revolutionary Committee.

The Bolsheviks are spreading propaganda against the war and the Provisional Government. My uncle thinks the war needs to be fought and won. The Bolsheviks command his division to march on Petrograd, where the government was to be overthrown. My uncle does not agree. He considers the Bolsheviks adventurists who will bring misfortune to Russia. The army is demoralized and unfit for combat. Before the July Offensive of 1917, Alexander Kerensky comes to the front and conducts a meeting. Among representatives from other divisions, my uncle reports on the situation in his own division, and his opinion of morale among soldiers and officers.

Once the July offensive collapsed, Iosef would have been killed by his fellow soldiers for supporting the war – had he not ended up in hospital again. The October Revolution found him still in hospital. The Civil War came and went, without his participation. Since then, Iosef had lived and worked in Leningrad.

When the Ribbentrop-Molotov Pact was signed, my uncle immediately predicted that there would be a war with the Nazis. When, on June 14, 1941, the state news agency (TASS) released a statement denying rumors of an imminent war with Germany, Iosef unequivocally declared that the statement was actually a warning in disguise and that people these days didn't know how to read newspapers. He added that he would enlist immediately when war was declared. His hatred for the Germans had, far from being extinguished, become more extreme with the Nazis' rise to power.

Actually, I remember, as a child, seeing a crowd of workers outside the newspaper headquarters. All of them were discussing the TASS statement, and many thought that war was unavoidable.

In the first days of the war, my uncle enlisted in the army as a volunteer, and was sent to the Baltic. His unit was forced into retreat, and did not come into direct contact with the Germans until they reached Pulkovo Heights outside of Leningrad. When my uncle exhorted his fellow soldiers to stand and fight, many replied that "Jews and Communists had better do the fighting." My uncle was horrified to think what might happen if he was taken prisoner, although based solely on his appearance, it was hard to tell whether he was Jewish or not.

The unit assumed a defensive position on Pulkovo Heights, and saw the enemy for the very first time. Several days passed. Multiple German attacks were successfully rebutted. In one of these battles, my uncle took a shrapnel wound to the arm. He made it to the field hospital, where they bandaged his arm, and sent him to hospital in Leningrad. The wards, and even the corridors, were full to bursting with wounded men. My uncle lay on the floor and watched untreated soldiers die beside him. Seeing that his own wound was becoming infected, he dragged himself to the operating room, after which he was transferred to another hospital in the Ural region. After the siege was broken in Leningrad, Iosef received an honorable discharge for disability, and returned home. When the war ended, he was given a small pension and got a job in a theater box office. I would spend time with my uncle every time I came to Leningrad on leave. We talked about the past, the present, and the future. I tried to learn from his rich life experience. After my discharge from the army in 1960, I often visited him, and he us, but more about that later.

And so, when I came to Leningrad on leave in 1949, I went straight to Uncle Iosef's place. He was a lifelong bachelor, but was nonetheless attractive to women. He lived in a fifty-square-foot room, which had once been the utility room of an elegant apartment in the city center. His neighbors were the city or district prosecutor – I don't remember which – and his family. The room's only window gave onto a wall, and even during the day you couldn't read without electric light. More often than not, I stayed out all day and only came back to sleep.

It was during this period of leave that I ran into my former classmate and fellow evacuee, Alya Grigoryeva. She had graduated teachers' college and was working in a nursery school. We spent the vacation together. Every evening we went either to the movies or to the theater. I only had a month in Leningrad, and my next leave wouldn't be for another year. I had taken an interest in Alya before, but now I decided not to waste any more time and made her a proposal of marriage. We registered at the city clerk's office and celebrated our wedding on November 1, 1949. Today, as I write these lines, marks our fortieth anniversary. A week after the wedding, I departed for my new posting in Chita province. My wife joined me three months later.

4 Air Force Service
1949–1960

Seven days on the train. It was my first time on the Trans-Siberian Railroad. As we traveled further east, the snow drifts became higher, the frosts more bitter, and the food situation more dire. We had our lunch in the restaurant carriage, which was always heaving with people. To avoid the long lines, we would buy provisions for breakfast and dinner at the station snack bars. It was always a rush to buy food and newspapers during the short stopping time. Things were made slightly easier if the train was standing at the first platform and you didn't have to cross through other trains, or even crawl under them.

Lulled by the noise of the tracks, I dozed, read, and admired the Siberian landscape, especially near Lake Baikal. After leaving Moscow, every new day had us in a new time zone. The time difference between Chita and the capital was six hours. My sense of day and night became confused. It was difficult to acclimatize. (It became even more confusing once I began flying home on leave. Then the time zones changed almost on the hour.)

Finally, I was in Chita, the regional capital. My fellow officers and I immediately presented ourselves at the district headquarters, where we learned the precise locations of our deployment. We were distributed among three regiments of a single division. Two regiments were based at an aerodrome at the Seventy-Seventh Passing Loop, and a third near the town of Borzya.

We spent the day in Chita, and then in the evening, we boarded a train to Otpor (across the border from Manchuria) and reached our final destination. We arrived early in the morning. It was dark, and there was an icy haze. The thermometer at the entrance to the station showed -55°C, and we were only in our military overcoats and leather boots. It was a mile from the station to the garrison, and we were driven there in the open back of a truck. At that time, the regiment had no bus at its disposal, only trucks. We were frozen to the bone.

The duty officer took us to the tactics room, where we got warmed up and began to look around. The room was covered in maps, models, and slogans. Among the usual ones about Stalin and the Party, one curious slogan had been carved into the blackboard with a knife: "An iron ass is better than a clever head!" This exhortation had more practical sense than all the others.

We awaited the arrival of our commander so that we could officially present ourselves for service.

Our regimental commander was Ilya Afanasyevich Cherkashin, a lieutenant colonel with three rows of ribbons. A bulky man of about forty, he spoke with a croaky bass and had a deep scar across his forehead.

I was assigned to the first squadron of the 350th Regiment. My squadron commander was Captain Vladimir Morozov. I will write more about him and Cherkashin later. With me in the first squadron were two of my fellow graduates, one of whom was Yuri Vasilyev, a Jew whose passport said he was Russian. With a Jewish physiognomy and a Russian surname, he had a strong desire to escape his Jewishness.

Another of my former classmates, Victor Zheleznov, ended up in the neighboring 22nd Krasnoznamenny Regiment. He was similar to Vasilyev in appearance, and was also registered as "Russian." This, however, had not prevented his deportation to the Transbaikal region and even aroused distrust in those surrounding him, as well as suspicion from the government. Later, the KGB would make sense of his and Vasilyev's biographies.

The fourth (undisguised) Jew from our graduating class, Berghaus, was assigned to the regiment based in the town of Borzya.

All three regiments were equipped with Yak-3 and Yak-9 planes, so we did not have to retrain.

All of the regiments' auxiliary buildings – other than the command headquarters, canteen, and officers' club – were dugouts of various sizes. Officers with families were provided with basic rooms in two-story houses, which had been quickly and poorly built in the 1920s. As the housing situation was strained (it always has been, throughout the USSR), we were accommodated at first in the local hotel – in an ordinary room with closely-spaced cots and nightstands. There was another room in the hotel with two cots, a closet and a rug, but that was for high-ranking officers only.

We were required to vacate the hotel when a delegation arrived from the regional capital. The chief of staff then ordered us to remove the clutter from an unused room and bring in supplies of firewood and coal. When we returned from duty in the evening, the stove was red-hot, and we fed it with fuel late into the night. Eventually, we went to bed. After two or three hours, we moved our cots closer to the stove and piled all our clothing on top of our blankets. By early morning, the temperature in our room was -10°C. When day broke, we saw that our windows were not only single-glazed but broken, and that there were huge cracks in the floor. The temperature in the basement was -55°C, just like it was outside.

When the most intense frosts set in, all the bottles of vodka in the garrison store burst. After that, they started ordering only pure spirit in winter, a simpler solution than heating the store. It's not hard to imagine what supply levels were like in that kind of weather, and how the storekeeper in her sheepskin coat would reluctantly draw her hands out of her woolly mittens in order to quickly weigh something on the scales, before warming them for a few seconds over a kerosene stove and tucking them away again.

Unable to face a return to the icebox, we opted to sleep in barracks or at the fire station, on whichever cots had been liberated by soldiers on watch duty.

After a week, I was given a thirty-square-foot room to share with First Lieutenant Boris Shatalin. Boris, a young man of twenty-eight, had been sent to the Transbaikal region from East Germany in punishment for alcohol abuse. Basically, everyone there was being punished in some way: whether for drunkenness or for being captured by the Germans, for bourgeois ancestors or for being Jewish. (In the early 1950s, you could have formed a Jewish division in ZabVO for each branch of the military.) But to return to Boris. When Boris was sober, he really was a first-class guy. We went hunting together and to the movies, and we read in the evenings. But when he came home drunk, he would grab his rifle and start shooting stray dogs through the window hatch. His buckshot would usually wound a dog or two, and then he would run outside and finish off the moaning animal at point-blank range.

To be clear: about a hundred feet from our window was a garbage heap, where not only dogs but cows liked to search for food. They picked out scraps and licked the insides of cans. Canned food was the most notable offering of our garrison store.

Boris's shooting was just about tolerable, but whenever I saw him heading to the door with an axe, I generally tried to restrain him. This happened several times a month. Two years later, Boris got married. His wife brought him under control and he changed for the better, settled down.

To give you a broader sense of the local geography: our aerodrome was home to two fighter regiments. They lived almost entirely in dugouts, and their readiness for combat was insured by two maintenance and training battalions. The garrison commander was Lieutenant Colonel Cherkashin, who was also commander of our regiment.

A mile and a half from us, on the other side of the railroad tracks, there was a tank division, commanded by twice-decorated Hero of the Soviet Union, General David Dragunsky. The tankmen had a large garrison with a post office, a spacious officers' club, a stadium, and several stores. We would go there quite often – especially the bachelors among us – in the hopes of "making a catch."

Between our two garrisons was what we called "trench town," a settlement of about twenty dugouts. The inhabitants of these dugouts were either political exiles or their descendants. Perhaps there were even some escaped convicts among them; I was never sure. They had vegetable patches and kept the cows who were always scavenging in the garrison rubbish dumps, for want of sufficient hay. They provided us with fresh milk and potatoes. Later, a Chinese couple appeared in the settlement and taught the locals to grow cucumbers and tomatoes. After that, the couple disappeared.

Seven miles to the north of us was a mechanized division. Seven miles to the south was a division of IL-10 stormtroopers. In short, the whole railroad line from Chita to Otpor was bristling with regiments and divisions, the most tactically important of which was the Sixth Tank Army.

Later, during training, we pilots would work together with the tankmen. In my first two years of service, whenever I looked down from my cockpit at the columns of tanks, I would feel a pang in my chest. But after that, I became so wrapped up in aviation that I forgot all about tanks.

To give you an even broader sense of the local geography: about 150 miles to the northwest of the Seventy-Seventh Passing Loop, on the banks of Lake Kenon, lay the town of Chita. At that time, soldiers and their families made up about 50 percent of the population. It was from Chita that we traveled west on leave – whether by air or land. Soon, a Moscow-Beijing courier train was put into service. About sixty miles south of the Passing Loop was the point where the USSR, China and Mongolia touched borders.

Though we were surrounded by rocky, treeless hills, there was a forest thirty miles north of our garrison where we would go hunting. About nine miles away was a small river where we would fish for carp. For more serious fishing, we would travel a distance of twenty miles to the larger Onon River.

The climate was continental to the extreme. The winters were long, with minimum temperatures of -60°C. The locals liked to joke: "Ten months of winter, and the rest is summer, summer, summer." The summers were short with sharp variations in temperature – which, in a single day, could fluctuate from +32°C at noon to +8°C at midnight. On the other hand, it was sunnier than Sochi, with very little precipitation. Any snowfall was blown about with sand by the wind. The winds were strong, and sandstorms were common.

Our garrison had its own power station, which was fueled first by wood and later by solar power, but fuel was not really the issue. The amount of electricity we received depended on how drunk the electricians were at any given time. When they were very drunk, we would all burn kerosene lamps.

The officers' club had its own generator and even a movie projector – but they were always showing three-year-old films we had already seen on leave. The only forms of recreation left to us were drinking, sex, and solitaire; fishing and hunting in the summer. The long winter nights, coupled with the periodic absence of electricity, significantly raised the garrisons' demand for condoms. If someone forgot to stock up on condoms in Chita, they would wash used ones and hang them by the stove to dry, just like underwear. The frequent deficit of condoms led to multiple abortions.

Now that the reader has at least a working knowledge of our setup, I will get to the heart of the matter: aviation. The bitter frosts meant that we were issued with fur clothing and shoes. After studying the flight zone within a two-hundred-mile radius, we passed our navigation exams, and began to fly the Yak-9 during the day, and a little later, the Po-2 ("corncob") at night. You don't have to be a pilot to imagine the closed, but not hermetically sealed cockpit of the Yak-9, where the temperature was the same as that of the surrounding air. Now imagine yourself in the open cockpit of the Po-2, with only a bit of plexiglass in front of you, and then in addition to the normal temperature, imagine the icy vortex of air during takeoff and landing. If it hadn't been for our fur masks, with openings for the eyes, nose, and mouth, we could hardly have survived the cold. Our eyes were protected by goggles. The openings around our noses and mouths would frost over, before freezing outright. We couldn't touch the controls with our bare hands, or else our skin would stick to the metal surface. It was possible to work only in fur gloves or mittens, which was very awkward, especially for the technical crew, who often suffered from frostbite.

My fellow graduates and I had only just begun to get a taste for pilot work when we received a summons from the regimental commander, who offered us the opportunity of transferring to the Zhukovsky Air Force Engineering Academy. We flatly refused. After all, if we had wanted to do ground work, we wouldn't have bothered learning to fly. The commander tried to fool us, saying that we would be able to work as test pilots. But we were well aware that only sons of high-ranking officials ever became test pilots.

My wife arrived in January 1950. Boris moved into a single room, while we remained in the thirty-foot room he and I had shared. We had a table, a bed, two nightstands, and four stools, two suitcases full of linen and a few pieces of china. Thus, our family life began. We started with practically nothing but were proud that we managed to do without help from our families – who in any case had their own problems to deal with. As there were no jobs for most officers' wives, garrison women mostly took care of the children and did the housekeeping. An important part of the latter was feeding the stove with fuel, which in our case was coal. Alya mastered this art completely, became a proficient stoker, and learned to clean the chimneys herself by taking apart and reassembling the brickwork.

Not far from our house (and not only ours), there was a curious attraction. Near the aforementioned garbage heap stood a public, one-hole toilet, constructed from the fuselage of an IL-2 fighter plane. There was never a line to get in there. The entrance faced away from the street, toward the field, but there was no door. So you can imagine how cozy it was in below-zero temperatures and the possible risks of disease. Another problem was that you had to be constantly vigilant. To prevent unwelcome disturbances, the toilet occupant would, at the sound of approaching footsteps, begin to whistle or sing their favorite melody, which would soon become familiar to all the building's inhabitants. Just as every radio tower has its own call signs, everyone who lived in our building had his or her own melody. Mine was:

> Oh, the roads, the dust and fog,
> Cold and fear, and the steppe grass...[1]

In September 1951, our first daughter was born. We called her Elizaveta in memory of my mother, and her birth was celebrated by the entire squadron.

---

[1]   A song by Novikov from the Second World War era.

Our neighbor put his eighty-square-foot room at our disposal for the evening. I made a trip to Chita and brought back a suitcase full of decent beverages and (for that time) more or less decent food. After the feast was over, we started a collective wrestling match. It was one of my youthful weaknesses, the tendency to wrestle when drunk.

In our own tiny room, we had to prepare food, do laundry, and bathe our daughter. At first, we didn't even have a bed or cot for her. She slept in an open suitcase on two stools. When Liza became a toddler, we often had to keep her from walking on the floor, as our red hot stove meant there was a huge discrepancy in temperature between ceiling (+30°C) and floor (+7°C). In the early hours of the morning, the temperature would drop, and the process of feeding the stove would begin. Whenever we opened the door, the room would fill with steam, as the corridor was totally unheated. Only a year later would we be given a larger room on the second floor with a heated corridor and a warmer floor.

When our second daughter Yuliya (named after my father) was born in April 1955, we were given two rooms of eighty and thirty square feet on the second floor.

We were not spoiled with luxurious living conditions, and I (unlike some) never asked for our conditions to be improved. My pilot work came first, and everything else took a back seat. Care for subordinates was a basic duty of officers at all levels of command. In this instance, by improving a subordinate's living conditions, an officer was only fulfilling his duty. There were some pilots who would fall "sick" to get out of flying or standing watch. Some wanted out of the air force entirely, and used alcoholism as an expedient. Logically, these pilots received the least attention and care.

There was one pilot in our regiment, Pyotr Belyakov, who wanted to leave the service. Back then, however, they didn't let people off just like that. What extremes did he not go to, in order to accomplish his goal? He discharged flares through the window panes in his room, came to the aerodrome staggering from inebriation, and so on. He put an end to his aviation career once and for all after lying down in a puddle next near the "Zabaykalets" restaurant in Chita, with a cigarette in his mouth, moving his arms and legs to imitate a steamboat. After being discharged, he worked as a trolleybus driver in Moscow.

Our deputy squadron commander Semyonov was an excellent pilot. His instincts were unparalleled... when it came to finding the nearest reservoir of vodka. I never saw him sober, not even in the cockpit. I doubt he ever had a dry day. Semyonov was short and of slight build. You could often see his wife – an amazon of a woman – dragging him home under one arm. He was soon discharged from the air force.

There was one regimental commander, Major Teryoshkin, who after a heavy bout of drinking fell asleep and choked on his own vomit.

Drinking was such an integral part of life in the air force that it is impossible not to write about it. Abstaining meant being the black sheep. You would be ostracized or trampled by the rest of the herd. You could only try to drink in smaller volumes or less frequently, if you were prepared to disregard all the usual strategies, e.g., "Do you respect me?" Unfortunately, I will have to return to this theme again and again. Not only has alcohol ruined many pilots, it is also a scourge of the society at large, ruining many good people.

In our current period of perestroika, right-wing nationalists and chauvinists are accusing the Jews of all possible sins, including getting the Russian people drunk. Anyone who is even slightly acquainted with the history of the Russian state knows that Russians were partial to alcohol long before the divisions of Poland, when the Russian Empire absorbed Poland's Jewish population along with its land. As early as the late seventeenth century, Tsar Aleksey Mikhaylovich, father of Peter I, issued a very telling piece of legislation. It began with the words: "Drunkards may not be driven from taverns without causing unrest." Gorbachev was evidently unaware of this ancient wisdom, or he would have avoided a grave error. Without improving the country's economic and social conditions, he introduced a wide-ranging temperance campaign, which not only dug the economy into a deeper hole, but made millions of people hostile to any kind of reform.

In early 1951, all squadrons in our regiment began to retrain on the La-7 and La-9 planes. The La-9 was our main aircraft, but we also did instrument training on the Yak-11. The La-9 was a plane which demanded an above-average level of technical skill and particular alertness at takeoff and landing.

The La-9 had an air-cooled, two-row radial engine. Its three-blade propeller created strong reactive torque, and use of the elevators created gyroscopic torque. With the smallest lapse in attention at takeoff or landing, the plane would flip over, doing serious damage to the landing gear and outer wing sections. In this way, the regiment ruined seven planes.

I, however, managed perfectly well and the La-9 became the first aircraft with which I felt a total sense of symbiosis. A reliable motor, four 23 mm cannons – powerful equipment for that time – and a comfortable cockpit; all this has left me with fond memories of the La-9.

January 1, 1952, found us in the Far East, in the town of Ussuriysk. We were meant to pick up some La-9s which were too old for Korea and fly them home to the Seventy-Seventh Passing Loop. We hung around there for a month, got the planes, and took them for a few rides, but command revised its plan and we ultimately returned on a passenger plane.

That year, I committed the most despicable act of my whole life: I opened and read someone else's mail. But let me begin at the beginning.

In each regiment, division, etc., there was an official with the title of "special division curator." At first I thought that he was the army's own counter-espionage agent. But later, I learned that he was a KGB agent, planted in the army. And that wasn't the worst of it. These special division curators acted like they owned the place. The special division first lieutenant made it seem like he was the regimental commander's principal assistant, and perhaps this was even the case until 1953. I will call him the "curator" for short.

One day, the curator approached me and asked me to come to his office that evening in such a way that no one else would see. His dugout was located near our squadron, about three hundred yards from our house. Officers usually spent summer evenings relaxing with their wives and children on the front porch. At the appointed time, I stood up and walked very conspicuously in the direction of the curator's dugout, reasoning that if I was arrested, people would know where I had gone. But everything turned out to be much simpler than that. The curator had something else in mind.

To begin with, he questioned me about various aspects of my background before launching on a discussion of foreign spy agencies and their insidious activities (on the level of propaganda). Then, he told me to come back again in few days' time, naming a backup date just in case. When I arrived for our second meeting, the curator introduced me to a colonel who was the special division curator for the whole air force. During our conversation, they revealed that the special division had a particular interest in Yuriy Vasilyev. They suspected him of espionage and of having relatives overseas – whose existence he denied, but with whom he was nonetheless in contact. As a member of the Komsomol, as an officer, and as a patriot, I was (according to the curator) obliged to help the government uncover Vasilyev's true nature. At the end of this conversation, I agreed to cooperate with them, and they presented me with a piece of paper, which I signed "Kazbek" (the colonel had suggested I choose a pseudonym, and as a pack of Kazbek cigarettes was then lying on the table, I chose Kazbek as my pseudonym).

At that time, I had not encountered much antisemitism myself, but had heard from friends and acquaintances in Leningrad that it was gaining strength.

My first task was to discover whether or not Vasilyev did have relatives overseas. It was not difficult for me to bring up the question in conversation, as we both served in the same squadron and saw each other almost daily.

I met the regimental curator several more times and made a written declaration to the effect that, judging by the content of my conversations with Vasilyev, he did not have any relatives overseas. This finding, and my intelligence work in general, were evidently unsatisfactory to the "organs" (the secret service).

When it became clear to me that Vasilyev did not have any overseas relatives, I began to doubt the validity of the special division's suspicions. The curator could not fail to notice how annoyed I was by his orders and how reluctant I was to meet with him. I could sense that he was looking to fabricate some kind of intrigue. As they would start saying later, "Bring me a man, and I'll find a crime."

The curator suggested I intercept one of the letters Vasilyev regularly received from Moscow. My naivety and lack of experience had led me to believe that letters were not monitored in peacetime. Besides, local KGB officials could always inspect our mail at any time.

The mail was brought to our squadron early in the morning and placed on a central table. It was hardly a challenge to come downstairs fifteen minutes early and read any letter in the pile, which is exactly what I did.

At my next meeting with the curator, I declared that on the basis of the letter's contents, Vasilyev had no overseas relatives. The curator was dissatisfied with my repeated negative findings. Perhaps he had been counting on the play of imagination, or had assumed that I would slander my friend, but I was not capable of such acts. I started to become agitated, and he saw that I was fed up with his game. I offered to enlist as a volunteer in the Korean War, to which the curator flatly replied, "When the need arises, this whole division will be sent to Korea." That was the end of our meetings.

My offer was inspired not so much by my dealings with the special division, which had taken a turn for the worse, as it was by a desire to test my strength as a pilot. By now I had achieved complete mastery of all the aircraft in garrison. What is more, I had a genuine wish to help North Korea defend itself against aggression from the South. You might say that I was filled with a sense of international comradeship. In any case, I believed the official rhetoric about the Korean War that was being spread at the time.

Later, after the Doctors' Plot, I surmised that they might have been preparing something similar on various levels of the army. After all, there was a high concentration of "individuals of Jewish nationality" (as we were officially called) in ZabVO back then. A "high degree of pollution," as the more antisemitic members of command liked to express it.

Flight training progressed according to plan. We practiced interceptions, dogfights, and airstrikes. We practiced landing in unfamiliar aerodromes. During our whole time flying the La-9, we did not experience a single motor failure in the whole regiment, which would have been unthinkable on any of the Yak planes.

We soon learned that we would be retraining on jet aircraft. In Korea, our MiG-15 jets were standing off against the American F-86 Sabre. We, however, were given out-of-date Yak-17s and quickly got the hang of them after studying the construction of the plane and its engine. After three forty-minute instruction flights, we were flying independently.

The Yak-17 was a weak machine with a weak engine, developed from the Yak-3 glider. Its engine was modeled on a captured German one. And although the Yak-17 had a maximum speed of 520 miles per hour – the La-9's was less than one hundred – it had significantly less range than the La-9. The Yak-17 was equipped with only four 23 mm cannons. Without drop tanks, you could only fly for thirty minutes at medium altitude before running out of fuel. And it had another serious deficiency: before starting the jet engine, you had to start a gasoline-powered motor, which would turn the jet engine's turbine shaft. In the keenest winter frosts, we had to heat the motors and engines with lamps. The lamps hummed and smoked, while the aerodrome came to resemble a gypsy camp. The motors had to be heated constantly, or there was no chance of combat readiness. As a result, the whole technical crew looked like chimney sweeps.

Watch was kept day and night by squadrons, often in the first state of readiness – that is, sitting in their cockpits. At the first sound of the alarm, they would fly up to intercept the "enemy." There was a feeling that the position in the East was serious, that the theater of war could be expanded to include China, where Soviet air bases were also located. If China got involved, there was a possibility that nuclear weapons would be used. For this reason, we were trained to fight bomber aircraft carrying nuclear bombs.

We played guessing games as to whether or not they would give us leave that year. They did. In my case, leave involved sixty days' travel there and back, but traveling by plane allowed us to save ten days. We spent twenty-five days in the Caucasus, and the rest in Leningrad. There, we learned of the further growth of antisemitism, of dismissals from work, of students finding it difficult to get into university. You could see a note of hostility in many people's eyes that was almost animal.

When I returned to the garrison and did my first watch duty, I had my first experience of antisemitism in the barracks. At "lights out," all the soldiers got into bed, however they continued talking loudly and arguing about something. Only the hall light – a single, dim bulb – was left on. When I entered the dormitory and ordered the men to stop talking, one of the soldiers loudly pronounced the word, "Zhyd (Yid)!" In response to the question, "Who said that?" I of course met with silence. "So there are fascists in the Komsomol?" No one said a word. The silence was tense. I walked up and down the rows of cots several times. Not a word. This had been the first murmur of antisemitism from below. It would be followed by louder murmurings from above. You can imagine how all this antisemitic sludge later floated to the surface during perestroika and glasnost.

The construction of new residential quarters began. On Saturdays and Sundays, we soldiers and officers alike would participate, preparing stone for the foundations. We would use RGD grenades (Soviet fragmentation grenades) to help us with the excavations. I took two grenades home with me just in case. They lay under my bed until the doctors were officially rehabilitated, after which I discharged one of them during training with my men (they didn't teach soldiers how to use grenades in the air force), and the second in a river, making about twenty little fish fly up in the air – the only time in my life I could have been accused of poaching.

"How naive!" to think that they could only come and arrest people at night, as they had in the 1930s. As if they didn't have other ways of arresting people, even in the workplace.

Time passed without any obvious manifestations of antisemitism of the kind I had experienced from the soldiers. The rumors being spread among ordinary people and by the KGB about the government's antisemitic policies did their dirty work poisoning people's souls. Those returning from leave told stories of the situation in Moscow, Leningrad, and other cities. Sometimes I would catch such storytellers unawares. They would cut off their stories in the middle of a sentence, and switch from the Jewish question to something else. I remember when our squadron's political officer[2] Nikolay Deryabin returned from Moscow and started talking about how they were firing Jews from work and refusing to admit them to higher education. Except that when he noticed me reading a newspaper nearby, he changed his satisfied tone to one of regret, and began to explain that the situation was only temporary, and in a few months things would start to improve.

Deryabin was right: in a few months, things did start to improve. And I believed. I believed that this was all a mistake, a distortion of national politics. I believed that there would be a change for the better, a return to the international principle. I believed this until 1967.

To celebrate the new year, 1953, we held a party in the officers' club. The tables were laid, there were amateur performances, dancing. After that, we returned to daily life in the aerodrome.

Then came the moment that would decide the whole Jewish question – the Doctors' Plot. The alleged "doctor-killers" were arrested, and vigilant Soviet patriot Lidiya Timashuk was awarded the Order of Lenin. I met this news with suspicion. I did not want to believe it, but nonetheless admitted the possibility that such a crime could have been committed. It never occurred to me that the KGB could fabricate such a "plot" entirely.

Otherwise, there were no obvious changes at the garrison, and work distracted my attention from the question of Jewishness.

During that period there were several accidents and tragedies in our division. One incident revealed a change in our relationship with Mongolia.

---

2   The deputy commander for political affairs.

There was a saying: "A chicken is not a bird, Mongolia is not overseas, a hundred rubles isn't money and a hundred miles isn't a distance." That's how it was on the far side of Baikal. We would strap a machine gun to the roof of a car and drive over the border to hunt for saiga antelopes. In the winter of 1953, one of our pilots, Chugunov, lost orientation, burnt up all his fuel, and had to make an emergency landing in Mongolian territory. Without stopping to think, our deputy division commander, Hero of the Soviet Union Colonel Bashkirov, immediately boarded a Po-2 plane, crossed the border, and landed beside the battered Yak-17. After taking such a liberty, Bashkirov was demoted and Mongolia was promoted – in the sense that now it was no longer a neighboring province, but a neighboring colony, with a border that had to be taken into account.

It was with mixed feelings that I learned of the death of the leader of all times and all nations. I had never in my life said, "Long live Stalin!" or pronounced a toast to Stalin. No, I'm lying – in 1949, on his seventieth birthday, I, along with some fellow cadets in Armavir, openly drank to the leader's health in view of the patrols, and were even proud of ourselves. That was the only time.

In March 1953, I stood in formation with the rest of the regiment as we were given the news of Stalin's death. Not only the funerary music, but the whole funerary atmosphere brought tears to my eyes. On the other hand, I felt a certain lightness. It seemed that change was near at hand, especially as far as the Jewish question was concerned.

Life continued. We were issued with MiG-15 planes. With each new class of fighter jet, the power of the engine increased, as did the rate of climb and other tactical and technical factors. Correspondingly, we pilots had to be more vigilant, increase our reaction speed, and make our actions automatic. Because of an increase in g-force we were, for the first time, issued with g-suits.

However, I often flew without connecting my suit to the aircraft's system. Even in extremely high-G, when my eyes went dark and there was ringing in my earmuffs, I felt I could control the plane "with my ass," as they used to say. I acclimatized myself to oxygen hunger as well, flying without my oxygen mask. In short, I used every single training flight to sharpen my piloting technique. Eventually, I became good enough that on both day and night flights in cloudy conditions (instrument flights) the arrows of all my flight instruments stood almost frozen on the right settings. When I made my first charted night flight in cloudy conditions, monitored by the division commander (on a Uti-MiG-15), the latter was so pleased with my flying that he allowed me not only to fly at night in cloudy conditions, but also, in contravention of all the existing rules, to train other pilots in such conditions.

A brief description of the division commander: Twice-decorated Hero of the Soviet Union, Colonel Nikolay Skomarokhov shot down thirty-two German planes during the war. He loved flying himself and introduced more challenging pilot training in some parts of the division. He also had a fierce hatred for all government workers. Due to an unpleasant episode during active service, his admission to the General Staff Academy was delayed. Through a friend in the staff, he had organized for his wife to be notified of his "death" at the front. For a long time, his "widow" had even received support money for their child. One day, fifteen years later, she boarded the riverboat *Nikolay Skomarokhov* and asked the captain to explain the name's provenance. Upon learning that her husband was still alive, she immediately wrote a letter to the Ministry of Defense. By then, Skomarokhov already had a new family. He had to return all the money paid to his "widow" and received a reprimand from the Party, before finally being admitted to the academy. In the 1960s, General Skomarokhov would command the air force in Eastern Europe.

The MiG-15 had one serious fault: spin recovery was complicated and came with a significant altitude loss. For training purposes, we initially practiced spin on a two-seater plane, but this ended rather quickly after the accident rate increased. There were several occasions of unintentional entry into spin. Some successfully recovered from it, while others had to parachute out of the plane. My classmate from Armavir, Sasha Koverchenko, recovered from spin, but did not have sufficient altitude to recover from dive. He crashed into a hill at a forty-degree angle, so that afterwards his grave was almost empty.

By the way, Sasha had been an avid hunter and his main problem in life had always been to get someone to lend him a car for his next hunting expedition. His requests usually met with refusal, which was strange considering the general enthusiasm for hunting. But after Sasha's death, his coffin was followed by a whole fleet of cars. It was too bad! It happens too often in Russia that the dead are accorded more respect than the living. A characteristic example is that of the academician Andrey Sakharov (blessed be his memory).

Training resumed two days later. We continued our combat readiness course. One morning, I was flying to air combat training with another pilot when I heard over the radio that there had been a fire on the aircraft of my wing commander, Lyosha Movchan. As I was approaching the aerodrome, I saw a column of fire. There was no sign of a parachute. Everyone thought that he had been killed. In ten minutes' time, the telephone rang: "Please come and collect your pilot, alive and unharmed." What a relief! What had happened was the following: The fire had started in the engine compartment. The fire extinguishing system was little help. Lyosha had decided to land. Flying over the neighboring aerodrome at a height of one thousand feet – the minimum height for ejection from a MiG-15 – he had noticed that the elevator control wasn't working (the tie rods had melted). Lyosha immediately ejected from the plane. The dynamic impact (when the parachute filled with air) and landing happened simultaneously. He landed on the neighboring aerodrome, next to a parking lot for IL-10 planes. Lyosha was the only pilot in the regiment who actually enjoyed parachute jumps, and this is what saved him. He had made around thirty jumps, when you could be exempted from parachute practice with only five jumps. Lyosha always jumped at the first opportunity and was a natural parachutist. This time, without waiting for his parachute to open automatically, he yanked on the ring without wasting a millisecond.

I made my seventh jump from an An-2 plane. There were ten pilots in the plane, all of whom were doing jump practice. We had only just exited the plane when the ragged wind began to blow stronger and we were carried toward the refuse pile of a scrap metal processing facility. One pilot broke both legs, another broke one leg, and the rest got away with bruises and deep cuts. I made a double somersault, during which I split my lip and hit my head hard. After that I made one more parachute jump, but that eighth jump was to be my last.

I joined the Party in December 1953 and was soon made secretary of my squadron's Komsomol organization. We made an attempt to hold alternative elections to the Komsomol bureau, but the political officer forbade it. Out of the five elected members, all five had been chosen in advance.

A word about the regimental political officer. During my service in the Transbaikal Region, the regiment went through three political officers. Lieutenant Colonel Ignatyev arrived from Germany under reprimand, which means that his regiment suffered more losses from drinking than from doing battle with the Germans. In our regiment he generally organized Komsomol and Party meetings, but his most significant initiative was to make us subscribe to voluntary (but really compulsory) government loans. In a speech before the regiment, he encouraged us to pledge 150–200 percent of our monthly wages, and, to set an example, was the first to pledge 200 percent. That night, anyone who had refused was called up and made to pledge. Flights were even temporarily halted once for this reason. After the pledge drive was over, Ignatyev decreased his own pledge to 100 percent and took the forms to the accounts department.

Ignatyev was replaced by Major Lyashko, who during his tenure as political officer placed the greatest emphasis on the moral purity of communists and Komsomol members. Lyashko delivered lectures on this theme and liked to give moral exhortations, especially to bachelors who often changed their girlfriends. Major Lyashko was discharged from the army after he sent his completely healthy wife to a mental hospital, and turned his own apartment into a brothel.

The third political officer was so colorless that I don't even remember his name. He could rarely be found in human company. More often, he sat in his office, sorting through paperwork. He was similar in appearance to Nikita Khrushchev.

You never saw any of the three in the cockpit of a plane, so they could hardly serve as an example for the men at the garrison. In general, the authority of the political officers was low.

In the staff building, there was a library of secret literature. Officers were allowed to reserve a book and read it at a table in the library itself. Few of us had any desire to go there – it mostly attracted members of command staff. In this library, I learned much about the testing of nuclear and thermonuclear weapons. The library was also the place where I became aware of what was really happening in the Korean War. From that time on, I began to read between the lines of Soviet newspapers, and would perfect this technique over the ensuing fifteen years.

Although we had many flight days, the yearly norm of fifty hours of flight per pilot was miserly. It was later increased to seventy hours per year. The aim was evidently to economize on fuel and ammunition, to extend the service life of the planes, and so on. They tried to compensate for quality with quantity – that is, there was a large number of planes and pilots – but training was sorely lacking. Good training would have required us to fly two or three times more than we did, and to practice shooting, especially aerial targets. We were trained on the ground at the aerodrome more often than in the air.

In addition, much depended on the regiment commander and the division. We would often come out to the aerodrome and learn that Cherkashin wasn't in the mood to fly, and after a short game of "boom" or "no boom," we would taxi back to the hardstand.

Lieutenant Colonel Cherkashin was a good person. Even if he could sometimes be caught swearing, he would always stop in time, and he never held a grudge. He had left school after fourth grade and did not mince his words. "The devil's democrat" was the mildest of his large array of abusive epithets. When Cherkashin surveyed the officers' quarters and found dirt in the kitchen or in the corridor, he would immediately begin berating the mistress of the house, "I have a mind to tear your skirt off and beat you with a damn broom, then you might learn to be tidy." He scolded soldiers and officers in the same way, before the whole regiment.

One time he went to the garrison store and requested a bar of chocolate for his son.

The storekeeper replied, "Ilya Afanasyevich, maybe you'd like two chocolate bars? After all, you have two sons."

"The older one [fifteen years old] needs a girl by now [he used a ruder word], not a chocolate bar."

There were officers' wives standing in line behind him, but that did not bother Lieutenant Colonel Cherkashin. And that was our commander. The soldiers gave him the nickname "Chapaev." Everyone accepted him as he was, as a given – even with a smile. No one complained about him; everyone understood what his upbringing had been and forgave the instances of meanness and rudeness.

During the war he had shot down a few German planes, for which he had been rewarded with medals. He had also shot down one of our own planes. When we were on a mission in the Far East, Cherkashin told us how it had happened. I reproduce the story in brief:

In 1943, his regiment (on Yaks) had been accompanying a large group of bombers on a mission. Suddenly, someone had screamed over the radio, "You're being attacked by Focke Wulfs from behind!" Cherkashin jerked around sharply and hit one of them, which immediately went down. Upon his return to the aerodrome, they wanted to make him a Hero of the Soviet Union for battering the German plane. But it soon came to light that the plane had been a Soviet La-5, which looked similar to a Focke Wulf. His division had not seen La-5s before, which had only appeared during the Battle of Stalingrad. It was a good thing that the La-5 pilot had managed to make a forced landing unharmed, and the affair was forgotten.

When he flew with the regiment, Cherkashin was always the first to take off and would soar into the distance as the rest of the regiment tried to catch up with their fierce commander. His orders over the radio were usually interspersed with profanities, for which he had been reprimanded several times by the air force commander. But his type was fairly common among commanders of the post-war period until academy-educated officers started coming up the ranks.

Time flies when you're absorbed in your work. We spent our next leave in the Caucasus and Leningrad. As we had limited opportunities to spend money at the garrison, we were always able to set aside a large part of it for leave. Apart from that, each of us would take loans from our friends before setting off from base.

After the establishment of trade relations with the People's Republic of China, Chinese fruit and other groceries appeared in our garrison store. We also used the dining carriage of the Moscow-Beijing express as a source of provisions. This is how we did it: a friend and I would drive (on my Izh-49 motorbike) to the railway station before ours, as the courier train didn't stop at the passing loop. He would climb into the dining carriage, and – while I drove fifteen miles to the next station – would buy all the necessary delicacies. Or at least, they seemed like delicacies to us.

In April 1955, my second daughter, Yuliya, was born. There was a change in my service life too: I was promoted to the rank of wing commander (a "wing" consists of four fighter planes).

In early October, the regimental commander summoned me and suggested I take a holiday in the Caucasus – or he would not give me leave until December. It seemed there was no choice.

The Red Grove sanatorium, in the mountains, about fifty miles from Sochi, was housed in a royal hunting lodge. After breakfast, the other officers and I would go to the solarium, where we would sunbathe and play cards.

After cards, we would go to the "Blue Danube" lounge and order bitter wine (there was no other) and have lunch. Then there would be more cards in a pagoda after lunch, followed by cards in the main building in the evening. They confiscated all the officers' documents on arrival to stop us from leaving early. And so we spent three weeks of forced holiday, not even allowed to go to Sochi, as all transport belonged to the sanatorium. All things come to an end, however, and we at last got free of this comfortable prison and returned to the garrison.

One day, they gathered all the pilots from both regiments and showed us a secret film about important tests that had been done in the Urals in 1954. The film showed the rifle corps taking up a defensive position. Dugouts, foxholes, trenches. Technical equipment was hidden in gun emplacements.

About five to ten miles out from the position was a large chalk circle with a cross in the center – an atomic bomb target. They demonstrated how they towed the bomb to the aircraft, accompanied by an escort of officers. The atomic bomb was carried by a Tu-4 plane, which was a copy of the American B-29. Around the chalk circle at various distances from the center, they put up various structures and positioned military equipment and domestic animals. Then, the tests began. Groups of IL-28 bombers struck their targets with ordinary bombs. Then, the Tu-4 dropped an atomic bomb of twenty kilotons. Fifteen minutes later, a parachute unit landed in the epicenter, and the rifle corps advanced toward the epicenter. All of these people were wearing protective suits and footwear and had their faces covered with gas masks. The corps units moved around in cars and armored vehicles.

We were later told, though it was not shown in the film, that a squadron on MiG planes had flown through the mushroom cloud, though the squadron commander had diverted his course, unable to take it. For this, he had been demoted and discharged from the army. After the tests ended, they began to deactivate troops and equipment. Nothing was shown or said of the consequences. But it is easy to imagine, especially after the Chernobyl disaster, the scale of the radiation poisoning and the fate of the participants.

In the spring, we were given brand new MiG-17s. The planes arrived in containers straight from the factory in Komsomolsk-on-Amur. The MiG-17 had improved tactical and technical features. The sweep angle of its wings had been increased to forty-five degrees, which improved its aerodynamic qualities, and it had a maximum speed of seven hundred miles per hour. After all the planes were unloaded and inventoried, we immediately began to fly.

In 1956, the Twentieth Congress of the Communist Party of the Soviet Union took place, which unmasked Stalin's cult of personality and his crimes. The materials that emerged opened people's eyes and made us reevaluate a great number of things. They also made us hopeful that life might change for the better on many levels of Soviet society.

How could one forget the words of Lenin, quoted in Bertram Wolfe's book, *Lenin and the Twentieth Century*: "For every hundred Bolsheviks, seventy are idiots, twenty-nine are crooks, and only one is a true socialist."

On October 4, 1956, Soviet troops entered Hungary to suppress the revolution. We could learn of the events in Hungary only through official (untrue) sources and from rumors people had heard on leave. At that time, the feeling of protest that would be present in 1968 had not yet taken hold, but there was an unpleasant aftertaste nonetheless.

I myself paid more attention to the Suez Crisis, and was upset by the rudeness of our government's "Note to Israel," in contrast to its correspondence with England and France. The USSR's attitude to smaller countries and ethnic minorities gave a good understanding of its political culture.

I was promoted to the rank of captain. A word about my professional ambition. There is a popular Russian proverb: "It's a lousy soldier who doesn't dream of becoming a general." I think that I was a good soldier, at least by peacetime standards. But I had a realistic sense of the opportunities available to me, not to mention my personality and other qualifications, and therefore did not dream of becoming a general. In fact, not only did I not dream of becoming a general, I had no desire to become one. After the war, and in the 1950s more specifically, those elevated to the rank of general were, among other things, graduates of a military academy. I had refused two offers to study at an academy. The first I have already described, and the second I will describe below.

If internationalism had been going strong in the 1920s and 1930s, the years following the Second World War saw an expansion of chauvinist and antisemitic attitudes, not only among ordinary people, but also in government policy. The rulers of our country stoked the fire of antisemitism so vigorously that they came close to inciting pogroms.

Even Lenin once wrote that whenever the reactionary faction found itself in a difficult position, it always pulled out its trump card – the Jewish question. Higher and mid-level government divisions cleansed themselves of ethnic "pollution." In other arenas, both social and economic, the glass ceiling was gradually lowered, and many Jews found themselves unable to rise beyond lower-level (sometimes mid-level) deputy or, in the case of academia, co-author.

This was how I assessed the opportunities available to me: the best I could hope for was deputy regimental commander, or divisional piloting technique inspector. No higher, although I could possibly have become a political officer of higher rank, since anyone who knew me or took any interest in my affairs were well aware that I could never allow myself to sink as low as the three aforementioned political officers.

Now for my second brush with military academy. One day, I was summoned to staff headquarters and read a telegram, which contained a personal offer to study at the Lenin Political Academy in Moscow. I immediately refused, arguing that political work would prevent me from flying. They tried to appease me by saying that the question of mandatory pilot training for regimental political officers and divisional political directors was currently under review. However, I stood my ground and would not give in.

The main reason for my refusal was the culture of dishonesty I had already got a sense of, not only from our political education, but from print media as well. I could never lie to soldiers and officers – that is, think one thing and teach them the opposite. What Ignatyev or Lyashko permitted themselves, I simply was not capable of. And in my case, it wouldn't be Dymshits the political officer who was lying, but Dymshits the Jew. The Jews would be lying.

Pre-revolutionary Russia was fairly unambiguous on the national question, and Stalin's tenure saw a revival of imperial politics based on the principle of divide and conquer. Russia may have let Kutuzov hand Moscow over to the French in 1812, but they would have never let Barclay de Tolly do the same. What Russia allowed the likes of Voroshilov, Budenny, and Timoshenko during the Second World War, no Jew would have ever been allowed, or even forgiven.

And so, due to the prevailing Soviet attitudes, I limited my own ambitions to divisional piloting technique inspector. Such a position would allow me practically unlimited flying time in all three regiments of the division and mostly exempt me from having to indoctrinate subordinates, which was hard to escape at any level of command, let alone in the political division.

After some time as a wing commander, I turned down an offer to become deputy squadron political officer. In this case I could not appeal to my desire to fly, as the squadron political officer spent as much time in the air as anyone else. If I had named the real reason for my refusal, I would at the very least have been thrown out of the Party and of aviation in general. Hiding one's true opinions was common among those who occupied any sort of position in that system.

After my refusal, the division political officer, Colonel Smolkov, began to view me with displeasure, and I soon found myself in a meeting with a member of the air force military council. With my personal file on the table before him, he devoted particular attention to the question of whether I had relatives overseas, and underlined something in red pencil.

Almost every year, each officer received a written evaluation from his immediate superior, which the officer would sign after being made aware of its contents. That year, "Likes to seek the truth" was listed among my negative qualities, however they forgot to put the word *truth* in quotation marks.

What could have been the reason for such an evaluation? In the first place, the speech I had made at a party meeting against excessive caution in pilot training. Combat readiness exercises had recently been simplified. It was bad enough that we had so little flight time per year. How could they neglect to teach us essential elements of important exercises?

In the second place, my refusal to sing in the choir. The regimental commander had decided to shock the whole army and create a pilot choir with mandatory participation. I duly arrived at choir practice, took my place in the first row, and demonstratively stood there with my mouth shut. Having obeyed the order to show up, I exercised my right to remain silent – appealing to our oath and code of conduct, as well as the fact that I was tone deaf, had no voice, and hated singing.

When the deputy commander of the 350th Regiment was transferred to the 22nd Regiment, he managed to get me transferred as well. The transfer meant little more than a change of immediate colleagues. Both regiments shared the same base, met daily in the mess hall and knew each other well. My place of employment moved less than half a mile away. We were flying the same MiG-17s. So, the move was quite seamless, and I started work immediately.

In a few months, a committee on combat readiness arrived from Moscow to inspect us. One of the committee members, a colonel, was also a piloting technique inspector. I don't know how to explain such special attention, but after inspecting the regiment's combat readiness, the commission inspected my wing, and then me personally, in all aspects of individual pilot training. The colonel tested my instrument flight and aerobatics skills, followed by my skill in shooting land and aerial targets. In all these categories, he awarded me five out of five. I hit the land target nineteen times out of twenty (the average is ten). In short, the inspector was satisfied, and even showed us how to do a double loop on the Uti-MiG-15, which at that time was usually only done in the parade division.

My workload increased unexpectedly after the deputy squadron commander stopped coming to work. It seemed that he was systematically "ill." In fact, he was down with a bout of drinking that lasted the whole year, until his discharge from the army. It fell to me to carry out his responsibilities, planning all the squadron's flights and flying with the squadron as an instructor.

If I had managed to avoid political work in the capacity of political officer, I could not refuse to act as squadron Party secretary, an elected position. The monthly Party meetings were compulsory, though most of them were conducted for appearance's sake. I did, however, manage to shorten the endlessly repetitive discussions by a few minutes for each year of my tenure.

My squadron commander, Konstantin Kolyshkin, put my name forward twice for the position of deputy squadron commander, but... I would discover why he failed to get me appointed only later, when we were flying two MiG-7s to be serviced in Chita and stopped to have lunch at a local restaurant. After a few drinks, Kolyshkin became talkative. He told me that the regimental commander, Colonel Shatalov, had flatly refused to appoint me, and moreover declared, "If Dymshits weren't a Jew, I would give him your job, but as it is, he'll be promoted only over my dead body."

I had heard rumors before of Shatalov's pathological antisemitism, and though I had never seen any evidence of it before, here was clear proof.

Shatalov was twelve to fifteen years older than me, and of frail constitution. His nervous system was shattered. Whenever he got wind of any kind of emergency, he would immediately lose consciousness and blood would start coming out of his nose. Shatalov once flew with me on an Uti-MiG-15 to assess my aerobatics skills. (Every pilot was assessed by a senior member of command at some time or other, depending on his rank.) In this situation, there were two ways to perform aerobatics maneuvers: smoothly, with moderate g-force, or else at the limit of the pilot's and the plane's physical capacity, to the point of blackout and wing deformation. During this flight, I got some of my own back for his antisemitism, flying with the kind of g-force that makes your eyes go dark, your face freeze in a grimace, and your body press into its seat with seven or eight times normal weight. When I parked the plane after the flight, Shatalov remained in the cockpit for another three minutes, unable to regulate his breathing. When he eventually climbed out, he was white as a sheet, and could barely stand on his feet. "Comrade Colonel (were we seriously comrades?!), allow me to receive my results!" I asked, according to protocol. He silently trudged back to the command point and put a "B" in my flight book. I think something might have got through to him.

Autumn of 1957 was upon us. My thirtieth birthday had already been and gone. I was beginning to feel my age a little, but a short rest after each flight generally brought me back to normal. And by a short rest, I mean two hours or so.

In October 1957, command offered to send me to Taganrog for an advanced tactical course in air combat. That was another matter – no politics there. So I immediately agreed. After taking my wife and children back to Leningrad, I continued on to Taganrog alone.

Taganrog is a large industrial city in Rostov province, on the shore of the Sea of Azov. The town's main attractions were Chekhov's little house, the Peter I monument, and an abundance of pretty girls. There was a local myth that when Peter I built a garrison here, he also supplied the soldiers with a selection of pretty girls from all over Russia. The soldiers married, settled down in Taganrog, and established a sense of pedigree which would be passed from generation to generation. Two hundred and fifty years later, or thereabouts, the town's main street on Saturdays and Sundays was a parade of beauties. After three months, my wife and children arrived and we moved into a rental apartment.

The course itself was intensive and at a high professional level. Such year-long courses were administered by the air force academy. We were indoors until spring, mastering about fifteen different subjects. We worked through land and air tactics at different scales, up to and including division level.

In spring we began our flight training. I flew over the sea for the first time, and over Donbass, which was obscured by a dome of smoke, flame, and soot.

We flew to Novocherkassk, where I became aware of the workers' hatred for Soviet officers. We landed near Krasnodar, where a group of Syrian pilots was in training. Our instructors told us stories of their poor level of preparation and strong inclination to prayer.

The possibility of leisure presented itself in Taganrog. The city was home to the cozy Chekhov Drama Theater, a few cinemas, a cultural center, and a nice park. There was even a beach on the Sea of Azov, but the water was very dirty.

Also in Taganrog, I learned of the death of my former flight school classmate, Agaryshev. In a state of drunkenness, he had argued with a friend, claiming that he'd knock the latter's tail off in a dogfight. The next day, after a troubled sleep, Agaryshev and his friend set off for the aerial combat zone. The friend, who had fought in Korea, began with a flip followed by a half-roll. Agaryshev couldn't react in time and crashed to the ground.

I made the acquaintance of one man who had taken down a friendly aircraft in the Far East. Oleg (not his real name) had been sitting in the cockpit on alert. At the sound of an alarm, he was commanded to intercept an aerial target. Oleg opened fire from three cannons and hit the "enemy" craft. Pleased with his success, he returned to the aerodrome, but forgot to flip his weapons deactivation switch. Steering the plane to a stop, he unintentionally discharged one of the cannons, blowing off the smokestack off a brick factory on the other side of the aerodrome. But that was nothing. Oleg's colleagues congratulated him in advance on what they assumed would be an Order of the Red Banner and ten thousand rubles for downing an enemy plane. But the enemy plane turned out to be a jet seaplane from a beryllium extraction plant, which no one at the base had seen before, and which had been flying without permission. All three of its crew members had died. Oleg was demoted. He went completely bald and mostly silent from anxiety.

At the end of the academic year, I passed my state exams with the highest grades in all theoretical and practical subjects, and received a congratulatory certificate.

Toward the end of 1958, I returned to the Seventy-Seventh Passing Loop, which had recently been renamed Bezrechnaya village. Not long before my return, the senior navigator of the neighboring regiment had died in a crash, and the new regimental commander, Colonel Nikolayev, was searching for an appropriate replacement. Shatalov was on leave at that time, and his deputies suggested that Nikolayev consider me. Nikolayev then invited me to an interview, and suggested I choose between two positions: squadron commander or regimental senior navigator. After taking a day to think and consult my colleagues, I gave Colonel Nikolayev my answer. A few days later, I embarked upon my new duties as senior navigator of the 350th Regiment. Afterwards I was told that when Shatalov returned from leave he was beside himself with anger and resentment that I had managed to slip through his antisemitic clutches. He was soon given an honorable discharge for reasons of poor health, and perhaps I had a role to play in that.

Living and working among antisemitic people has one positive side effect: antisemitism makes you more competitive. If you want any job that hasn't already been closed to you by secret instruction or by someone like Shatalov standing in the way, you have to be the best at whatever it is you do. You have to really stand out from the crowd.

A small clarification about the position of senior regimental navigator. In aviation, there are people whose professional specialty is navigation. These specialist navigators are most often found on bombers or transport aircraft in military aviation, and on passenger liners in civilian aviation. A fighter pilot, flying a one-seater plane, performs the navigator's function himself.

But there are also fighter pilots who perform the duty of navigator. In this case, the navigator flies just like all the other pilots, but on top of that he has a whole pile of responsibilities. The senior regimental navigator is responsible for the navigational training of the whole flight corps, conducting training and assessment on land and in the air. Furthermore, the senior navigator is responsible for the navigational apparatus on board each aircraft as well as for the air control work conducted by the CP (command point). The workload was considerable, but the work itself was interesting and enabled me to fly more often as an instructor. I don't know about these days, but back then there was a saying: "The more you fly, the longer you fly."

I tried to fulfil my new responsibilities as expediently as possible. To become acquainted with all the new aspects of the job, I had to work a twelve-hour day, but in general things were going well. In the first eight months of 1959, I spent 159 hours in the air, in contrast to a yearly regimental average of seventy hours. That's the kind of air time it takes to train a pilot properly.

In autumn of 1959 my fate took a sharp turn. The Ministry of Defense had an official regulation limiting service in the Transbaikal region to five years, after which there should be a change of posting. (However, this regulation was rarely carried out, as most officers were sent to the region in punishment for some offense.) So it was that, after ten years of service, I was reassigned to the North Caucasus Military District.

I was sad to be leaving the regiment where I had begun my Siberian service. I was used to the people there and had a good working relationship with the commander. Colonel Nikolayev tried to dissuade me, seducing me with the possibility of becoming deputy squadron commander. He also revealed that the regiment would soon be moving to a base near Irkutsk, where work and leisure conditions would be much better. We took a joint trip there two days later. The aerodrome, near Belaya railway station, really was first class. The living quarters were fitted out with modern conveniences, including television. As there was no satellite television at that time, we watched the local Irkutsk channel. All around were forests and rivers – that is, hunting and fishing.

But I wanted to convince myself that the time of state-sponsored antisemitism had passed. For this reason, I agreed to the transfer to the village of Zimovniki in Rostov province. I flew right up until the final hour before going straight from the aerodrome to change clothes, gather my wife and children, and board the train.

In 1960, once I had the measure of the regiment and its command, I would regret my decision. But by then it was too late. As they say in such cases, "Everything you don't do is for the best." And it was true. In 1961, the regiment that I had left (one of the country's best air defense regiments) would be disbanded in disgrace for mass alcoholism and fighting in the ranks. But I would only find out what had happened two years later.

For the time being, I was in Zimovniki. Rain. Sticky mud. The garrison was about two miles from the rail station. I phoned the regiment and asked them to send a car, but it got stuck along the way. We eventually got there, with great difficulty, on a tow truck. There were wrecked cars lying in ditches on either side of the road. We were lucky. It was often impossible to get by without a tractor.

Here was the garrison. We were given two rooms to live in. Here, we had running water – whereas in Siberia we had hauled it in buckets. There was even an indoor bath, but we weren't allowed to use it, as the pipes had been laid near the building and there was no drainage system.

There had been a tragedy in the regiment one month before my arrival: a young pilot had crashed while flying at night. The regiment and squadron commanders responsible had been removed from their positions. This set fear upon the administration and led to a decrease in flying hours, which had already been low. This was a second order regiment, which meant that its intake consisted mostly of recent flight school graduates, who were then re-posted to other regiments after an initial period of training. In November 1959, I received the new rank of major.

My relationship with command got off to a bad start, for one because of the substandard accommodation, and later because of their reluctance to fly. Only toward spring did I get into a normal rhythm. But I hadn't flown twenty-five hours when I was offered another position in Astrakhan, with the opportunity to fly the Su-7, a new model of aircraft. I accepted, and was supposed to fly over in a few days for a preliminary meeting.

But suddenly all flights were cancelled, and according to a new law which decreased the size of the armed forces by 1,200,000 people, half of aviation was made redundant. MiG-15s were sent for reprocessing as winged missiles with half a ton of explosives. Khrushchev was placing his emphasis on missiles and atomic submarines. But in the wars that were being fought closer to home, aviation was necessary. In Vietnam, for instance, American aviation was completely dominating the field. Any number of Soviet surface-to-air missiles couldn't stop the mass bombings. Our anti-aircraft missiles paled in comparison to American electronic equipment.

Our regiment was one of those destined for demobilization. It had deserved that fate. Most of its young pilots were transferred to other bases and the rest were discharged. Soon only the command was left, whose future was to be decided by a commission from Moscow. We five remaining senior officers decided to put aside our former disagreements and take a breather. We went fishing and into town, we swam and sunbathed. We spent our evenings around a table outside, playing cards and discussing various issues. In June, the regimental party boss came back from a congress with details of the Powers incident. Even before Powers, American intelligence planes had penetrated Soviet airspace fairly often. Some of them went down over the sea, that is, they were hit over neutral waters. But our fighter planes (until the MiG-21 was developed) were unable to hit the American U-2. The maximum altitude of the MiG-19 was one mile lower than that of the U-2.

On May 1, 1960, Powers took to the sky above Pakistan with the aim of photographing intercontinental ballistic missiles in the Ural region. Soviet anti-aircraft radar intercepted the U-2, and several fighter units were deployed, but without result. A wing of MiG-19s was deployed near Sverdlovsk, but it could only fly under the U-2, and was powerless to take action. As the U-2 drew closer to an area of anti-aircraft missile activity, the fighter planes were given the command to return to base. Three planes veered out of formation and turned back, while a fourth remained beneath the U-2, trying to reach it. When the air is atmospheric, clean, and uncharged, it creates a false impression of distance. It seems that your goal is right in front of you, even if it is a mile off. You only have to pull the lever all the way toward you and you're down to minimum speed. In a few minutes, you're losing height, the aircraft becomes unstable, and you've gone into tailspin, dropping from a height of four or five miles.

The remaining MiG-19 pilot was ordered to retreat twice more, but he was either unreasonably stubborn, or after a medal and the cash reward that came with it. He did not obey the command. The first anti-aircraft missile shattered his MiG-19 to bits, and he died instantly. The second missile missed the U-2 by a hair, exploded, and its fragments took down the plane. Powers parachuted to land. He was later swapped for a Soviet spy.

The commission arrived from Moscow: a few colonels with a general in the lead. They took up residence in the staff headquarters, surrounded themselves with a wall of paperwork, and started calling each of us up, one by one. The regimental commander Andrienko agreed to transfer to land work. The rest expressed a wish to discharge. Then my turn came. When they asked me whether or not I wanted to stay in aviation, I answered that I didn't want to serve in another regiment like the present one. After my answer was analyzed, and after I rejected the offer of becoming a squadron commander in Tikhoretskoye, the commission entered their conclusion in my file: "Does not object to demobilization."

I waited another carefree month for their final decision. Then, upon receiving my documents and a decent sum of money, I set off for Leningrad with my family, where a "trial by fire" awaited me.

And so my life in the army came to an end. In a few days I became an officer of the reserves and received a military pension for twenty-three years of service, taking into account the extra years added for air force pilots.

5 Civilian Life

1960–May 1967

My nomadic army life had come to an end. When we arrived in Leningrad, it seemed to me that we would live there permanently, to the end of our days. At that time, there was no other place I wanted to live, and Alya certainly wasn't going anywhere else. She was born in Leningrad, and her mother, two sisters, and brother were still living there.

As I explained before, my family's room had been requisitioned after my mother's death, so we had to stay with my wife's relatives. Alya's brother lived with his wife, two children, and mother in two rooms of a communal apartment. When we arrived, the five of them moved into one large room, while Alya and I and our two girls were given the thirty-square-foot room next door. It was the third such room in which I had lived.

At that time, it was mandatory to have a registered place of residence, especially in large cities. However, after the reduction of the armed forces, a former serviceman could register in Moscow, Leningrad, or Kiev only if he or his parents had residential property in that city, or if he was conscripted into the army from that city. Because I did not satisfy any of these conditions, I started making the rounds of various bureaucratic institutions. I started with a legal consultation. My lawyer advised me to give some money to the right person, "grease the palm," as they say, and the problem would be solved. However, the lawyer warned that in this case I would end up bankrupt. Since the four of us had nothing but the clothes on our backs, I was unwilling to throw away my whole pension on a bribe - not to mention the moral side of the question.

Without a registered address, I couldn't get a job. As they used to say, "Without papers, you're just a booger on a person's nose. With papers, you're a person." As I had some savings as well as my pension of ninety-six rubles per month to live on, I had the luxury of being able to solve the problem aboveboard. At some of the government departments I visited, I met former officers whose situation was similar to my own but who didn't have pensions. Such people would lose hope after a month or two and leave Leningrad.

All my efforts to convince the government officials that we had no other place to live ran up against the conditions decreed by the law. Their standard answer was, "Yes, theoretically you're right, but legally you're wrong." Two months of bureaucracy passed without result.

And then I had a piece of good luck. Another condition was added, granting registration if the parents of the applicant's spouse had residential property. We were immediately registered, after which we were put on the waiting list for an apartment of our own. According to the same set of regulations, demobilized soldiers were meant to be granted accommodation within a period of six months.

Now I had to solve the problem of work. I went first to the Leningrad office of Aeroflot, but they were only taking on reserve pilots from Leningrad Military District who had put their names down while still awaiting discharge. Next, I decided to find out if I could work at an aviation club or DOSAAF (Voluntary Society for the Cooperation of Army, Aviation, and Navy). I went to an information office and took my place in line. When my turn came, I asked for the addresses of these organizations. Behind me in line stood a dutiful citizen of about fifty. Upon hearing my request, she immediately butted in, "Don't give him those addresses, they're secret."

I replied, "Calm down, citizen! If there's a war, Leningrad will be nuclear target number two." This obviously had such a calming effect on her that she froze with her mouth open, and couldn't say another word.

I received the addresses I needed and went to the institutions in question. However, I couldn't find anything appropriate at any of them, as there was no pilot work available. Someone suggested I give speeches to youth groups about aviation, but I declined.

We could not live on my pension alone and were beginning to eat into our reserves. I had to find work quickly. At flight school I had been certified as a pilot-technician, which enabled me to get work at a factory as a radio regulator. So, I worked, and also made periodic appearances at Aeroflot, where I became a frequent visitor to the human resources department.

Our older daughter was going to school. My wife stayed at home with our younger daughter. I went to work, but I also needed a way of occupying my spare time. Many demobilized officers on a pension spent their free hours drinking, playing cards and dominoes, and visiting prostitutes, but that held no appeal for me. The entrance exams had finished at all the universities except for Leningrad Agricultural Institute. An old school friend of mine worked at the institute and suggested I should take a course there. I submitted a part-time application to the department of agriculture electrification. After studying for two months, I passed the entrance exams. Though I had no real desire to study or to earn a diploma, I had hopes of eventually finding work as a pilot and decided to bide my time by working and studying in parallel.

Five-and-a-half months after our arrival in Leningrad, we were given a two-room apartment of about one hundred square feet in one of the new, Khrushchev-era buildings. Such an apartment was beyond the wildest dreams of a Soviet family like ours. We bought furniture and all the other household goods we needed. You could say that our family was settled.

In February 1961, I made yet another appearance at the Aeroflot human resources department. Kotrekhov, the human resources manager, told me that I could either do ground work at the Leningrad airport, or go to Murmansk, Arkhangelsk, or Uzbekistan and work immediately as a pilot. I said I would give my answer in two days' time. On my way out of the office, I met and struck up a conversation with an Aeroflot pilot, who advised me not to go anywhere, but rather invite Kotrekhov to lunch, get him blind drunk, then give him two or three hundred rubles, and I would be guaranteed a pilot job in Leningrad. The same advice as I had been given about registration. After the army, all this seemed foreign and unpleasant.

In two days' time I came to Kotrekhov's office again, and asked, "If I go to Uzbekistan, when and on what condition will you find me a job in Leningrad, since my family is here?"

"When you become captain of an aircraft," he answered.

So I left my job at the factory and bought a plane ticket. In early April 1961, I flew to Tashkent, Uzbekistan. My flight landed in the evening. I looked around the city center, but as there were no available rooms in any of the hotels I had to go back to the airport, where I slept on a folding bed. In the morning I set out for Aeroflot's Uzbekistan Bureau, where they told me to go to Bukhara.

In Bukhara there was an independent squadron of An-2s and a flight of Yak-12s, and the squadron commander Bakalo was also in charge of the airport. After acquainting himself with my resume, he signed me on as a pilot.

Once I had done the necessary paperwork, I moved into the pilots' house – a Finnish-style wooden structure – with a group of discharged officers from different parts of the USSR. In two months we set out for Tashkent, where we were taught to fly the An-2. After retraining, depending on our flight experience and training results, we were qualified as first and second pilots and distributed among various Uzbek airports. I returned to Bukhara and began to work as captain (first pilot) of an An-2 on local flights.

I wrote a letter to Kotrekhov, and received the reply, "I will transfer you once you start flying with passengers. Right now there are no openings."

In order to fly with passengers, I had to complete one hundred hours of cargo flight. The time it took to meet this requirement generally depended on how much cargo there was to transport. We – that is, my second pilot and I – decided to take initiative. We made contact with businesses and organizations who we thought might have cargo, then delivered this cargo to various towns and settlements, even to desert expeditions, or groups of workers who were drilling wells. We even made a couple of trips to Kazakhstan.

There was a geological expedition from Leningrad in Bukhara at that time, several of whose members I knew. One of them told me a sad story about a Jew who had worked with them as a chauffeur. Heavy drinking was a daily occurrence in the group; they bought vodka in crates. But there was this Jewish kid with them who didn't drink, and whose main goal was to save up for a car. The salary they offered was decent. However, the other members of the expedition constantly teased him, asking if he "respected" them, and so on. They made fun of him and humiliated him until he finally started drinking with the group. He took to drinking so hard that he became an alcoholic. Then his well-meaning colleagues unanimously decided to send him to forced rehabilitation, and off he went.

I completed my hundred hours of cargo flights, and began to make my first passenger flights. Once more, I sent a letter to Kotrekhov, and soon received the reply, "No openings. I will transfer you to Leningrad in spring."

All this time, I was flying the An-2. The plane was reliable, could hold eleven or twelve passengers, and allowed you to take off and land in tight corners.

The summer was hot in Bukhara, but because the air was so dry, it was a more bearable heat than in the Caucasus or on the Mediterranean. In the summer of 1961, we had two days when the temperature got up to 49°C, but the rest of the time it stayed around 30 to 35°C. There could be sandstorms;

but after the Siberian frosts, I was mainly focused on warming myself in the Central Asian sun.

Best of all in summer were morning and evening flights. The motor didn't overheat, and when you gained altitude, the temperature inside the plane was quite pleasant. Flying in the middle of the day, the cylinder heads and engine oil would reach maximum temperature immediately after takeoff. I had to slow down and fly at a lower altitude. Heated by both the sun and the motor, the temperature inside the plane could get up to 60ºC. We never turned the fans on because they simply circulated hot air. It was a good thing that our passengers were undemanding and accustomed to the heat. Often before a flight they would pray and thank Khrushchev for air travel. After loading their bundles, carpets, and such onto the plane, they would take their seats and you could see them melt with satisfaction. It made sense. There were places in Uzbekistan that, a year before, you could only get to by camel. Thanks be to Allah and Nikita Sergeyevich!

When we transported cargo, we would undress and fly in our underwear. With passengers, of course, we would wear our uniforms – though we were allowed to remove our ties.

I often flew along the Bukhara-Qarshi-Uchkuduk route. There were uranium mines in Uchkuduk. The miners were convicts with prison terms of over ten years. Those who worked above ground were prisoners with shorter sentences from various parts of the Soviet Union. Their only goal was to save up for an apartment, car, or dacha, and get as far away from the source of radiation as possible. You could only gain access to the mine with a special pass, and visitors were transported in a single, dedicated train carriage. The other carriages were set aside for uranium ore. Those who traveled to Uchkuduk by air also needed a special pass.

One time, I had just finished a scheduled flight to Uchkuduk when I received an additional assignment. I was told to prepare for boarding, and a police wagon drove up to the plane. Three prisoners were shunted out of the wagon, handcuffed, and brought on board. The senior officer told me that one of the prisoners was the former director of a collective farm, the second was his accountant, and the third was brigadier of the same collective farm. Together, they had robbed the farm of a million rubles, on the principle that "everything that belongs to the collective farm also belongs to me." After receiving maximum prison sentences they were being sent to the uranium mines, never to return.

The pilots' house sat on the edge of a suburban collective farm that was almost equidistant from the airport and the city of Bukhara, two miles in either direction. Cotton fields surrounded us on all sides. If you surveyed the territory from a plane, it became immediately obvious that where there was water, there was life and greenery. The rest was sand. In places you could see dried up salt lakes, which were very convenient landing pads in the desert.

The brigadier of our collective farm lived very close to us. His second wife lived across the street. Both his first and second wives each had five children, and seemed as if they weren't going to stop at five. These grimy children played all together, surrounded by a swarm of pesky flies.

The brigadier sold us fresh milk and eggs. If we let a jar of milk or water stand for any length of time, a layer of clay sediment, half an inch thick, would soon form at the bottom. We had to boil everything. Generally, we had our breakfast and lunch at the airport restaurant. After a hot, exhausting day, it was nice in the evenings to drink a piyala of hot green tea, or a bottle of dry wine from the fridge.

There was another local route from Bukhara to Tamdy. Tamdy, a small town in the sands of Kazakhstan, was famous for its herds of stray dogs. It was less than 150 miles from Bukhara, but after driving there and back by car, you had to take the motor in for repair, thanks to the sand and its destructive effects. For this reason, we usually flew there – driving over the sand only in very special cases.

After work, we would usually spend our evenings at home. Sometimes, we would go to town to see a movie, walk in the park, or visit a cafe. The younger pilots went to Bukhara much more often.

There was another pilot from Leningrad in our company, a real Don Juan. On his wedding night he managed to sleep with one of his wife's friends. I could tell endless stories of his exploits, but that's not the point. One night, he returned from town in only his underwear and socks. It seemed that after escorting his girlfriend home, he had been walking alone in a dark corner of the old city when he saw a group of four men walking toward him. They asked him for a light, but before he could take his lighter out of his pocket, he felt a blow to the head. He awoke half-naked, with blood on his face and scalp. The street was empty. He dragged himself to the police station, where they bandaged him up. He told them what had happened. He had been robbed of his suit, watch, shoes, and even shirt. At the police station they drew up a report and informed him that he was not the first person to have been robbed in this way.

After this incident, a colleague and I made low-caliber revolvers. Anyone who came back from town late and alone carried one of these homemade weapons with him, more for a sense of security than for any practical purpose. It took several months before the robbers were apprehended. They turned out to be soldiers who liked to go on nighttime raids dressed in civilian clothes.

In a few days' time, I and a few others were sent to Samarkand, where we finished our night flight training on the An-2. During our time there, a crazy thing happened. An IL-14 commercial flight was returning to Tashkent from Bukhara with thirty-two passengers on board, several of whom were members of the Bukhara air squadron. Near Samarkand, one of the motors began to fail. It so happened that the captain of the aircraft was flying as captain for the very first time. Up until then he had been co-pilot. He should have landed at an aerodrome near Samarkand, but out of concern for his reputation, the pilot did not want to make a forced landing, and decided to fly all the way to Tashkent. In a few minutes, the motor broke down completely, but he decided to keep going with only one motor. It was the middle of the day. The motor, working at maximum speed, overheated, and the aircraft gradually lost altitude. In that case, he could have landed outside of the aerodrome. There were cotton fields for miles around. But… Losing not only altitude but speed, the captain made a mistake that would have been unforgivable even for a cadet. Twenty miles from Tashkent, from a height of sixty to seventy feet, he suffered a sudden loss of speed and crashed to the ground. All the crew and half the passengers died. The rest were wounded with varying levels of seriousness.

After finishing my night flight course, I returned to Bukhara, where I continued to fly local routes. Though Bukhara is a regional center in Uzbekistan, there was not a single Uzbek pilot at Bukhara Airport, and only one Kyrgyz pilot. During my time in the air force, I had never met a pilot from Central Asia. What could be the reason? I don't know.

A word about the Kyrgyz pilot. I once witnessed how he crashed a plane and almost killed himself. It was his second crash. The first was on a Po-2 (a biplane). While flying on assignment once, he had seen an oasis with a single, tall tree and a herd of sheep grazing around it. Deciding to give the sheep and their shepherds a bit of a fright, he flew close to the ground, rose up again, dove and… crashed into that stupid tree. The frightened shepherds dragged him out of the wreckage, dug a grave for their fellow Muslim, and prepared to wait until sunrise, when they might bury him. It was then that a group of geologists appeared on a rover. Upon learning what the matter was, they checked the pilot's vitals and found that he was still alive. After administering first aid, the geologists sent the wounded man to hospital. The kid was lucky. He was allowed to fly again after a year, and then, after a few years' experience on the Yak-12, he decided to have a bit of fun again.

This time, he was meant to deliver several cages of white mice to an epidemiology station. However, after dropping to a low altitude, he lost focus and drove his nose into the velvet sands. As he crawled out of the shattered plane, he took with him a flare gun and several rockets. In a few hours, a search for the missing aircraft began. Hearing motor noises, he discharged the missiles, which expedited the process. The pilot was taken to the hospital with an injured spine and serious contusions. I know nothing about his subsequent fate. Perhaps he was allowed to fly again, for the sake of the "local cohort." There was a generally condescending attitude to the natives in Bukhara. People called them "donkeys," "flatbreads," and other offensive things.

The scourge of the urban and rural populations of Uzbekistan was cotton picking. Most of the "white gold" was picked by hand. People were encouraged to work the cotton on their days off, as well as being forcibly taken from work on weekdays – and this did not exclude the employees of Aeroflot. Women and children made up most of the workforce, while the local men spent most of their time in cafes or at the bazaar. In order to get them to come to work, the government would ambush them. A unit of policemen would surround the bazaar, grab the men, put them on a truck, and drive them to the cotton fields to help the women and children. There was, of course, little to be gained from such help.

Rural Uzbek women gave birth to many children, worked, kept house, and at thirty or thirty-five looked twenty years older.

Canal irrigation was widespread in Uzbekistan. When it came time to irrigate the cotton fields, the gate of the Bukhara dam was opened, and water rushed freely through the canals to the fields, trees, and lawns of the city. For a while after the gate was closed, puddles of water remained in the principal canals of the system. Fish flowed into the canals together with the water. We fished in these puddles, going after rather large catfish and bream. Though it was tricky to catch and hold onto a fish with your hands, we would catch a whole bucketful and cook a generous fish dinner for all the pilots in our house.

During my work in Bukhara I flew to Leningrad twice on holiday. I would spend two or three days with my family before returning to work. During my second trip from Tashkent to Moscow in 1962, our plane was caught in a powerful storm. As I was sitting in the engineer's place, between the two pilots, and a little behind them, I could see and feel all the tragedy of the situation. There were 120 passengers on board. You can imagine how bad it must have been for them, especially at the rear of the plane, considering that we pilots were being shaken out of our seats. The aircraft's navigator saw on the radar that we were surrounded on all sides by stormy conditions. Even the emergency aerodrome was closed for that very reason. The dispatcher in Moscow did not allow us to change course for a long time, as there were other planes above and below us. The situation was only aggravated by the fact that the flight was a direct one and fuel was getting low. It was a good thing that we were on a Tu-104. It was developed from the Tu-16, so its strong construction withstood the storm (though I had heard of an instance in which two Tu-16s had crashed in similar weather conditions, en route to Irkutsk). If we had been flying an IL-18, an accident would have been unavoidable. After landing, the captain, white as a sheet, said that he had already prepared for the end. As they say, all's well that ends well. The Almighty must have remembered that he still needed me for June 1970, and refused the sacrifice from Aeroflot. I had a bottle of cognac with me, and we drank, then and there, to celebrate the flight's safe conclusion. The stewardesses joined in.

Civilian aviation never gave me the same amount of pleasure I had known as a fighter pilot. In a fighter jet, pilot and plane meld into a single organism, and aerobatics are like a pleasant dream. I have had more than one dream in which, pushing off from the ground with my feet, I have floated lightly up into the air and completed various maneuvers with a feeling of total satisfaction. Perhaps flight is a kind of drug. The pilot usually takes pleasure from flying, after which he feels a desire, even a need, to fly again. But flight is also work, and the work isn't easy, even if you love it.

I don't want to say that flying a civilian aircraft is the same thing as driving a bus, but there is a certain resemblance. The size of an airliner and its cockpit prevent the pilot from feeling at one with the plane, as he can in a fighter aircraft. There is a single working principle on passenger flights: to deliver the passengers safely to their destination. A fighter pilot has more variety in his work: aerobatics, shooting, dogfights, interceptions, group flights, etc. And flights themselves are always full of action, more dynamic. In any thirty minutes, you could complete some complicated aerobatics maneuvers in the flight zone, shoot an aerial target, then whiz over to the shooting range to practice on land targets. Whereas in civilian aviation, during the same thirty minutes, you might fly X miles in a straight line, usually on autopilot. So, the size of the plane has a significant effect on how it feels to fly.

I think you could apply the same logic to a country. When your motherland is vast and immeasurable, it is hard to imagine, if you live in Brest, that Sakhalin is also your motherland, or living in Arkhangelsk, that Kushka is also your motherland. Perhaps there's an optimal size that allows inhabitants of a country to feel comfortable in it. But most important, in my opinion, is the feeling that you need your country, and that your country needs you. Then you know that the country is your motherland. And despite a whole series of negative events, I still felt that the USSR was my motherland.

In the summer of 1962, I was meant to fly to Lvov, pick up a new, Polish-manufactured An-2, and fly it back to Bukhara. On the way back from Moscow, I dropped into Leningrad, and went straight to Kotrekhov at the human resources department. The promised spring had passed, and I was met with the same answer: "There are no openings. Fly another year in Uzbekistan."

It became clear to me that all Kotrekhov's promises had been false, and there was no point hoping for a transfer. Alya categorically refused to move to Bukhara. So I decided to hand in my resignation.

While I was delivering the An-2 from Lvov to Bukhara, a small adventure occurred. My second pilot was the Don Juan type I mentioned earlier. At the hotel, he met a cougar with sadistic tendencies. She left him with his nose on, but one night with her left him covered in bruises. Though the trip was three days in total, no lotions could help him erase the marks of infidelity. When he got home, he received a beating from his wife, which left him with another bruise under his eye.

When I returned to Bukhara, I handed in my notice. But it wasn't going to be that easy. The airport director refused to accept my resignation. It was only after the city prosecutor put pressure on him that he agreed to sign it. I bought a ticket to Leningrad, said goodbye to my colleagues, and was back home in a few hours.

Alya now had a job as a kindergarten teacher and had gone on a school trip to the countryside, taking our daughters with her. After paying a visit to the family in Zelenogorsk, I began my search for work.

I unexpectedly received notice from the Agricultural Institute that if I didn't pass my first-year exams in the next two months, I would be expelled. This meant that I had some hard studying ahead of me, as I had only been able to do a fraction of the coursework in Bukhara. Sleeping only five hours a night, I spent the rest of my time either looking for work or studying. In two months, I passed my exams and pass-fail assessments – all but one, which was German. But with only one fail, they let me matriculate to the next year.

On my way back from the Elektrosila factory, where I had just been offered work as a technician, I met one of my former colleagues from ZabVO. Anatoliy had been discharged a year later than I had and lived three hundred feet from my front door. We got to talking, and I told him about my problems. He told me what had happened to the regiment after I had left for Taganrog. A few days later, Anatoliy helped me get a job at an instrumentation factory, where his friend worked as a contract administrator for the air force. Before that, I had been to the same factory twice, but had been told twice that they did not need any more workers. I began work on an aircraft instrument assembly line, while also continuing my studies at the Agricultural Institute.

When I was doing tactical training in Taganrog, they led an excursion for officers to a combine factory. That was the first time I had seen large-scale manufacturing. The visit left an unpleasant aftertaste. The conveyor belt hadn't been working. The workers unhurriedly brought various parts over to the assembly line, then stood in groups and smoked. I decided that this must be an exception to the rule. When I became a laboratory technician after the army, I didn't spend much time in the workshops themselves. Now, as a worker in a large assembly plant, with more than three hundred employees, I had the opportunity to learn about manufacturing. To begin with, I learned to assemble and regulate combined aircraft navigation instruments. But I was bothered by the absence of rhythm. The pace of work followed an established system. The first ten days of the month were sleepy. In the second, things started warming up. The last ten days were fever pitch. As the month came to an end, we would work overtime and often at night. Discipline was low and the defect rate was high. In the best cases, we fixed defective parts ourselves before assembly, and in the worst, discarded them.

We used medicinal alcohol to sanitize certain items, but 50 percent of which was used for personal consumption. The plant director, Vasilyev, was frequently carried into his office in a state of incapacity. You could run into him more often in the warehouse, where the alcohol was kept, than in the assembly plant. He was eventually sent to a rehabilitation clinic. At the factory, alcohol was a stronger currency than the ruble, and we used it to pay for various small favors.

The factory also made instruments for spaceships. My acquaintance worked at the plant where they were made and had been on several work trips to the cosmodrome. He told me how, even before Yuriy Gagarin's space flight, two cosmonauts had died on the ground. He had seen their graves at the cosmodrome. By the way, in 1962, I sent an application to the cosmonaut training center, but received the response: "At present, we are not accepting applications."

Can anyone really imagine what it would have been like if the first Soviet cosmonaut had not been ethnically Russian? I'm not even talking about a Jew. Even a Ukrainian or Belorussian with the best credentials couldn't possibly have been the first in that "happy family of equal nations," the Soviet Union.

While working at the factory, I made periodic visits to the Aeroflot human resources department, but was always told, "No openings."

I wrote a letter to Khrushchev, which was redirected to the Leningrad Communist Party Regional Committee. After that, I had a conversation with the deputy secretary of the regional committee, who promised to help me find pilot work, but this promise turned out to be as empty as Kotrekhov's had been.

A little while later, I ran into a former colleague from Bukhara while riding the bus. With the help of influential relatives, he had been able to get a job at the Leningrad airport and was now flying as second pilot on a Tu-104. We went together to the airport, and he took me to the place where a squadron of An-2s was housed. The squadron commander examined my flight papers, and we talked business for a while before he agreed to take me on as a pilot and signed a document to that effect. I returned immediately to the Aeroflot office, as documents of hire could only be processed at the human resources department. But my meeting with Kotrekhov resulted in the usual response, "No openings."

It was at this time that I learned of the death of my best friend Boris Avdeev. I once met Lyosha Movchan, the enthusiastic parachute jumper, when he was traveling through Leningrad on leave, and he told me what had happened. During a weather reconnaissance flight on a Su-7 in Perm province, Boris could not find the landing strip, due to rain and low cloud cover. While trying to find the landing strip visually on his third landing attempt, he crashed into a hill on approach to the aerodrome and died.

After finishing my third year at the Agricultural Institute, I became a factory engineer. As my engineering work mostly centered on the instruments I had put together on the assembly line, from the first bolt to the last, I generally had about two extra hours of work time, which I used for reading technical literature and doing coursework.

Alya got a job at the same factory, in a laboratory where they tested measuring instruments. Our daughters were both at school. In general, life became a steady stream of daily worries and responsibilities. We went to the theater sometimes, to the movies more often, read books, watched television, celebrated public and family holidays. There were no indicators of serious changes in our family life. My fifth-year exams were approaching. Spring of 1967 was also approaching.

6 The Hijack Affair

May 1967–June 1970

Spring. I had to pass my exams and pass-fail assessments for fifth year. And at the same time (namely, May 1967), the situation in the Middle East was becoming more acute. I did not start listening to western radio stations ("enemy voices") until armed conflict began, but I followed the situation closely in the Soviet press. Even before the war, Egyptian president Nasser, Hero of the Soviet Union, declared that Israel was a tumor on Arab land, which must be destroyed. He made this announcement in Moscow. And yet, the Soviet government did not react – in tacit agreement. Though the USSR had played an important role in accepting the UN resolution to make Israel a state, it had made a sharp turn in the direction of the Arab countries, and was now arming Egypt and Syria, the most extreme of them. In May 1967, I had no concept of the main factors on both sides, which would decide the outcome of the war. The newspaper articles I read gave me an impression of pan-Arab unity, of an Arab advantage in resources, not to mention a fortyfold advantage in numbers. It seems that I already knew about Soviet misinformation and propaganda, but I still let them deceive me.

Nasser declared a blockade of the Israeli port of Eilat, which was already an act of aggression. His blockade of the Aqaba Gulf, his demand that UN troops leave the Sinai Peninsula were not only *not* condemned by the Soviet press – they were not even subject to criticism. The reverse was true: everything was turned on its head. Israel was accused of exacerbating the situation in the Middle East. In mid-May, Nasser gave a speech at one of the aerodromes on the Sinai Peninsula and declared that the time had come to settle accounts with Israel. There was a feeling of approaching war.

For some reason, the position of Israel seemed to me to be similar to that of Republican Spain in the 1930s. For the first time, I felt personal responsibility for the Jewish state and understood the danger she was in, surrounded by enemies. If I had been given the opportunity to go to Israel as a volunteer, as thousands of volunteers from different countries had gone to fight in Spain, I would have gone. But I was still not ready to leave the Soviet Union for good.

I prepared for and took my exams, but my thoughts were thousands of miles away from Leningrad, and I was worried not for my exam results but for that little country.

The news that war had begun greeted me as I was on my way to the Institute, and its patent falseness made me worried. That same evening, I began to listen to "The Voice of Israel" on the radio. I also began to visit the Leningrad Central Lecture Hall and never missed a lecture about the international situation. I was impressed by the large number of Jewish audience members. Evidently, many were concerned for the future of Israel.

The Six-Day War ended with an Israeli victory, and we could calm down. But immediately Soviet propaganda kicked in with a bitter campaign against Israel and Zionism, comparable perhaps only to what had been during the war with fascist Germany. There was a greater and greater feeling of antagonism and pathological hatred for the Jewish nation in general, and not just Israel. The Soviet Union, followed by its satellite countries, ended diplomatic relations with Israel. The USSR had not made a break with the dictatorial and reactionary regimes of Africa and Latin America. At that time, Israel and Lebanon were the only democratic countries in the Middle East. It is important to note that diplomatic relations do not necessarily signal agreement with a country's internal and foreign policies, but rather acknowledge a government's right to existence.

After what Nazi Germany had done, the Russian government could not openly pose the "Jewish question" in the same way, and therefore they left it up to the Arabs.

Now, after the Sabra and Shatila massacre, it is easier to imagine what the fate of Israeli Jews would have been if the Arabs, supported by the so-called "socialist" camp, had been able to realize their brutal plan of driving the Jews into the sea.

I tried to distract myself from Soviet propaganda. It was clear that what I was reading in the papers were not the personal opinions of antisemitic journalists – or not *just* their personal opinions – but rather the government's position. Everything fell back into place. This was when a whole series of questions presented themselves to me, which would not allow me to write everything off as error or mis-estimation: What kind of political and governmental system am I living in? What is the government's attitude to minority groups? Can I continue to live in the USSR?

Since I had spent all forty years of my life in the Soviet Union, was a member of the Communist Party, and considered the USSR my motherland, it was imperative that I answer these painful questions and make the corresponding decisions.

At this point, you might ask if I had ever had such thoughts before? Yes, after the Doctors' Plot and especially after the publication of documents from the Twentieth Party Congress. But I had never before desired to leave the USSR.

When I sat down to tackle these questions, I began on the level of words. Union of Soviet Socialist Republics. What kind of union was it, if the majority of republics had been taken by force, both before and after 1917? The union was purely formal. Internationalism and equality of nations were a fiction. For that reason, I decided that I was living in the Russian Empire – and more precisely, on the territory of the metropole, as a second-class citizen.

There was no Soviet power as such. The local Soviets operated on the level of roof or sidewalk repair. The Supreme Soviets unanimously approved or rejected proposals on orders from the top. The Empire was ruled by a dictator, or a small group of people, in the name of the working class and its front rank, the Communist Party. In short, after Lenin, the Soviets played no role in national government.

As for socialism, not only had it *not* been established, but the very idea of a socialist society had been discredited. In pointed contrast to Marx's idea that socialism would prevail in all, or most countries, Russia had all but proved the impossibility of a socialist victory in a single, enormous country – what is more, a country completely unprepared for socialism. The Bolsheviks saved the Russian Empire from dissolution and made an attempt to put the theory of permanent revolution into practice. But then Stalin liquidated the Bolsheviks and set government politics on the imperialistic path of expansion. Within the country, the imperialist, chauvinist policy of divide and conquer was enacted. The totalitarian regime turned its "citizens" into serfs at best, and during the time of Stalin, into slaves. The regime destroyed public morale. Indifference, alcoholism, theft, and corruption flourished. For several years I had been drafting a letter to the Central Committee of the Communist Party on the way things stood in the army and the manufacturing industry. In the spring of 1967, I stopped writing it and even destroyed my notes.

I came to the conclusion that I would not and could not continue to live in the USSR. The USSR/Russian Empire was not my motherland, and I had to abandon it.

Now, in the age of perestroika and glasnost, there is no need to justify myself. But back then I had to prove the truth of these convictions to myself. Soviet print media, radio, and television revealed a significant swathe of Soviet history. The fewer blanks in the history books, the more black (bloody) pages. Twelve years later, the same rhetoric was repeating itself: "Power to the Soviets! Factories to the Workers! Land to the Peasants!"

Some may ask, "But surely it's possible to live in an empire, under a totalitarian regime, and even in the position of a peasant?" Of course it is. People lived in the British, French, Turkish, and Austro-Hungarian Empires. But when the government conducts antisemitic politics and it is possible to leave, then it is better to run from such a country, especially when there is a Jewish state to run to. Hundreds of thousands of Jews left tsarist Russia after the pogroms. Hundreds of thousands left and are still leaving, not the Soviet Union, but the Russian Empire, with its long, tragic history with the "Jewish question."

I felt foreign in the USSR, unable to live in this "evil empire," as Ronald Reagan later called it. Though the evil reached its apogee under Stalin, it had been born much earlier. In the middle of the previous century, Russia had become Europe's gendarme, the epicenter of reactionary politics worldwide. That was when Karl Marx came up with the epithet, "empire of evil." We can only hope that Mikhail Gorbachev will be able to transform it into a democratic, civilized country. It will be a long and difficult road, but the alternative could have tragic consequences – not only for Russia.

After making my decision to leave Russia, I had to decide what to do about my family, friends, and work; to weigh my chances of success, and understand what would await me in the case of failure; to consider the problems that would await me in Israel, and they would be many – work, language, climate, and other things. All these questions had to be examined in parallel to the technical question of how to get across the Russian border and into Israel?

There was no question of a legal exit. My idea of what Russia's land borders were like was drawn not only from films, such as *Locked Border*, *On the Border*, and others, but from a measure of personal experience. There was a forbidden zone, fifteen miles wide, along the land borders, where the local population would immediately inform on any stranger who appeared. Even the beaches of the Black Sea were cleared of sunbathers in the evenings and placed under strobe-light surveillance.

The air borders were more familiar to me. I had even flown along the Chinese border at an altitude of forty-five thousand feet, clearly entering Chinese airspace – but that had been the assignment. On other occasions, I could have easily flown to Japan or Turkey, but the thought had never even entered my mind.

Initially, I considered two means of crossing the border. The first was to rent a dacha on the Karelian Isthmus and build a hot air balloon, using the combined hot air from four blow torches. The problem of where to find appropriate materials was immediately raised. What is more, the size of the balloon would have attracted general attention long before it had filled with air, and the organs would have had their way with the "amateur aerialist."

The second idea was to assemble an airplane. At the aerodrome garbage dump in Samarkand, I had seen not only separate parts, but whole decommissioned planes, whose resources had been exhausted. With the help of some properly paid technicians, you could make one of those planes airworthy. But what was possible in Uzbekistan would have been impossible in Leningrad, for the same reason it would have been impossible to build a hot air balloon. Two visits to an aircraft hangar convinced me of that.

I continued to work at the instrumentation factory. After the Six-Day War, I was called upon a few times to lead discussions in the party line on the situation in the Middle East. Though I listed the Central Lecture Hall and the weekly paper *Beyond the Border* as my official sources, I was really using information I had heard from "The Voice of Israel" and the BBC. My audiences listened with interest. There was nothing of the kind in the Soviet pro-Arab media, and the new version was not only more interesting but inspired more trust. I was asked to give more presentations. In addition to the Middle Eastern theme, I spoke about the situation in Indonesia. The first division had lost its habitual caution.

When I told Alya that I had decided to leave the country, I was met with total incomprehension. This led to a family conflict.

In late February 1979, in an interview for the eighty-ninth edition of the magazine *Circle*, Alya describe the situation thus:

You see, it was a very, very difficult family drama. Because, when he decided we had to move to Israel, I was totally against it. And tried with all my might to hold him back. Israel was so far away, it might have been another planet. And I couldn't leave. My mother was dying. To leave her would have been as good as killing her.

I tried to convince my wife that we had to leave Russia for the sake of our children. They could end up in concentration camps, and at the very least would always be second-class citizens. But even after Alya's mother died, I received the answer, "No, Russia is my motherland, and I will never leave."

It was probably a huge mistake not to discuss the matter with my daughters. I assumed they would want to stay with their mother. Perhaps, with their help, the family problem would have been solved much faster and with less pain, although I have my doubts on the last count.

The year 1968 was underway. I was in my sixth year of studies at the Institute and would soon have to defend my thesis project. While still employed as an engineer at the factory, I made the decision to leave my job, so that none of my friends would have to answer for my future actions (which is what usually happened in such cases).

Then came the news that Yuriy Gagarin, the first cosmonaut, had died. And once more we were inundated with lies. About a year later, I heard the actual details of Gagarin's death from a government division pilot. At that time, the government division serviced not only government and politburo ministers, but also cosmonauts, which is why the pilots of this division were a rich and reliable source of information.

This is what the pilot told me: Yuriy Gagarin arrived at the aerodrome to conduct a series of training flights. When he approached his plane, a MiG-15 technician informed him that the craft was ready for takeoff. Seeing that Gagarin was drunk, the technician told him that he was not able to let him on board the plane in such a state. Gagarin responded with insults and abuse, and when the technician informed the regimental commander, Colonel Seryogin, of the situation, Seryogin felt unable to forbid the first cosmonaut from flying. He proposed to Gagarin that they fly together to the flight zone, to do aerobatics maneuvers on the Uti-MiG-15, claiming that in any case the plane needed to be taken for a ride after repairs.

And so, the first infraction (and the first cause of death): flight in a state of inebriation (slow reaction time).

Pilots usually conclude a series of aerobatics maneuvers with a steep spiral, flip, or dive. In all three kinds of descent, there is a sharp increase in speed. The aircraft can reach about six hundred miles per hour, even when maneuvers are being conducted slowly. This is when some of the unpleasant qualities of the MiG-15 begin to show themselves: an opposite roll reaction, and a spontaneous, scarcely noticeable rotation around the longitudinal axis of the plane during dive.

Gagarin, in the front seat of the plane, was unable to control it, and seeing that the ground was fast approaching, decided to eject. But he only managed to remove the canopy (which was found separately from the plane). The plane did not explode, but rather fell into a bog. Its fragments were removed with great difficulty. The second cause of death was, therefore, a serious error in pilot technique during descent.

Gagarin's third infraction (and perhaps the third cause of death) was his disregard of the Uti-MiG-15 piloting technique instructions, which state that the pilot in the rear seat should be the first to eject. When Yuriy Gagarin removed the canopy, without informing Seryogin of his decision to leave the aircraft, a current of air hit Seryogin in the face, depriving him not only of the ability to control the plane, but of ejecting from the plane himself – as there was no division between front and rear seats in the upper part of the plane.

So perished two colonels, two Heroes of the Soviet Union – the first cosmonaut, who had little experience flying and a great deal of experience carousing, and Seryogin, an experienced fighter pilot, who was powerless to prevent catastrophe in a world where everything is permitted to the few.

And even though alcohol was an acknowledged cause of pilot deaths, even in the decades preceding glasnost (while drunkenness in aviation had been widespread in the forties and fifties, mandatory breath checks were introduced in the sixties, to be conducted before each flight), this cause was difficult to acknowledge in Gagarin's case, as he was an international celebrity.

In the early hours of August 21, 1968, the combined troops of the Warsaw Pact (with the exception of Romania) invaded Czechoslovakia. Twenty-three years after Soviet tanks had liberated Prague from the Germans, Soviet tanks appeared once more in the streets of Prague. I was worried for Czechoslovakia, which had tried to democratize its government. I ended up arguing about this

with the secretary of the Communist Party Regional Committee. His principle justification for the introduction of armed forces into Czechoslovakia
were the deaths of 120,000 soldiers during the liberation of Czechoslovakia in
1945. The suffocated "Prague Spring" confirmed the rightness of my judge-
ments about the Russian Empire.

I graduated from the Institute with a degree in electrical engineering. It
was a weight off my shoulders.

After many unsuccessful conversations and arguments with Alya about
leaving Russia, I filed for divorce in the peoples' court. I thought, not without
justification, that would relieve my wife of responsibility for her husband's
actions, and my children, for their father's actions. "Incompatible personalities" was the most common reason for divorce in Russia, allowing couples to
separate without too much trouble.

Around that time, a friend asked me to help a Jewish girl get a job in my
factory. She had graduated from a technical college in Leningrad that special-
ized in instrumentation. I made some inquiries in the quality control department, where they needed a worker with her qualifications. I gave the division
manager her resume, and he agreed to take her on. But when they saw from
her appearance and her documents that she was Jewish, they immediately
remembered that they had promised the job to another girl.

I went to another division, where the manager, a middle-aged Russian
woman, openly admitted that she needed a worker but blushed when she told
me that the first division and human resources had reprimanded her for her
division's high "pollution" level – that is, its large number of Jewish employees. For that reason, it would have been hopeless for the girl even to apply. I
don't know if that was her first brush with "internationalism," but in any case
it was a lesson that had to be learned.

In 1968, I went on several work trips. There was a fighter plane base at the
airport in Gudauta. There, they showed and told me what the results of the
Six-Day War had been. Earlier, the planes had stood parked in a single line,
but after Israel had destroyed most of the Egyptian, Syrian, and Jordanian
fleets on the ground, it was decided to dig trenches to accommodate the aircraft, which made work more difficult, but also made it easier to relax.

In 1968, almost nine years after my departure from ZabVO, I found myself
there again at the Ukkurey air base. Once upon a time, there had been an out-
of-the way cargo aerodrome in the same place, where a regiment of IL-10

stormtroopers had been based. As a result of the conflict over Damansky Island, a large amount of construction began along the Chinese border. A huge concrete landing strip had been laid at the aerodrome in Ukkurey. Instead of wooden houses, five-story housing blocks were built. They also put up a fancy officers' house, a hotel, shops, and even an atelier. The base was made to accommodate two transport aviation regiments as well as one regiment of fighter pilots. The Chinese gave us the necessary push to transform our military bases and furnish the garrisons properly, not even to mention the transfer of further divisions to the East. As I heard at one lecture, the sum spent on strengthening the border with China was equal to the whole military budget for 1943. Military bases once more populated Chita province and Mongolia. Traveling in the region, I noticed an abundance of alcoholics. While riding a bus to the train station, I chatted with a couple of officers from the Ukkurey garrison. I told them that I had once served in the region and landed in their aerodrome. They openly shared their concern about the low level of discipline in the army. Desertions, drunkenness, and fighting had become common occurrences. As one of them expressed it, if war was to break out, we would have another 1941 on our hands. There was a marked conservatism of thought. Until 1968, the military high command was still thinking in World War II terms, as if there were no missiles or nuclear weapons that could destroy all living organisms on earth.

An interesting thing took place during a trip to a base near Arkhangelsk. I arrived in the evening and went straight to the garrison hotel. The orderly showed me to a room with five cots, where four drunk officers were sitting at a table playing cards. On the table were a bottle of vodka and some snacks. Their purple faces made it clear to the orderly that there wasn't room for anyone else. Their eyes traveled from me to the orderly and back to me again. The orderly showed me to another room and left. In a few minutes she returned, muttering under her breath, "damned antisemites." Evidently, a more open conversation had taken place between her and the officers than had been possible in my presence.

Though the situation was already pretty clear to me, I decided to conduct an experiment. A certain military institution (we'll call it N…) was looking to hire an electrical engineer. I called the human resources department and told them everything about myself except for my Jewish ethnicity. They proposed that I come to an interview at their office, to which I replied that since I lived far away, I needed to know for sure that my biographical and professional profile was acceptable to them. Receiving an affirmative reply, I said that I would be with them in an hour. Indeed, I was only a five-minute walk away. After strolling for an hour in Victory Park, I entered the lobby and called the human resources department. I was met by two men, the head of the human resources department and some colonel. One look at me and a formal scan of my documents was enough for them to decide, "You are not what we are looking for." I smiled and asked, "My qualifications aren't appropriate?" No answer. Only the colonel lowered his eyes, as if to say, "Does he really need us to explain it to him? He's not a child."

In June of 1969, I went on vacation with my daughters. We rented a room in Yevpatoriya (Crimea). After twenty-five days, Alya came to replace me, and they spent another three weeks in Crimea.

A few days after my return from vacation, I realized my intention of quitting my job at the factory and got a job at a poultry farming trust which had its offices in the Smolny Palace, together with all the regional government organizations. All the most important regional officials were concentrated here. As senior electrical engineer, my primary concern was supplying electricity to the poultry factories of Leningrad province and, in particular, to two new ones that were being built.

One of my former army colleagues told me an interesting story about a friend of his, who I will refer to as "the friend." So this friend, a fighter pilot, had been accepted at the air force command academy before 1967. When the academy announced that they were selecting students to be trained as cosmonauts, forty officers put their names down, of whom the commission chose three, including the friend. They had a conversation with the air force commander, who told them to finish their studies at the academy, after which they would be transferred to the cosmonaut training center. But in the end there was no transfer. The friend graduated from the academy with high grades, which gave him the right to choose his posting. But at that time, the Six-Day War had already taken place and left its mark on Soviet lawlessness and so-called "internationalism." The friend was not even asked to indicate a preference and sent to ZabVO, and not as a pilot but as the assistant regimental engineer. The friend wrote complaint after complaint, but was never able to return to pilot work. Eventually, he was made contract administrator at an aircraft assembly plant. One evening, he was having dinner with an acquaintance, and "when the wine goes in, the secrets come out." The acquaintance, who worked at the Military Commissariat, told him that after 1967, a secret order had been issued that "individuals of Jewish ethnicity" should not be employed as pilots.

After that story, a reckless thought came into my head: to get a confirmation of the story from the Aeroflot human resources manager for the Northwest region, Kotrekhov. I called him on the phone, and pretended to be the Regional Committee deputy secretary, with whom I had once had a conversation about pilot work (I have forgotten his name). The conversation went more or less like this:

"Hello! This is (surname), deputy secretary of the Regional Committee. Mark Dymshits contacted me about his search for work. I believe he communicated with you over a period of eight years, but nonetheless was unable to find pilot work. My son is also a pilot, and I understand Dymshits's position. Comrade Kotrekhov, how can you explain such a situation?"

"You see, comrade secretary," Kotrekhov replied, "at the moment we have the maximum number of pilots on the books, and I have explained the situation to Dymshits more than once."

"But, Comrade Kotrekhov, he is a communist with good qualifications. Eight years is a terribly long time to wait," I continued, trying to give my voice an authoritative tone.

"There is one more reason, comrade secretary." After a short pause, he continued, "There is the Instruction of 1967, which I can't infract, as much as I might want to help him."

"What Instruction is that?" I raised my voice.

"I can't tell you the number right now, but believe me, there was a weighty reason for refusing Dymshits's request, even if there had been an opening."

"All right. I will clarify the situation, and if necessary will contact you again. Goodbye." I hurried to end the conversation before Kotrekhov could offer to find the number of the instruction and call the Regional Committee deputy secretary himself. In that case he would have been immediately able to identify who had called him.

I never learned the number of the instruction, and could not bring myself to call Kotrekhov a second time. Besides, was the number really necessary, when all aspects of Russian life were controlled not by laws, but by instructions, both secret and not-so-secret?

Only now, in the age of perestroika, has the question of the rule of law been raised, but the process of establishing it will be a long one.

Short notices appeared in the paper about Cuban hijackings of American passenger planes. The question arose, why couldn't I use the same method to fly across the border? In the USA, all possible measures were taken for the safety of passengers and crew, which was why even with a fake grenade or pistol it was possible to force the crew to fly in the desired direction. In the Russian Empire, on flights close to the border, the crew would be armed and was meant to take all possible measures to stop the hijacker, putting passengers' lives and the plane itself at risk. For that reason it was impossible for one person to carry out such an intention. You had to find another two or three people.

So the problem of a "team" came about. I had a few Jewish friends in Leningrad, and I began to sound them out on the Israel question. But even my hints made them react as if I had asked them to come with me to another planet.

I went to Leningrad Synagogue several times. I circled around it, in the hopes of meeting young Jews and perhaps making friends. I could never bring myself to go inside the synagogue, imagining that it was under KGB control. At that time I didn't even know that people came there to pray on Friday evenings and Saturdays. And really, what did I know then about Jewish traditions and history, Judaism itself, or the Hebrew language? Almost nothing. I had grown up in a Russian environment, served in the army and worked among Russians. My Jewish friends were just as assimilated as I was. It is hard to approximate our level of assimilation as a percentage, but you could say about ninety-five. In short, I was Jewish only biologically and bureaucratically.

Until I could find comrades who could help me hijack a plane, I decided at least to find a Hebrew textbook and dictionary. I looked in all the bookshops, not only in the center of Leningrad, but also on the outskirts. I thought that something might have been left hanging around from the 1930s. But the booksellers had either never heard of such a language, or stared at me as if I had asked them to sell me something forbidden. And that was practically how it was: Hebrew was banned. The last dictionary, edited by Shapiro, had been published in 1962. Other than that, I found no Hebrew publications in any of the stores.

I told this story to one of my friends from the wartime evacuation period, and he told me that he knew someone called Venya who had managed to get hold of a dictionary for a short time. This friend arranged for me to meet Venya on the street. Venya gave me the dictionary for two weeks, and promised to introduce me to Hillel Butman, who would be able to give me a Hebrew textbook.

Some time later, we – that is, Venya and I – went to visit Butman, and that was how I met Hillel. I never saw Venya again, but Hillel Butman and I agreed to meet. He gave me the textbook *Elef milim* (A thousand words), and I began to study from it after work. After a few short meetings with Butman, I reached the conclusion that he wanted to get to Israel as passionately as I did and that he might be receptive to my idea of hijacking an airplane. Hillel already knew my background, and how after the army, I had flown An-2s in civilian aviation.

One evening in late October, we found ourselves walking down a deserted street, and I proposed to Butman that we take control of an An-2 in the air and fly it over the border. To accomplish this, we would need three or four more active people, and together with our families, there would be eleven or twelve of us. We could hijack the plane near Leningrad, cross the Finnish border, and land in Sweden. Or, we could hijack the plane near Yerevan in Armenia and fly to Turkey. From Sweden or Turkey the plane would return to Russia, and we would continue on to Israel. The details could be discussed later, but that was the idea in principle. Hillel promised to think about it, to weigh up the pros and cons, as well as to ask the advice of some trustworthy friends. For the moment, he advised me to attend the ulpan at Misha Korenblit's apartment. The Hebrew teacher was Lev Korenblit, who despite his surname was no relative of Misha's.

At one of our meetings, Hillel introduced me to Shlomo Drezner, who had served in ZabVO just like me. We got talking about my air force service, about Chita province. It was clear that they were trying to get a sense of my character, naturally enough. There was a real possibility that after my service in ZabVO, I could be a KGB agent. One of my fellow airmen, deputy squadron commander Nikolay Deryabin, had joined the ranks of the KGB after the army.

Later, the author of *Fascism under a Blue Star*, the judophobe Evseev, would write that they only had to put a bottle of cognac on the table and I immediately agreed to hijack the airplane. It was liars like him that turned the whole Soviet Union into a swamp of lies.

In December 1969, the army reserves were called up for training, which was conducted in classrooms. One overzealous lecturer, a "general" of lightning-fast victories, made pronouncements that in the case of war, Soviet tanks could be on the Atlantic coast of Spain in a week. We wouldn't even need to change the treads on the caterpillar tracks. They were designed to withstand precisely such a journey – across the whole of Western Europe. We would march through Finland and take the rest of Scandinavia in three days. It seemed that the lecturer, a lieutenant colonel, was stuck in a Second World War mindset – just like that woman at the information office. As if there weren't any weapons of mass destruction! It is hard to believe, and in fact the lecturer was only saying what he had been told to say. It was probably just propaganda. Of course, in the absence of nuclear weapons, such propaganda might even have been justified, considering the USSR's huge number of tanks (around fifty thousand). But was the West really going to rely on conventional weaponry? The use of weapons of mass destruction would lead to an international catastrophe, far worse than 1941 or 1945.

My next meeting with Hillel led to a serious complication of my original plan. He proposed to hijack a large passenger liner, which would be full of only Jewish passengers, fly it to Sweden, hold a press conference, drum up interest for our cause, and in so doing, throw open the borders of Russia for aliyah. I found Hillel's plan both alarming and enticing. It was alarming for two reasons: In the first place, where could we find that many Jewish passengers if I hadn't been able to find any? In the second place, I had never flown a large passenger jet. Only once, in the army, had I practiced landing an IL-14 blind (using instruments). This was my only experience.

True, pilot technique in the air varies little from aircraft to aircraft. You have to know how the cockpit is fitted out, at the very least you have to know enough to keep you in the air. Later, I studied the cockpit of the Tu-124 at the Leningrad Public Library, where there were albums on all the different civilian aircraft in the USSR. Different classes of aircraft differ significantly when it comes to preparation for landing and the landing itself. Whenever I flew as a passenger, I always sat next to the window and during landing tried to determine our distance from the earth. I became quite precise, that is, I could determine almost exactly the moment when the plane wheels touched the runway. A few times, during flights from Bukhara to Leningrad and back, sitting in the cockpit, I was able to observe how the pilots carried out landing procedure, and in that way was able to gain some experience.

Hillel's plan was seductive because, if successful, it really would open the gates for other Jews who wanted to leave the USSR for Israel. Even in the case of failure and arrest, it would be impossible to hide the court case from society at large, and the result could be the same as if we were successful.

In the case of interception, it would be more difficult for the government to shoot down a passenger liner than a small An-2. However, the quiet An-2 (with a maximum speed of 155 miles per hour), flying low to the ground, would be harder both to detect and to shoot down. In that area I had significant experience: of interception at different altitudes, and of shooting aerial targets.

In short, we reached a unanimous conclusion that we should hijack a liner. Hillel promised to discuss the plan with some of his friends. If they agreed, he would begin selecting the passengers, and I would begin my technical training.

I have written that Hillel asked advice and discussed our plan with his friends. Of course, I wondered who these "friends" were. How reliable were they? But I didn't ask Hillel. I had no other choice and in that sense was totally dependent on him. Through my studies at the ulpan, I began to understand that some organization was probably necessary to make these Hebrew and history classes possible. Although the ulpans were forced to operate underground, I couldn't see anything unlawful in them. It seemed to me that their place should be in the Palaces of Culture, where people took classes in English, French, and other languages. Hillel didn't tell me about the Leningrad Zionist Organization – the "friends" with whom he was discussing our plan. But I was satisfied that there were Jews ready to take such a step and decided not to ask too many questions. I thought that the less I knew about anything unconnected to the plane hijacking, the better. I used the same logic when I told Alya:,"The less you know, the better for you, for the children, and for the cause."

Three months had passed since my first meeting with Hillel, but our preparations were unpardonably slow. I felt that the logistics of hijacking a passenger liner was getting us into time trouble. The longer our preparations went on, and the more people were encouraged to join us, the greater our chance of failure became. But there was an important goal before us! I even fantasized, dreamed about 1.5 million Jews emigrating to Israel, which would mean ten military divisions.

Towards the end, we met in a group of three: Mikhail Korenblit, Hillel Butman, and I. Hillel and Misha conducted meetings with candidates to be passengers on our flight. We also made three reconnaissance flights: Misha to Kishenev, Hillel to Riga, and I to Moscow. I flew with my former colleague from Bukhara, so I was able to sit in the cockpit there and back.

During these reconnaissance flights, we noticed that although the door to the cockpit was left open, the cabin crew monitored movements in the direction of the cockpit. From my position inside the cockpit, I observed that the crew was given pistols but kept them in the navigator's case.

At that time, we didn't yet know that there had already been one attempt to hijack a Li-2 ("Douglas") plane, after which increased security measures had been introduced. In 1968, a female dissident decided to leave the USSR for political reasons. She convinced her husband to come with her, as well as her brother Yuriy Vasilyev, who had served in the army as a parachutist. All three of them, armed with a machine gun, a pistol, and a false grenade, boarded a Li-2 passenger aircraft somewhere in the northwest USSR. During the flight, two of them set off for the cockpit. The stewardess, noticing that one of them had a machine gun under his coat, managed to slam the door shut. The cockpit door only had a handle on the pilot side. One of the three brandished the false grenade at the passengers, telling them not to leave their seats. The twenty-four passengers, among whom were several naval officers, thought for some reason that the hijackers were robbers and started hiding their rings, earrings, money, and watches.

Pushing the stewardess aside, two of the hijackers were left standing in front of the closed cockpit door. One of them shot a round with the machine gun, hoping to hit the inner lock, but the door did not open. The co-pilot was injured. The crew began shooting back through the door, wounding one of the hijackers and knocking out the machine gun. The captain informed the passengers via radio of the situation on board and received the order to land at an aerodrome in the middle of a field. When the plane came to a stop after landing, the three hijackers jumped out and tried to hide in the forest. But even before landing, the aerodrome had been surrounded by soldiers. The woman's husband was killed in the crossfire. Yuriy Vasilyev and his sister were captured and brought to trial.

I met Vasilyev as a prisoner in 1972, which was when I learned of the above events. It is good to learn from the mistakes of others, but we did not have the opportunity to extract a lesson from that particular incident, as there was nothing written about it in the press.

In March 1970, we developed a plan to hijack a large passenger plane along the Leningrad-Murmansk line, a plan which had begun to seem like the plot of a detective novel and had been given the code name "Wedding." There was even a bride and groom selected for the charade. This name was to be retained until the very end of our epic.

The problem of finding enough Jewish passengers really slowed us down. I demanded that the date of the flight be fixed and that Hillel take a holiday from work in order to expedite the selection of passengers. We chose May 2 as our date. Hillel refused to take a holiday, and this allowed me to conclude that Hillel was hesitant. He'd miss his holiday in any case. Though this meant that he was still thinking about his summer holidays, I had no other choice and decided not to discuss the matter further.

That same month, a parallel plan began to be developed. The KGB had already found out about our preparations, but I would only learn that from an investigator in the Leningrad prison. We had four months at our disposal before the "Chekists" (the secret police)[1] found out about us and began to act. And even at that relaxed tempo, the KGB got its act together sooner than we did.

The day we had chosen for our act, May 2, was a state holiday, and therefore convenient for all participants. May 2 was, furthermore, a beloved holiday among heavy drinkers. If vigilance in the Air Defense increased in the lead-up to May 1, on May 2, some guys would come out to watch duty with serious hangovers, while others would wait until after watch duty to begin their celebrations.

In March, I had a serious discussion with Alya. Regardless of the divorce, I continued living in the same apartment, and not only doing my share of the household chores but also fulfilling my conjugal duties. But suddenly, she

---

[1]   In Russian, the name of the Soviet political-punitive organization created by the Bolsheviks on December 20, 1917, was *Chrezvichaynaya Komissiya*, thus "Cheka" for short. It was the first Soviet secret police, known for its brutal tortures, murders, and executions. This term entered the vernacular as slang even after the agency was replaced by the NKVD and finally the KGB.

put the question to me tougher: either I forget about Israel, or we put an end to our cohabitation. Since I wouldn't be needing a permanent residence after May 2, there was no need for us to trade in our apartment for two smaller ones. I decided to rent a room, and on April 1 moved in next door to Misha Korenblit.

My March conversation with Alya swam up in my memory when I learned from the investigator that they had discovered our hijacking plan in that same month. Perhaps the investigator knew what had passed between me and Alya, and mentioned March in order to increase my suspicions.

Time passed slowly, and I was unable to speed up our preparations. I decided to leave my job and join the process of selecting passengers from among Hillel's friends. Out of four, only one had agreed. I think that was a good percentage.

At the end of March, Hillel Butman, Misha Korenblit, Edik Kuznetsov, and I met up in one of our apartments. We discussed everything pertaining to Operation Wedding, including the question of weaponry. I was anxious for us to have firearms, arguing that in the event something went wrong, they could shoot us up like pheasants. Hillel was categorically against this, to the point of refusing to take part in the hijacking. We decided that we would only use weapons for intimidation. At this meeting, I met Edik for the first time. Together, we went to Leningrad airport to determine the flight number and departure time of our flight to Murmansk. Hillel gave a correct estimation of this meeting in his book. I quote:

> That evening, I lost control over Operation Wedding. Mark Dymshits and Edik Kuznetsov exchanged addresses during their trip to the airport. After that, they could continue to act without me. What is more, as neither of them was a member of the Organization, they were least likely to consider its interests.[2]

That evening, I would add, confirmed my desire to see Operation Wedding through in one form or another. There was less than a month left until our agreed date. The mood was rising. And suddenly, like a bolt from the blue, on April 11, at one of our regular meetings, Butman revealed that

---

[2]   *Leningrad to Jerusalem with a Long Layover* (Heb., 1981), 155.

the committee had decided to ask Israel about the wisdom of conducting Operation Wedding. If Israel gave permission, we would carry out the operation, but if not, we would give it up – and for the moment we would set it aside until Israel's answer came.

In the first place, Hillel should not have mentioned the committee, but had obviously chosen to name the committee instead of his "friends" to give their decision more weight. In the second place, after five months of preparation, how could he just walk away from our goal like that? It was clear that the Israel question was a ploy – because no government would sanction the hijacking of a plane. Maybe only governments like Libya or Iraq. I immediately told Hillel that the answer would be negative, and that as citizens of the USSR (albeit only nominally), we had to make our own decisions.

But I was also mistaken, as Israel's reply would only be the harbinger of more serious problems (a "fatal medicine"). Either a positive or negative answer would make Israel complicit in the preparation of a "terrorist act," something I would learn only after arriving in Israel. Back then, I firmly believed that there was no use waiting, that Hillel and his friends had only had enough courage for five months of preparation, and that I had to get together with Edik and start all over again.

If I had been religious, I would have appealed to the Almighty. That whole time, I had a feeling of external pressure to bring Operation Wedding to a conclusion, as if a voice was hovering somewhere above my head, saying, "You must, you must." I think that was a consequence of my air force service.

As Edik Kuznetsov and I were in agreement, I traveled to Riga at the end of April. I had never been to the Baltic states before, and therefore had a desire to see the city, in addition to our business meeting. I went to his and Sylva's place, and took Edik outside for a talk. After that, we went inside again, and I was introduced to Yosef Mendelevich. Yosef was the first religious Jew I had ever met (not counting my grandmother). He agreed to show me around Riga, and we began our tour with the synagogue. In Leningrad, I had always been afraid to go into the synagogue, assuming it was under KGB surveillance. And here I was in Riga, about to visit the synagogue. I overreacted, expressed myself rudely, and we quickly went outside. After taking a walk along some of the central streets, which reminded me of Leningrad, we drove to the forest, where we discussed the proposed hijacking. We chose a date for our next meeting, and I returned to Leningrad.

As an aside, yesterday, December 16, 1989, I learned of the death of Andrey Dmitrievich Sakharov – a great humanist and academician, the honor and conscience of Russia. Can anyone in Russia measure up to him? I don't think so. In general, I have the feeling that for every democrat in Russia there are a thousand enemies of freedom. Sakharov supported our fight to reach Israel. Sakharov petitioned the chairman of the Supreme Soviet Presidium, Podgorny, to commute our death sentences, categorically refusing to believe that we had betrayed our motherland. Not only Russia, but the whole human race, has lost a great man and a Nobel laureate.

On May 1, I was invited by Hillel Butman to a gathering at his apartment. Sylva and Edik had arrived from Riga. Yuriy Fyodorov had arrived from Moscow. I lived in the same area as Hillel. We drank a round of vodka and chatted. Then, Edik, Hillel, and I went outside to discuss Operation Wedding. Israel's response had still not come, and the only ones waiting for it were those who were using it to inform their decision. For Edik and me, the response had no significance, since we did not belong to the Organization and had not sought Israel's consent.

Hillel confronted us with three conditions: To carry out our own hijacking, "without getting the Jews mixed up in it" – which meant that a majority of the participants had to be non-Jewish; once we had reached Sweden, to coordinate our further actions with the Israeli embassy; and to give the Organization advance warning.

Again, we were not members of the Organization, which meant that these conditions were a matter of form. In future, we would make our own decisions.

Of course, Hillel himself could have left the Organization and continued to cooperate with us. It would have even been possible for the Organization to sign a formal exclusion notice, based on his participation in the operation. True, it was hard to throw off the KGB's plans with a few pieces of paper. The KGB could even call the words of Lenin anti-Soviet when they needed to arrest someone – Yakov Suslensky, for example.

Then I thought that perhaps Butman had wanted to conduct the hijacking by proxy, but I soon rejected this idea. At the end of the day, the Organization meant more to him than Operation Wedding, and he didn't want to put his family and friends at risk.

I quote several lines from Hillel's book:

It was a tough conversation. Tomorrow, May 2, should have been D-Day. Now everything was being put off. Everything was left hanging. And what is more, I felt a wall of distance grow between us. If Israel's answer was 'no,' then the participants of Operation Wedding who were also members of the Organization would desist. But the others... How would Mark and Edik behave in the case of a negative response? There was no way of telling. I had already ceded control over Operation Wedding.[3]

Next, we had another three-person meeting, but with a different group. Right there on the street outside Butman's building, Fyodorov, Kuznetsov, and I discussed our further actions. We decided to continue our preparations. I took it upon myself to look for other options. Edik Kuznetsov would lead the search for passengers in Riga. We would communicate by telephone, keeping in mind the possibility of being wiretapped.

Edik proposed to keep the Zionist committee ignorant of all our actions. His caution was not unfounded. At the Zionist Organization conference of May 4, 1970, Ben Tovbin threatened Butman that if the latter didn't cease his preparations for the hijacking, he, Tovbin, would personally inform the KGB. I learned that from Butman's book much later. At the time, I was only struck by Kuznetsov's excessive caution. Fyodorov said nothing. We parted with hope and faith.

Did I think what might await us in the case of arrest? Of course I did. I had read about trials, prison, and labor camps in Solzhenitsyn's writings. I weighed up the living conditions against my own abilities. I endured physical pain fairly well. I had experience with hunger, and was no stranger to extreme cold, heat, and lack of air. My weak spot was sleep deprivation, which meant that night interrogations could be an effective means of humiliation and exhaustion. But a man could also refuse to respond, fall asleep, or lose consciousness. That was also a way out. I was prepared for all these things.

On the level of society, I thought there would be a public trial and an international furor. The longer our sentences, the louder the furor would be. Shorter sentences would result in less attention and a smaller likelihood of aliyah. In

---

[3]   *Leningrad to Jerusalem with a Long Layover*, 189.

those days, I was afraid they might arrest us at our various homes and try us secretly, and separately, in regional courts. I was even afraid of frightening the KGB, in the event I discovered they were on our trail. Which they were.

Putting myself in the place of KGB officer, I sketched the following scenarios for myself:

1. I know about the proposed hijacking and I want to prevent an international hullaballoo and a mass exit of Soviet Jews. I call up each of the participants individually and tell them, "We know everything you are planning. Do you want to go to prison?" "No." "Then we will give you forty-eight hours to pack up and get on a plane for Israel. The air will be clearer. But if any of you are slow to leave, we'll arrest you. Is that clear?" "Clear." In that way, I could get fifty to sixty families out of the Soviet Union, and everything would calm down for a year or two.

2. I know about the proposed hijacking. I arrest each of the participants at his or her home. During the investigation I act like a traditional hostage taker and offer the Jewish prisoners to Israel in exchange for some kind of product, technology, or loan, and in a couple of years the exchange of goods takes place. (At that time, I had no idea how cruel and bloodthirsty they really were, that they might want to set fear upon the Soviet Jewish population. But more about that later. I would learn that lesson later.)

3. I know everything. I make arrests at the aerodrome. There is a trial, followed by short prison sentences and no media attention. Quite the reverse; I decide to make the organs, the trial, and the whole system look humane and fair. I offer to exchange the hijackers (as in version No. 2) for our own "progressive" freedom fighters, who have been rotting away in capitalist prisons.

I had not considered that the world was irrational, and that the organs might act against common sense in favor of their own corrupt interests.

I returned from rose-colored fantasies to real life. On May 19, I went to see Alya and wish her happy birthday. She asked if I had given up yet on my plan to get to Israel. I answered that I was still looking for a way. "I can't live here," I told her, "I can't breathe in this atmosphere of lies and hate."

Alya said that she would talk to our daughters and come back with an answer. She wanted to keep our family together, and said that everything would become clear once she had talked to Liza and Yuliya. Liza would turn nineteen that year, and Yuliya was fifteen.

So, May 19, 1970, would be the day that decided the fate of my family. Either they would come with me to Israel, or I would lose them for a long time, perhaps forever.

I returned to my apartment (on the far side of the Neva) with mixed feelings. I was tortured by one question: why, after refusing categorically to leave Russia, had Alya suddenly decided to keep the family together? I decided to put off any more thinking to the next day, when I would have her reply. That night seemed like an eternity. I couldn't get the questions out of my head, but kept putting off the answer until the next day.

On May 20, I went to meet Alya. We went for a walk along Novoizmaylovsky Prospect and sat down on a bench. There were no passersby, no one to bother us. It was chilly and wet. Alya told me that after a lengthy discussion with our daughters, she had decided to stay with me, to keep our family together, and whatever happened would happen. She and the girls understood, of course, that it was illegal to leave the USSR and had nonetheless made up their minds to try.

I did not ask for the details of their conversation, and Alya talked in general terms. I could sense – it was obvious – that the decision had been difficult for them to make. Our whole meeting was tense. You could imagine how they must have felt. After all, this wasn't just a trip out of town.

I told Alya that I would go back to my apartment, pack my things, and move back in tomorrow.

I went back to my rented room, sat down on the folding bed, and began to consider the situation. On the one hand, I was glad that my wife and children would be with me. On the other hand, what if we were arrested? I didn't want to give them any information about the plan, let alone its details. If that happened, they could also risk prison.

But it was also possible that Alya was working for the KGB. The following scenario drew itself in my imagination: The KGB became aware of our idea, and perhaps even our plan for May 2. They began to investigate us, but nothing happened. They most likely became aware of the Organization's rejection of our plan. But then, they wondered, what were we planning next? Then, the KGB called up Alya and maybe even the children as well.

They say to Alya, "Alevtina Ivanovna, we know what your former husband and his associates are planning. They want to do great harm to our motherland, which I do not doubt is also your motherland. For such a crime they may answer with their lives. I imagine that you are not indifferent to your husband's fate. We can return him to you and spare his life, but you must help us. If you agree to cooperate with us, for the sake of our motherland and your family, I will give you further instructions. You will not find them complicated."

"To save his life and return him to the family, I would do anything," Alya replies. "Russia has always been and will always be my motherland."

"All right, Alevtina Ivanovna," the KGB officer continues, "agree to emigrate to Israel with your husband, and inform us of his intentions. Here is our telephone number, call at any time. Your agreement might lead your husband to suspicion, so be careful. Thanks to your cooperation, Alevtina Ivanovna, we will prevent a crime from taking place, and you will regain your husband, and your daughters their father. I hope that your former spouse has not become too set in his anti-Soviet ways. Tell no one about our conversation. I wish you luck! As they say, 'God bless!'"

I asked myself what I should do if that was really the case. Tell Edik and Yura about my suspicions? But I had no proof. What would it change? I would only set everybody's nerves on edge. Could I spy on Alya? But what if I was being spied on? Then we would all be arrested at home – the least desirable outcome. I racked my brains for two hours thinking over all of this, and concluded that I should cast off all suspicions, continue to look for a new way to hijack an airplane, and maintain my connection with Riga.

On May 21, I had an unplanned meeting with Hillel Butman and Lev Korenblit near the building where I rented a room and studied at the ulpan. We found an empty lot. As the weather was cloudy with spitting rain, there was no one on the street, and consequently no one bothered us. Hillel and Lev began the conversation by informing me that Israel had answered in the negative, that Israel was contending with air piracy and Arab terrorism, and that Operation Wedding would only be harmful to Israel. Both Hillel and Lev led me to understand that the Organization was worried by our intentions and was in a state of alarm.

I replied that I was not a member of the Organization and would not submit to its decisions, that they had embroiled Israel in our affair, and their response could never have been "yes." I considered our plan to be beneficial and would not turn my back on it now.

"But Mark," Hillel said, "could you at least warn us when you decide to act, so we can take the necessary safety measures?"

To which I replied, "Consider yourselves warned."

In his book *Leningrad to Jerusalem with a Long Layover*, Hillel does not mention this important meeting, and I think not by chance. It was this meeting that put an end to our communication regarding Operation Wedding.

I will quote Hillel's closing speech at his trial:

> The only time was the May 22 [sic], when Lev Lvovich and I tried to talk him out of it, shouted at him, demanded that he drop the idea, and Dymshits said, 'Well, consider yourselves warned!' If you can call that a warning – even though at that point he had no concrete plan, and made no secret of that – I really am guilty of failing to react to his warning as a true Soviet citizen should have. I simply didn't take him seriously.[4]

Of course, Hillel had been perfectly aware that a "true Soviet citizen" would warn the KGB. You can cut him some slack, considering he was speaking in front of the court and wanted to get away with a shorter sentence. But it was foolish of him to call my warning anything less than serious. Lev Lvovich took the warning seriously.

After that, our conversation became heated. It was as if we were speaking different languages and moved by different feelings. At the end of that difficult meeting, I packed my bags, paid my landlady, hailed a taxi, and returned home to my family.

Only after that meeting did I begin to feel the danger presented by the Organization. I understood that after my warning, there would be further attempts to persuade me to back down. I thought that Butman understood how determined I was to see the operation through to its conclusion. After all, Butman had proposed an analogous plan, to hijack a large passenger plane.

4　　Abram Rozhansky, ed. *Anti-Jewish Trials in the Soviet Union*, vol. 1, *1969–1971* (Jerusalem: Hebrew University Centre for Research and Documentation of East European Jewry, 1979), 451.

This plan was to have been carried out not for us, but for the common good, for aliyah. It had never even entered my mind to dispute Butman's plan, or to doubt his and his friends' determination.

The risk was great, but the goal was also great. For the sake of such a goal one could, and should, as far as I was concerned, risk a great deal. I quote Butman:

> The escape of a few people was, for us, not a question of their personal destinies, but a possible solution to the national problem in the USSR, and our contribution to the battle for Israel...The Operation could become the Organization's swan song. But we created the Organization in order to accomplish specific goals, not to keep ourselves alive. We must sing our swan song to the end.[5]

But when the going got tough, none of those who had agreed to the hijacking in theory wanted to make their contribution and sing their swan song. In general, members of the intelligentsia are cautious, risk averse, and indecisive, and most Jews in the Russian diaspora were similarly afflicted. Most of the intelligentsia was inclined to endlessly discuss actions that might present mortal risk, but they would never make a decision, let alone carry out such an action. And for that, you couldn't blame them. But I should have been aware of these qualities and not tried to involve the intelligentsia in such an action.

The Jewish intelligentsia in the Russian Empire did much to revive Jewish traditions, history, and language as well as popular support for Israel. But Operation Wedding was not for them.

This might sound a little boastful, but in Russia, pilots were said to be a mixture of "concentrated willpower and the ability to take risks." These qualities were encouraged in aviation. Perhaps they explain the large percentage of pilots who have participated in government coups and other adventures. You just can't expect such qualities from people who have worked all their lives in factories and civilian institutions. Back then, I didn't consider and had no way of considering this factor, as I didn't know many of Butman's friends.

I began to think about the ethical side of the operation, considering how things stood in the USSR, when the principle of "the end justifies the means"

---

[5]   *Leningrad to Jerusalem with a Long Layover*, 132.

was the norm for society and even more so for the regime. We lived in a state that was immune to the rule of law, where laws were neither respected nor fulfilled. The principle of "hold on and don't let go" did not enable us to leave Russia legally. Hijacking a plane in a democratic, civilized country would be considered a terrorist act, motivated by political or financial aims. But in our case, hijacking a plane was a way to leave the Soviet Union, which had signed the Declaration of Human Rights without carrying out its requirements.

Now that perestroika and glasnost have come to Russia, and it is possible to leave in an almost normal way, would it even occur to anyone to hijack a plane? Of course not!

From words to deeds. We needed to develop a new plan of action. I returned to my first idea of hijacking an An-2. It would not be a problem to find twelve passengers, not like it had been a year ago. Riga wasn't Leningrad, and the regime there hadn't managed to cripple people with fear in the same way. Edik confidently declared that in Riga there would be a surplus of willing participants. If I had known the people of Riga from the very beginning, our preparations might have lasted no longer than two or three weeks. But that's all hypothetical…

I tried to remember what the night watch had been like at Bukhara airport. One cripple with a Berdan rifle would come in the evening, as the working day was ending, and would guard the airport through the night – utility rooms, aircraft parking, storerooms. He always arrived drunk, or would bring vodka and a snack with him. Because he was missing one leg, and had no prosthesis, he would move around on crutches, and his mobility after his usual dose of alcohol was limited to the edges of his raincoat, which he spread out on the ground. If you gave him an extra bottle, you wouldn't even have to tie him up or gag him.

Apart from the security guard, the airport also had a dispatcher on night duty. The Bukhara airport did not operate at night, but its aerodrome could be used in the event of an emergency. During my time in Bukhara, the aerodrome was not once used to land a plane at night. Girls would usually come to the dispatch point by night, turning it into a little brothel. Planes were parked on the other side of the airfield. That was how things stood at Bukhara airport in 1961–62.

But it was already 1970, and Leningrad was not Bukhara. Here the rules were completely different to how they were in Central Asia. We would have to study Smolny airport and find answers to all possible questions, including where they kept the aircraft batteries in the event they took them off the planes overnight.

On May 23, Sylva, Edik, and I went on a reconnaissance mission. We took the train to Smolny station and approached the hardstand from the forest behind. It grew dark. At the edge of the hardstand was a watch tower with a guard in it. Communications and signal wires had been trained to the top of the tower. There was a rope drawn along the hardstand, which was guarded by several German shepherds on chains. There were dogs every fifty yards. Strobe lights illuminated the whole hardstand. We observed for a while from the bushes before heading back. On our way, we decided that this version wasn't going to work.

Whereas Hillel Butman and Lev Korenblit had tried to make me give up the operation, Sylva Zalmanson made me promise not to abandon the operation for at least a year. I refused to give a year's guarantee, but I promised to do all I could to find a viable option.

A day later, I decided to get a job, any job, at Smolny airport, and study all the possibilities of hijacking an An-2 on the ground or in the air. Then we could develop a new plan.

On May 26, on prior agreement with Butman, I came at lunchtime to the factory where he worked.

After the committee had refused their support, the plan to hijack a large plane faded away on its own. But this did not mean that the operation was off the agenda. For the Leningrad Zionist Organization, perhaps. But for me, the guys from Riga, Yura Fyodorov, and Aleksey Murzhenko, not one bit. The situation was the same as it had been five days earlier, when I had given my warning. Besides, I had promised to continue my search for a Plan B. I would have to play a game of cat and mouse with Hillel.

We met. I told him that I hadn't yet worked out a new plan, but that I had moved back in with my family. I chose not to mention the fact that my family had agreed to travel with me to Israel. Nor did I mention what kind of work I was looking for and why. Hillel offered to petition Israel on my family's behalf. As little as a week ago, I would have refused immediately. But as things stood now, due to my warning and our new relationship, I began to squirm for the first time in my life.

I answered that there was no way the government would let me leave. I was certain of that. Even now, looking back, I imagine that I would have spent no less than fifteen years waiting for an exit visa. Hillel argued that he and fellow Organization member Solomon Drezner knew the same state secrets as I did, but I did not count these arguments as serious. Though Drezner may have known the particulars of the MiG-15, its prototype had already been delivered to England during the Korean War – though it remained a state secret in Russia. Even the 1898/1931 model of the three-line rifle was a state secret, as were crime statistics in the Russian Empire. But such "secrets" only existed in order to hide the real state of things, that is, how far we lagged behind the West, as well as making it possible to charge anyone with the crime of divulging "secrets."

I, unlike Drezner, was familiar with actually secret maps of anti-aircraft defense in the Transbaikal and North Caucasus Military Districts – much more to the point than any information about the MiG-15 or the number of murders in a given area of Leningrad.

But it wasn't those concerns which held me back. Rather, I knew that the process of lodging a petition would eat up time I needed to prepare. After the results of a petition came through, there could be no further discussion of the hijacking. In order to avoid a discussion of whether or not they would let us go, however, I gave Hillel the necessary information to petition for myself, Alya, and the girls. What I privately thought to myself was this: now we need to speed up our search for Plan B-time was ticking. We had only two or three months at our disposal.

At that meeting with Hillel, I didn't get antsy, nor did I shout as I had the last time. I behaved with caution, so that no one from the Organization would have any reason to go to the KGB. But you couldn't slip away from Butman. He insisted that I give up on Operation Wedding in principle, even if a viable Plan B were to reveal itself. Hillel so wanted to hear me say "Yes," without the risk of confusing his desire with reality, but he already knew me. Later, he would write: "After deciding that his place was in Israel, Mark, with his character, was bound to fight to the very end. And he did."[6]

If our previous conversation had been demanding, this one seemed diplomatic, with elements of blackmail. Hillel asked me to give him an answer. I said that I needed to think first. In order to be totally clear on my position, Butman made a sneaky move. He suggested I sign a telegram expressing my

---

6   *Leningrad to Jerusalem with a Long Layover,* 126.

sympathy for the victims of a recent Arab terrorist attack on a bus of children. I said that I would answer that question in the evening as well.

Now I had to wrack my brains: how could I avoid frightening them, while at the same time not allowing their caution to lapse?

That evening, I answered the two questions. To the first, I answered yes. This answer calmed them down, while also giving me a few months for Plan B. To the second, I answered No. This answer was meant to make them think, to put them on their guard. I could not answer yes to the second question, or I would immediately find myself in time trouble. I would only have several days at my disposal.

Later, two days before the hijacking attempt, I gave them another warning. But more about that later.

In the early morning of June 1, 1970, I set out for Smolny airport with the aim of finding a job. Before going to the human resources department, I went to the waiting room and began to examine the flights of local airlines. I noticed that on June 1, the new flight 179 from Leningrad to Sortavala via Priozersk, was commencing service. Next to the timetable of flights hung a scheme of all the routes. Flipping through them, I noticed that flight 179 came closest to the Finnish border. I knew nothing about the airport in Priozersk, where the plane made its stopover, and this knowledge was essential.

I immediately approached the ticket desk and bought a ticket. There were only a few minutes left until boarding began. I walked outside and waited for the announcement. In a few minutes, exactly one hour before departure, the pilot came out of the dispatch room and asked those of us who were standing there, "Is anyone here flying on flight 179?"

I answered in the affirmative, and went up to him.

"Since there's only one passenger, we don't want to taxi up to the airport building," the pilot said. "If it's no trouble for you, I would request that you accompany me to the plane on foot."

I replied that as I had no luggage, just a newspaper, I was ready to go. We crossed the airfield, toward the hardstand where several An-2s were parked. We walked along the hardstand as if we were out for a morning stroll. The weather was beautiful, and my overall mood was high. A Plan B was hatching.

"Will we be flying on an aeroplane like that one, with two wings?" I asked the pilot. "Were aeroplanes like that in use before the war?"

The co-pilot answered my questions seriously. "These are new planes. A plane with two wings is called a biplane. Its large wing area allows it to take off and land where space is limited. And generally, we don't call them 'aeroplanes' anymore. We use the Russian word, *samolet* [airplane]."

"And this *samolet*," the pilot continued, playing the role of guide, "is the personal aircraft of Secretary Tolstikov of the Party Regional Committee. Look how lovely it is inside."

The pilot opened the door of the plane. It really had been tastefully done. I had seen scores of aircraft in Uzbekistan and flown An-2s, but this was the first time I had seen such a comfortable interior.

We approached our aircraft. The captain was already in the cockpit, and the co-pilot took his place. The door to the cockpit was wide open, and passenger seats ranged along the sides of the plane (a far cry from the plush chairs in the governor's jet). I sat beside the door and glanced at the fuel meter. There were about 250 gallons of fuel left, which would serve us for about 550 miles. Not bad. The An-2's fuel capacity was just over three hundred gallons.

The captain radioed the dispatch point and turned on the motor. We taxied out of our parking spot, crossed the runway, and approached the boarding area. At this point, the motor was turned off. I thought that we might be about to take on more passengers, but no one showed up. The pilots left the aircraft and I with them. The co-pilot said he hoped I wasn't in a hurry. "We have received a command to take a navigator on board," he explained. "This is our first flight to Sortavala, and without a navigator they won't let us go." Both pilots went off to the dispatch room, while I spent fifteen minutes walking around the plane. At last, the three of them appeared: the captain in front, the co-pilot behind him, and about fifty feet behind them trailed the navigator, quite a beefy guy. The captain sat in his seat, the navigator sat in the co-pilot's seat, and the co-pilot sat opposite me by the open door to the cockpit.

We took off and attained cruising altitude. My attention was divided between the instruments and land orientation points, which I observed through the porthole. At the same time, I asked stupid questions, like, "Do planes really always fly along the railroad lines?"

"How small the people are, just like ants!" I exclaimed in surprise, remembering the old story: A passenger who is flying for the first time sits next to the window. After its engines are turned on, the plane slowly taxies to the runway, where it waits in line behind another plane. Before takeoff, the engines begin to revolve with greater speed. At which point the passenger looks out the porthole, nudges his neighbor, an experienced flyer, and says, "Look how small the people are, just like ants!" "Those are ants," answers his neighbor. "We're still on the ground."

The co-pilot started getting bored of my stupid questions, stood up, scratched his head, and went into the cockpit. After rummaging around between the seats for a while, he returned to his place opposite from me. A TT pistol had appeared in his hands. I gave no sign of surprise, pretended total indifference, and continued to examine the scenery beneath us. The co-pilot took out the magazine with cartridges. Holding the pistol like a snake, he began to turn, poke, disassemble. Discreetly observing his inept manipulations, I thought that with such "specialists" we wouldn't be needing actual firearms. The co-pilot fiddled with the pistol for ten minutes before returning it to the cockpit. Then, as he had nothing to do, he came back, yawned loudly, and dropped off to sleep.

I continued to examine the terrain, as well as the flight instruments – trying to recover my old skills after an eight-year break. We skirted around some kind of forbidden zone, then returned to our course. Here was Priozersk. We landed, taxied up to a rustic wooden house. Everyone got out of the plane. A man came out of the house, and asked the pilot if everything was all right. "Yes," replied the pilot. "Tell the dispatcher that we have no passengers for the next leg."

I set off in the direction of town, but after two hundred yards, sat down on a bench to watch the crew. In a few minutes, they were back on the plane and bound for Sortavala. I watched the houses on the edge of the aerodrome for half an hour, while supposedly reading a newspaper, then took off for a walk around it. Next to the aerodrome were a cemetery and a pine wood. Cows were grazing on the edge of the forest. No radar, no radio. Only one telephone in the wooden house, which was obviously inhabited by the man from before, whose job it was to keep an eye on the airfield and keep telephone contact with the airport.

We could not have hoped for better.

After this examination, I went into the town of Priozersk, where I boarded a bus back to Leningrad. On the way, I thought over all the elements of our plan. As 1:5 (one inch to five miles) maps were secret, and 1:10 were only for professional use, I had to buy a 1:25 map of the whole northwestern USSR at a kiosk. That same day, I called Edik in Riga, and told him that he must come to Leningrad on June 8, as we had earlier agreed.

Later, some of our group members began to wonder whether flight 179 had been put into operation by the KGB, or whether it flew every year during the summer. Perhaps both things were true. Our plan was desirable for the KGB as it was for us.

Six months from now, June 15, 1990, will mark the twentieth anniversary of the arrests. Perhaps they (the organs) will release their files on the affair, following the example of Great Britain. In the meanwhile, we can only make assumptions and propose our own versions. If we imagine that the flight was added on purpose and that the KGB was counting on my visit to Smolny airport, the question still arises: Why did they need to demonstrate to me that the crew was armed? That way, they could have put us off Operation Wedding.

That evidence could be refuted in the following way. The KGB knew of our plan beginning in March 1970. A group was formed to investigate us and take any necessary measures. A grand plan was formed, of arrests, trials, striking fear into Soviet Jews. The KGB needed a significant case, which would demonstrate the necessity of their existence in the face of domestic enemies, and for that they would need support from all sides as well as an unlimited budget. In the lower ranks of the KGB, they were counting on medals and rewards, ranks and promotions. Some were thinking of state interests, but mostly they were thinking of what they'd be doing in a year's time. The song that went "think first about Motherland, then about yourself" was, after all, only a song. KGB officers at that time were extremely cynical and no less anti-Soviet.

And suddenly, I appeared at Smolny airport alone, and immediately bought a ticket for flight 179.

Perhaps what happened was something like the following. Dymshits – obviously a maniac or fanatic of some kind – notices that he is being followed. Knowing he has fallen into a trap, he decides to hijack the plane alone. In that case, he risks spoiling the KGB's plans. He has to be given a fright, a reason to gather his friends together for a proper showdown. Then we (that is, the KGB) can take them all in. We will prove that our unlimited budget is not in vain, including the 15 percent of confiscated property we take from the MVD – in the sense that we steal all of their lucrative cases. But I digress.

So, according to this version, they would have summoned the crew to the dispatch point, reinforced it with a navigator (probably a KGB agent), and demonstrated that they had weapons on board.

However, I had only been doing reconnaissance. What is more, I knew that flights in the border zone had to be equipped with firearms, and that the first flight on a new route had to be manned by a navigator. In short, the above factors failed to impress me. The reverse, in fact. On the one hand, I saw how inexperienced the co-pilot was with weapons. On the other hand, the sign of the TT pistol reminded me of my own magazine and cartridges from the army, which I decided to take with me.

Now from assumptions and hypotheses to what really happened. As I had been the only passenger to Priozersk, I worried that a lack of passengers might lead them to cancel the flight. For this reason, I asked Yuliya to fly to Priozersk with a girlfriend. We had to show Aeroflot (or the KGB) that there was demand. On June 4, Yulia and her friend took flight 179, doubling its previous number of passengers. On June 8, there were six passengers from the KGB and three from our group. So you could say that demand for the flight was increasing.

In Leningrad, I was visited not only by Edik Kuznetsov but also by Yura Fyodorov. In basic terms, I explained Plan B to them. As there were now more willing participants than there were seats on the plane, we had to create a second group. The plan, in brief, went like this:

We would buy twelve tickets for flight 179. Another four would take the train to Priozersk and wait for our plane to land at the aerodrome. Upon arrival in Priozersk, the main group would seize and tie up the pilots. I would get behind the control wheel, taxi toward the woods – where we would leave the pilots – pick up our other four group members and fly through Finland to the Swedish town of Boden.

On Monday, June 8, three of us set off on another reconnaissance flight from Smolny airport. We boarded individually, as if we were strangers. This time, we were accompanied by six "farmers." These burly KGB agents, dressed in padded jackets, were making sure that we three didn't try to make a run for it. The three of us really could have thrown off the "big case" they had prepared.

We flew on the Secretary Tolstikov's plane. In such an important matter, it made sense to be flying the best An-2 in the region. The door to the cockpit stayed open the whole flight, which was standard practice. I noticed that this time, we had only 180 gallons of fuel, which would not have been enough to get us to Sweden. That possibility also had to be taken into account.

The "farmers" also pretended not to know each other. One of them, who had his arm in a cast, could hardly sit still. He was obviously itching to give one of us a blow to the head with his fake "broken arm." The KGB agents had to contain the anger they felt toward the enemies of the "very, very best regime" in the whole world. Their instructions evidently permitted them to act only in the case of an obvious hijacking attempt.

Another "farmer" with an empty basket spent the whole flight hunched over, his hand thrust deep into his right pocket. This agent must have wanted to put his pistol into action, but again, the instructions got in the way. Instructions, in the KGB, are more important and more reliable than law. I couldn't see the any other agents, as they were all sitting behind me.

Of course, it would have been easy to arrest the three of us. But it wouldn't have been enough for a "big case." Small-scale gratitude, a few medals "for valor in combat," nothing more. But they wanted more. We only needed to be stalled a little... It was only a matter of time!

> Comrade officers, with a little forbearance, we will build a case on the level of the Doctors' Plot. These Jewish bastards are looking to make a break from our loving family of friendly nations. We'll show them Israel! We'll show them so much Israel, they'll forget it ever existed! We gave their small nation a whole province at the expense of the great Russian nation, but they're always complaining. Give these bourgeois Jewish nationalists their Israel, and they'll have a base for world domination...

That was how Leningrad KGB chief Lieutenant General Nosyrev began his brief, after receiving preliminary instructions from his boss in Moscow, Andropov.

As I write these lines, the Romanian nation has just overthrown a bloody dictatorship. Nicolae Ceausescu and his wife Elena, who added their own bloody chapter to the Soviet story, have been executed. The Romanian KGB, or Securitate, showed the whole world what the role of such organizations in so-called "socialist" countries really is.

But I will return to the events of June 8, 1970. We flew into Priozersk. We had a look around. At intervals of twenty or thirty feet, Yura, Edik, and I walked in the direction of the town. Our six farmer-bodyguards got confused and didn't know where to go. Evidently, they were here for the first time, and their instructions had not entered into such small details. After taking a minute to collect themselves, they set off in the opposite direction to Priozersk, and left us in peace.

Once we were alone, we walked together and began to discuss our plan. We passed a lone "Volga," parked on the side of the road. Two men were loitering around the car's raised hood. Yura's practiced eye immediately determined that these were KGB agents. Edik confirmed this. I was gaining the impression that guys in operations were typecast. Their appearance was so similar that they could have been blood brothers. Even without Edik and Yura's experience, I could not say anything against their suspicions, and silently agreed.

We boarded a suburban train. There was no one in the carriage to stop us from discussing our new plan. On the way to Leningrad, we discussed all the details and reached a unanimous decision: this was the plan for us. We decided to buy up all twelve tickets for flight 179 on Monday, June 15. We immediately decided who the passengers would be. The second group would take a train to Priozersk on the evening of June 14. There, in the forest by the aerodrome, this group would wait for our plane to arrive. While they were waiting, they would prepare a hiding place for the bound and gagged pilots.

When we, the first twelve passengers, flew into the Priozersk aerodrome and the co-pilot went to the door to let passengers out, two or three of us would grab his arms and bind him. Simultaneously, another three people would attack the captain, who usually stays in the cockpit for another fifteen to twenty seconds after landing. I would take the wheel and taxi over to the forest, where the second group would be waiting for us. We would put the bound pilots in sleeping bags and put gags in their mouths. We even decided that if either of them were wounded, Mary Hanoch, a nurse who was part of the Riga cohort, would give them tetanus injections.

Edik suggested that we take their photo ID cards. The USSR would definitely demand that Sweden return us escapees, alleging that we had committed murder. The KGB would dredge up some pictures of dead alcoholics, and that's when we'd need photos of the actual pilots to use as counterevidence.

We discussed the question of how many passengers would come. The An-2 usually accommodates twelve passengers, but could hold twenty people without any danger. There would be sixteen of us without luggage. Since we would leave the two pilots on the ground, and during the flight to Priozersk we would consume a quantity of fuel equal to the weight of two people, our weight from Priozersk would be the same as our initial weight setting out from Leningrad.

It would take ten minutes to reach the Finnish border at a speed of one hundred miles per hour. We would fly low (twenty to thirty feet), out of radar range. If we were detected, the nearest military aerodrome was located between Leningrad and Priozersk. In the time it would take to contact the aerodrome and mobilize a unit of fighter planes from second alertness level, we would have already made it across the border.

Of course, the Finnish border was no obstacle for the USSR. If the fighter planes were able to detect and intercept us, which would be quite hard to do, as their radar screens would show only static close to the ground, I would make contact with them on channel four. I would communicate to them that two armed terrorists had hijacked the plane and were forcing us to divert course to Finland. There were women and children on board.

We imagined that KGB agents felt themselves quite at home in Helsinki. Besides, Finland had an agreement with the USSR that the former would return any escapees. Considering all of these factors, there was little chance that they would shoot us down. Of course, if they found out that there were only Jews on board, they could shoot us down even over Finnish territory, without experiencing the least pang of conscience. That was, of course, if they were able to hit us! It isn't so easy to contend with a low-flying, slow-moving target.

If all went according to plan, we would land at the aerodrome in Boden. If we didn't have enough fuel to get to Sweden, we would land on an open part of the highway, or in a suitable field. Then, we would need to walk through the forest to the Swedish border. In this eventuality, we took a small supply of groceries and water. We imagined that the border between Finland and Sweden would be purely symbolic.

In Sweden, we would ask for political asylum and appear at a press conference. The latter we had made no plans for, but we understood how unavoidable and important it was. We imagined that we might face trial in Sweden.

Considering all the reasons for our flight and the conditions which led to it, we imagined that we might be given short or nominal sentences. It would then present little difficulty to get from Sweden to Israel on a commercial flight.

Edik thought that if we were arrested in Russia and tried, we would be sentenced to ten years of hard labor. Even with his experience of the criminal justice system, he never considered the possibility of execution – or perhaps he didn't want to frighten his fellow participants.

We solved the problem of provisions, equipment, and such. We agreed to meet on the afternoon of June 14 near the aerodrome in Priozersk and confirm the final details of the operation. In the remaining days, Edik completed preparations and determined who of the cohort from Riga was going to do what.

After arriving in Leningrad, we bought a few tickets for June 15 at two different ticket kiosks. We went back to my place, had dinner, drank a shot of vodka to our collective success, and parted until the 14th.

On June 10, the participants gathered at Smerli park in Riga to discuss all the operational details. Yosef Mendelevich had made two copies of the "Testament" – our message to the public. Edik edited it for style, and in this new form it was to reach the attention of society at large as well as all the Jews of the Russian Empire. I would like to reproduce it here entirely.

> "Move! Flee the land of the north! [...]
> Move, Tziyon! You who are living with the daughter of Babylon, escape!"
> (Zechariah 2:10–1)
> We, nine Jews living in the Soviet Union, are making an attempt to leave the territory of this state without asking the government for permission. We belong to those tens of thousands of Jews who, over the course of many years, have been informing the relevant government agencies of their wish to repatriate to Israel.
> With consistently monstrous hypocrisy, perverting human, international, and even Soviet laws, the government continues to refuse us the right to leave. We are haughtily informed that we will rot here, without ever setting eyes on our Fatherland. Jews who wish to become citizens of Israel are subjected, in the USSR,

to various kinds of surveillance, even arrests. As a foreign element in this country, we are constantly under threat of events such as those of the 1940s and 50s, when the politics of religious genocide reached its apotheosis in the physical elimination of Jews. The only future in store for us here is spiritual assimilation – in the best case.

All of the Communist government's attempts to "solve the Jewish question" are in vain. They must understand, at last, that it is not in their power to decide the fate of the Jewish nation. With our actions, we hope to draw the attention of those who run the Soviet government to these eternal truths, and to the inescapable tragedy of Jewish life in the USSR. We would like to tell them that it is in their interests to let our people go Home.

We also appeal to international organizations, first of all to the UN, and to Mr U Thant[7] personally. Mr U Thant, the Jews of the Soviet Union have appealed to you more than once with pleas for help. But, evidently, the fate of a whole nation is an indifferent matter to you. You always find a way to avoid addressing our problems. You never responded to our letters, although we placed great hopes in you. You pass judgement on measures taken by Israel to defend its own existence, and you care little for us. Or are you simply afraid to challenge the interests of a great power? But in that case, who needs you? What gives you the right to speak in the name of the world's peoples? We demand that you take the necessary steps to stop this continued violation of human freedoms, to improve the plight of three million Soviet Jews. We have had enough bloody lessons, falling on the roofs of our nation.

Jews of the world! Your sacred duty is to fight for the freedom of your brothers in the USSR. Know that the fate of Russian Jews, whether they will continue to live or cease to exist, depends on you. We feel a sharp hunger for freedom, for her blessings, which have become ordinary for you. We call upon you to use them to the full; to use them in defense of our rights. And until then, until we have freedom, you must continue to build our Jewish House

---

[7] The third secretary-general of the United Nations.

and represent us in the place where we so long to be. We are
moved by the desire to live in our Motherland and share her fate.

> Mendelevich, Yosef; Riga
> Zalmanson, Israel; Riga
> Zalmanson, Wolf; Riga
> Kuznetsov, Eduard; Riga
> Altman, Anatoliy; Chernovitsy
> Dymshits, Mark; Leningrad
> Hanoch, Leib; Riga
> Penson, Boris; Riga

P.S. We appeal to you all with a request to care for our near
and dear ones, in the event we are unsuccessful, and protect them
from the repercussions of our act. It is worth underlining that our
actions do not pose any danger to those not directly involved. At
the moment our plane rises into the sky, we will be its only passengers and crew.

On the day when our plans were being discussed in Riga, and the various
roles assigned, I very nearly got myself into an unpleasant situation. This is
what happened. I was walking up to a bus stop near Victory Park. At the same
time, from the other side of the street, a man of about thirty with a wrestler's
build approached the bus stop with a woman on either arm. His purple face
and bloodshot eyes made it clear that he was boozy.

It was rush hour, people were returning home from work, and as a result,
there were many people at the bus stop. After the war, Leningrad had ceased
to be the kind of city where people lined up for the bus or tram and took their
seats calmly, in order. Those born and bred in Leningrad had dissolved into
the mass of people who had arrived from the surrounding countryside.

When the sixty-three bus approached the curb, everyone threw themselves
toward the doors and a crush ensued. The gentleman I mentioned before
ended up sitting beside me, and letting out a vodka-scented belch, he pro-
claimed quite loudly, "Are you butting in ahead of me, Abram?"

"Who gave you right of way, Ivan?" I answered with another question, in
Odessa style.

He hadn't expected such a cocky answer, and his purple face assumed a
terrible grimace. He would have started a fight, but the two women grabbed

hold of him, and in any case we were in a tightly packed bus. There was little room to raise an arm, let alone start a fight. Then, I could only think that this humdrum antisemite could get me locked up for two weeks, which would put our group in a difficult position. I should have kept my mouth shut.

Later, I thought that the KGB agents on our case could have released me from jail under any pretext – anything not to lose their "big case." But at the time, I just sighed with relief when the incident had run its course. The guy couldn't even look at me. He was probably thinking, if he was capable of thought, that these Yids needed to be stamped out, they'd got too cocky, but it'd be fine, we'd get 'em in the end.

In the apartment next door to us lived a police captain with his wife. I didn't know them well, only by sight, but we greeted each other in the hall. On the morning of the following day, we could hear a banging on the wall. Of course, it would have been fine if they had only needed to beat in a couple of nails to hang a rug or a picture, but all day?! I suggested to Alya that they might be installing a listening device in the wall. This wasn't so easy to do in concrete. Alya kept silent. In the afternoon, I rang the neighbors' doorbell. The door was opened by a pretty woman I had never seen before, in a little dressing gown, with tousled hair, and a flushed, sweaty face. I was forced to apologize, and say that I had got the wrong apartment.

Later, remembering that moment, I surmised that apart from setting up a listening station in the next room, they had also made room for a brothel.

We had to think over the potential consequences of our action one more time, not only on the social level, but also on the family level. What would await us when we arrived in Sweden? What would await us if we were arrested?

I walked out onto Novoizmaylovsky Prospect. How it had changed in ten years. Ours was one of the first families to move into the new buildings. At that time, there were no sidewalks, only ditches and mud. There were no streetlights. And now there were lawns, trees, alleys with benches on either side of the road. The street was well lit. I sat down on the same bench where Alya and I had talked twenty days ago and began once more to think over each element of Operation Wedding.

Back when I first told Hillel my idea, I imagined that our chances of success were ninety to ninety-five out of a hundred. But our chances grew slimmer and slimmer with each month, until on June 11, 1970, I guessed that they were more like five or ten out of a hundred. But as our chances of personal success, that is, a successful hijacking attempt, were lessening, I felt that our chances of social success were growing in direct proportion. By this I mean our chances of inciting the global community to fight for aliyah.

Again, the question of my wife's allegiance swam before me. If my suspicions were true, then the KGB would have promised to free me from prison before the others; that is, I would have an advantage over my comrades. However, I swore to myself on that bench that I would not take a single step to be released earlier than the others.

What is more, I decided that in the case of arrest, I would explain the reasons which had led me to hijack the plane. If I was to lie, play games, renounce the idea, renounce Israel for the sake of getting a shorter term, we would look like common criminals in the eyes of the world, and our main goal would not be achieved. If the trial was open, we would have to use our time on the stand to make sure Soviet Jews, and the world at large, knew as much as possible about our actions and their goal.

On that very day, June 11, I imagined that if my wife was cooperating with the KGB, she and my daughters would be released immediately, and if she was not cooperating with them, they would be tried and given nominal sentences.

So, we Jews were prepared for the worst. But what about Yura and Aleksey? I thought they must have had a better idea of the situation than we did, having gone through the criminal justice system as young men. They knew what they were getting themselves into. By the way, this question continued to worry me even later in Israel, after we Jews had been released and they remained in the camps.

If we got to Sweden, we would ask for political asylum and conduct a press conference, at which we would reveal the situation of Jews in the Russian Empire. But that would not exempt us from a court case. The men would probably be given small sentences, and the women would most likely be freed. But then, what would they have to live on? We had to take money with us. At that time, I was totally lost when it came to finance. Later, the KGB would spread rumors that we had suitcases full of gold, but it had not even occurred to me to swap my Soviet money for gold trinkets.

I had one thousand rubles. I called an old school friend (from first grade), and told him that I needed five hundred rubles. At our meeting, I told my friend that I planned to travel to Georgia, where it would be possible to pay for an Israeli visa. I gave him some valuables as a security, and said that if I returned, I would collect them and give back his five hundred rubles. Of course, I had no intention of returning.

I initially wanted to burn the television and radio before leaving our apartment, but later I decided to leave everything as it was – to give "Big Brother" a material stake in our departure.

On June 12, Arye and Mary Hanoch arrived from Riga. In the afternoon, I had scarcely made it home when Misha Korenblit arrived. Without realizing that Arye and Mary had gone out, I closed the door to the bedrooms, and invited Misha through to the kitchen. This visit, two (and a half) days before the event, was the last thing I needed. Misha asked me to sign a secret letter to U Thant. I refused. My reception of him and my refusal to sign the letter gave Misha grounds for suspicion and concern. As I was seeing him out, he asked me:

"Are you going through with it?"

"Yes"

"When?"

"On Monday."

"Call me a few hours before."

"All right. I'll call." We agreed on a code word.

Hillel describes this visit in his book but doesn't mention that I named the date. From his account, it seems like the Organization didn't have time to prepare for the searches that ensued.

On May 21, I had warned Hillel Butman and Lev Korenblit that I would continue with the hijacking. On May 26, I refused to sign the telegram. Now, on June 12, I had refused to sign the letter, and named the date of Operation Wedding. But this, evidently, was not enough. I still had to promise to phone Misha and tell him what time we were leaving.

In three hours, I destroyed all my notes, letters, and certificates – in short, all my papers. There was nothing anti-Soviet there, but I didn't want to leave personal information for the KGB.

How much time does it take to call or visit thirty or forty friends? I think one day is enough. In that same time frame, you can certainly hide or destroy literature and papers, and the Organization had two days.

What was the reason for their lack of speed (to put it mildly)? I think there were two reasons. First, they mistook what they wanted for reality. Summer was vacation time. No one wanted to deal with the operation, even though it had been on the cards before. It was precisely for this reason that they had contacted Israel, to get it called off. They imagined that the rest of us would get worried and drop it. A comparison with June 1941 involuntarily comes to mind, or perhaps even more so with the eve of the Yom Kippur War. Of course, the comparison is a stretch; the scale and the consequences were very different. The Israeli leaders, especially Moshe Dayan, made the people believe that the Arabs wouldn't be able to start a war for at least ten years. The people after all, did not want war. Intelligence data were interpreted and made to suit their wishes. They were so reluctant to go to war that they not only failed to make preventative strikes, but they began mobilization much too late. And later, they would justify themselves by appealing to the unexpectedness, the suddenness of it all, the lack of time.

Second, the word *balagan* (puppet show), which is widespread in Israel, has now been replaced in Russia by the word *bardak*, signifying disorder, laxity, unpunctuality, and so on. An all-embracing term. Misha called Lasal Kaminsky and told him of his suspicions, but neglected to mention the date of the operation. Lasal did not have time to confirm Misha's suspicions. And everything came to a grinding halt. The (conservative) Organization was not prepared to act in an emergency.

In the evening of June 13, a tall, broad-shouldered man with the exhausted face of a former convict appeared on my doorstep. I opened the door, stared at the stranger, and waited for him to speak. "Mendel Bodnya," he introduced himself. I invited him inside. Evidently in response to the astonished look on my face, he crooked his arm and showed off his steely muscles. I got dressed and followed him outside.

"The guys from Riga sent me," he began. "I know what's going on. But I wanted to clear a few points up."

As we walked along the street, I answered all his questions. Toward the end of the conversation, Mendel said that he was ready to join our group, even if the chances of success were only five out of a hundred. He said that he would spend the night at a friend's place before making his way to Smolny airport in the morning.

June 14 was an eventful day. The Riga group arrived in Leningrad under KGB surveillance. In the afternoon, on the edge of the forest near the aerodrome, we confirmed the details of the hijack as two KGB officers watched us from their black Volga. Black cars were considered prestigious in Russia. All the prominent Party members (as well as the KGB) drove around in black limousines. I'm not sure why the KGB decided to follow us in such an obvious way. Perhaps they couldn't change their plan in the last few days and had decided to scare us off, before arresting us at home. The opportunity had been theirs since March. Perhaps they thought there wouldn't be enough material for a "big case." Or perhaps it was much simpler than that, and they were just being sloppy like so many others. Until the case materials are released, we will never know.

From the airport, Edik and I returned to Leningrad. The rest of the Riga crew spent the night in the forest. We had to take the second group to Finland Station, where they would board a train to Priozersk. We almost missed the last train. We were looking for Mary, and Mary was looking for a lemon. She was pregnant and had a craving for something sour. The group entered the carriage a minute before the train pulled out.

Next, we had agreed to meet Yura Fyodorov and Aleksey Murzhenko outside the station. We went outside, and walked along the facade. Lenin, from the roof of his armored car, was pointing toward the south, but we were aiming to go north first. We would have fulfilled his wish and turned south, but fate (or the Almighty) had something else in store for us.

Eventually, Yura and Aleksey appeared. They were walking toward us with a tail – as we later learned – of KGB agents from Moscow. Our guys had brought pretenders from the capital with them. Now the KGB would have to divide honors between the Leningrad and Moscow branches. This was a time of feverish competition for ranks and medals. "To each his own."

Yura gave a sign, and we walked past them. Edik and I went back to my apartment, while Fyodorov and Murzhenko zigzagged around Leningrad until one in the morning, trying to throw off their tail. They didn't show up at my place until two.

Perhaps the KGB psychologists had advised them to exhaust us with surveillance and trailing, so it would be easy to take us later, when we were armed to the teeth. The KGB would later spread rumors that we had been armed with machine guns. It was often the case that they began to believe in their own fictions.

The night before the operation I managed to sleep about two hours. Then we had a quick breakfast and began to gather our things. "Is it worth taking this thing?" I asked, picking up a homemade revolver. Yura asked me to give it to him, which I did. At least that way it could be used for intimidation, as well as for crossing the Swedish border.

It was time to go. In groups of two and three, we went to meet our fate, and not only ours. "What has the coming day prepared for me [us]?" (Pushkin, *Evgeniy Onegin*).

There was not a single cloud in the sky in the early morning of June 15. If we had code-named our operation "Wedding," the KGB could have called theirs "Clear Skies Over Leningrad." On days like that, you could go out of town and fish or just stroll. With backpacks and a guitar, we might have been heading to our dacha. I had sent our suitcase with necessary possessions to Priozersk with the second group. In it was a map with our intended route, and a magazine with cartridges for a TT pistol.

As previously agreed, I found the nearest payphone and called Misha Korenblit. No answer. Later, I would learn that his apartment had been searched earlier that morning, and Misha had revealed all the details of the Leningrad Zionist conference of June 13, 1970.

I called Butman. Eva Butman answered. I told her that Misha wasn't picking up, but to pass on the message that "Marusya was going to the doctor's in two and a half hours."

My last few hours of freedom. Later I would learn the correct term: "In the big zone." We arrived at Finland Station, then took a taxi to the airport. Again, we saw two black Volgas on the side of the road.

All the operation's participants, individually and in groups, had gathered in front of the airport building. The waiting area was surrounded by trees, bushes, grass. Our family found a spot under a tree. There was some time until boarding, so we arranged a second breakfast. Now, I suppose, is the time to list all the participants of the operation and say something about each of them.

Boarding the An-2 were

1. Anatoliy Altman. Born 9/19/41 in Kirsanov, Tambov province. Jewish. Secondary education. No party affiliation. Submitted a visa application in Odessa, but was refused. Resettled in Riga. Worked first as a carpenter, later as a machinist.
2. Mendel Bodnya. Born 12/24/37 in Latvia. Jewish. Secondary education. No party affiliation. Refused an exit visa, despite the fact that

his mother lived in Israel. Worked at the Riga bread factory. Athlete. Disabled.

3. Mark Dymshits. Born 5/10/27 in Lozovaya, Ukraine. Jewish. Higher education. Excluded from the Party after arrest. Served in the air force, later worked for Aeroflot, at a factory, and as senior engineer at a poultry farming trust.

4. Alevtina Dymshits. Born 5/10/27 in Leningrad. No party affiliation. Secondary education. Russian. Worked as a kindergarten teacher, then as a laboratory technician.

5. Elizaveta Dymshits. Born 9/21/51 in Zabaikalye. Secondary technical education. Worked at a factory that made leather handbags.

6. Yuliya Dymshits. Born in Zabaikalye, 4/25/55. No party affiliation. At the time of her arrest, had completed the eighth grade.

7. Yuriy Fyodorov. Born 6/14/1943 in Yaroslavl province. Russian. Studied at technical college. In 1962, was sentenced to five years for allegedly anti-Soviet activity. Worked as a laboratory technician.

8. Eduard Kuznetsov. Born 1/29/1939 in Moscow to a Russian mother and Jewish father. Secondary education. No party affiliation. Had previously served a seven-year prison sentence for allegedly anti-Soviet activity. Worked as a hospital administrator.

9. Yosef Mendelevich. Born 8/3/47 in Riga, to an observant Jewish family. No party affiliation. Was refused an exit visa to Israel several times. Worked as a hospital orderly.

10. Aleksey Murzhenko. Born 11/24/42 in Lozovaya. Ukrainian. Secondary education. No party affiliation. In 1962, was sentenced to six years for allegedly anti-Soviet activity.

11. Wolf Zalmanson. Born 11/2/39 in Riga. Higher education. Engineer. Jewish. At the time of his arrest was a lieutenant in the army.

12. Israel Zalmanson. Born 3/13/49 in Riga. Jewish. No party affiliation. At the time of his arrest had finished four years of university study.

Waiting in Priozersk were

1. Leib (Arye) Hanoch. Born 10/4/1944 in Mordovia, to an observant Jewish family. Moved to Riga in 1968, where he applied for an exit

visa and was refused. Worked as an electrician at a factory, while simultaneously studying at technical college.

2. Mary Hanoch. Born 9/21/50 in Riga. Jewish. At the time of her arrest had finished three years of university studies in biology. Worked as a laboratory technician at the university.

3. Boris Penson. Born 1/2/46 in Tashkent. Jewish. No party affiliation. Lived in Riga. Secondary education. Worked as a designer.

4. Sylva Zalmanson. Born 10/25/44 in Repyevo village, Novosibirsk province. Jewish. Higher education. Worked as an engineer at a factory in Riga. Was refused an exit visa to Israel several times. Married Eduard Kuznetsov in 1970.

Now that I have listed all the participants, I will return to the events of June 15, 1970. I had been to Smolny airport before; my first reconnaissance flight had been on June 1, and three of us made another flight on June 3. But I had barely seen anyone in the waiting area outside, let alone the twelve who gathered there on the morning of June 15 like film extras. Many were wearing suits with ties, carrying briefcases. You could say we were festively dressed. Perhaps the Leningrad Communist Party Regional Committee and KGB, as well as their Moscow competitors, were already licking their chops, anticipating the shower of awards that was coming their way. In short, I had never seen a group like ours on a domestic flight.

And our five chances out of a hundred melted like the morning fog in the rays of the summer sun. It became clear that they would take us here. They wouldn't want to take any risks and arrest us in Priozersk during the hijacking itself. There were about fifteen minutes left before boarding. Should I warn my wife and daughters? Prepare them? Thoughts and images of what might happen next flashed through my brain. No, it wasn't worth frightening them. They wouldn't leave, even if I warned them. Everything had to run its course.

While we sat under the tree snacking, we somehow managed to miss the boarding announcement for flight 179, if there had been one. Suddenly, Yosef Mendelevich ran up to us, panting, and said that boarding had begun. I looked at my watch. They had evidently started five minutes early. The KGB wasn't wasting any time. Yosef ran to the boarding gate. I took my backpack and set out for the plane at a clip. My wife and children were behind me.

I went through the gate, raised my head, and the whole panorama of our arrest unfurled before my eyes. In that very second, they grabbed my arms. I heard a shot to the right, and managed to jerk my head to the left before the whole load of sand and gas landed on my right temple, instead of in my eye. I was in shock for a second. Then they threw me to the ground. Two men twisted my arms back and handcuffed me. Another pair of agents twisted my legs so that my heels would end up facing outward. The agent responsible for my left leg was especially energetic in his twisting. He must have had sadistic inclinations.

"What are you breaking my leg for, asshole?" I asked, naively.

"What else am I supposed to do with you?" my young torturer replied.

And it's true that this was his work, his bread and butter, perhaps with red caviar. This arrest might have earned him his first medal "for valor in combat." There were "shock workers" in every profession, even the KGB. In my time, I had been a shock worker in both aviation and in the factory. Admittedly, after events in Tbilisi, when they hacked people to bits with infantry spades, this guy began to look like a humanitarian.

They set me on my feet. Blood was dripping down my cheek, but there was no pain – not like what I'd felt when those guys from the MVD almost blinded me with a belt buckle when I was a cadet. I looked at my family. My daughters stood on either side of my wife. They were completely frozen. They were flanked by KGB agents. Why was Alya so calm? She hadn't covered her eyes or started crying. It was as if she had expected this scene. Perhaps she had been warned of the arrest? At that moment I was almost convinced that she had cooperated with the KGB. Only later, in Israel, did I learn that she had been paralyzed with shock.

All of our guys were handcuffed, with their hands behind their backs. Some had their hands tied with rope (a deficit). There were machine guns all around, soldiers with dogs, KGB officers in civilian clothes. The scene was worthy of the Bolshoy or at least a movie screen. The achievement of the KGB in this instance was measured by the scale of the scene and the number of actors.

The black Volgas began to roll in. I moved my arms and one of my handcuffs came unlocked.

"What kind of a botch job is this?" I exclaimed.

"Those are American-made handcuffs," an officer replied with patriotic aplomb.

They tied my hands with rope and led me up to one of the cars. We drove to the barracks on the opposite side of the aerodrome. I was led into a classroom, where they began to search and inventory my possessions. On the table where they began to unload the contents of my backpack lay a small gold-colored chain. The KGB agents wanted to include it in the inventory of my possessions, but I managed to convince them that the chain was not mine. They could have written that I was attempting to take part of the Russian Empire's gold reserves out of the country. Later, we would learn that following our arrest, the KGB began to spread rumors about suitcases of gold. Leningrad KGB Investigator, Captain Vitaliy Nikolayevich Ryabchuk, presided over the search procedures. He presented me with an arrest warrant, which accused me of treason by attempting escape overseas on a hijacked aircraft.

When they finished the inventory, they put me back in the black Volga. I was sandwiched between two KGB officers. At the front were the chauffer and the investigator.

We drove up to the gray building on Liteyny Prospect that is well known to all residents of Leningrad. After my discharge from the army, I had received my Leningrad residence permit there from the office of the MVD Commander. Two torture organizations under a single roof. Now I was to make the acquaintance of the most powerful organization in the country, the so-called "competent organs" – the Leningrad branch of the KGB.

On the level of execution they had worked well, professionally, with panache. Now we would have a chance to rate the work of their intellectual center, that is, those who had planned their operation in parallel to ours. We will have to wait. Time will tell who will emerge the winner. Everyone knows how hard it is to wait for justice, and then be forced to catch up. But in Russia we were trained to do just that. In our case, we didn't have a choice. We had done our part, at least until the trial. The KGB had also accomplished the first part of its plan. Now a new stage of combat would begin, where a leading role would be played by international organizations and Jews from the diaspora. How Israel would behave, I had little idea. If they rose to fight for aliyah and our freedom, we would emerge the winners. If they remained silent and pretended that nothing serious had happened, the KGB would win as well as the whole Russian Empire, or prison of nations.

Lenin coined that phrase to describe tsarist Russia. But back then you could go to any police station, request the necessary documents, and in two weeks you could leave for any country in the world. However, from about 1925 to 1970, only a few invalids, pensioners, and defectors managed to break free from the "loving family of free nations." The sovereignty of the republics wasn't even up for discussion. Later, I would meet Levko Lukyanenko in prison, who had been initially condemned to death, then to fifteen years of labor camps. His guilt consisted of nothing more than calling for a referendum on Ukraine's independence from the USSR, which did not contradict the Soviet constitution.

If the KGB succeeded in setting fear upon Soviet Jews, and the world remained silent, our operation and my role in it could very easily look like a provocation. This was my greatest fear, from the time of my arrest until I heard that the aliyah had begun. You live and you learn, as they say.

7 Leningrad KGB Prison
June 1970–December 1970

They led me through a maze of corridors to the office of the investigative bureau chief. On the way there, we made a brief visit to the bathroom. The ropes were removed from my hands.

"Wash off the blood and sand. We don't want the chief to see you looking like that," said Captain Ryabchuk, evidently concerned about my appearance.

We entered the spacious office of Investigative Bureau Chief Colonel Barkov. The tables were arranged in a T-formation, at the center of which sat the colonel himself in uniform. Several other KGB officers were present. Investigator Ryabchuk stood next to me.

After opening my file, Barkov began. "How could you, a Party member, make up your mind to hijack an airplane?" he asked.

Still ignorant of prison formalities, I asked Barkov, "How should I address you?"

"Comrade, for now," Barkov answered, with a measure of doubt.

"All right. Comrade colonel, how can a socialist country treat ethnic minorities so poorly?" I answered, question for question.

There were a few seconds of silence. Barkov was shuffling papers in my file. He was evidently reading something. Then, he said, "You had a good career in the army. Attained the rank of major in eleven years of service as an officer. But nevertheless, you chose to commit a crime."

"I became a major after ten years of service as an officer, if we are going to be precise," I corrected the colonel, as if that detail had any relation to our operation and its consequences.

"All the more so," Barkov continued. "You also chose inveterate anti-Soviet agitators as your associates. Did you not know that Kuznetsov, Fyodorov, and Murzhenko have criminal records?"

"For me that was meaningless," I replied, as an unserious thought flashed through my head. Without them, our group would have been an assembly of model Soviet citizens.

"You must take a lawyer." The colonel had evidently decided to create an impression of concern.

"I don't need a lawyer," I refused, unsurprisingly, considering my lack of experience with the law. I imagined that a lawyer would have little significance in such an affair.

Here, the investigator spoke up. "Comrade colonel, for offenses which carry a sentence of death, a lawyer is mandatory."

"Very well, we will assign you a lawyer. It will cost no more than twenty-five rubles," Barkov informed me, evidently concerned for my financial position.

It became clear to me that they had already planned the court case and chosen lawyers for us all. Pevsner, who was assigned to me, took five hundred rubles (four months' salary) from my wife instead of the promised twenty-five, without blinking an eye. Alya was forced to borrow all of her sister's savings in order to pay the lawyer, as the money we had saved for our journey had been confiscated. Now, Pevsner is living in the USA. Perhaps he pats himself on the back sometimes, thinking of the good deal he got out of the "hijacking affair," thanks to which he was able to move to the States.

Barkov, evidently pleased by the results of the day, ordered his subordinates to take me away. "Let him have a rest," he said.

However, my valiant investigator, Captain Ryabchuk, decided to strike while the iron was hot. "Mark Yulievich, ten or fifteen minutes more of your time, and then you will be taken to your cell," Ryabchuk informed me, in a friendly way, as we left Barkov's office. They took me to an empty room. Ryabchuk immediately began to question me about the names of the other participants. I couldn't remember all of them, but with Ryabchuk's help, we came up with a list of twelve names.

"Is that all? But Mark Yulievich, what about the group in Priozersk?" asked Ryabchuk, his face melting into a self-satisfied smile.

"I don't know anything about them," I said, and wasn't lying. I really knew nothing of what had happened to them.

"They got here even before you. They were in such a hurry that they left your suitcase in the train."

Together, we put together a list of the second group. I hadn't met a few of them until the day before the operation, so I didn't remember their surnames.

"Why did you have a magazine and cartridges in your suitcase?"

"Just in case. Flight crews are armed with TT pistols," I responded, thinking that the magazine could have been the reason why they'd almost blown
my ear off during the arrest, assuming that I was armed.

"Very well, Mark Yulievich, that should be enough for today," Ryabchuk
concluded and called the guards. The satisfied smile never left his round face.

I, on the other hand, had little reason to smile. I would smile much later,
when the first fruits of our operation began to appear, when the aliyah began.

Two guards came in to the room. Rather than carrying out Barkov's
instruction to let me rest, they led me down what seemed like an endless
series of passages and corridors to the prison's processing area. They took
my mugshots and fingerprints, filled out a form, noted my characteristics,
searched me and my clothes – that is, they did all the usual things. Then
another journey through the prison labyrinth to my new place of residence,
where I would spend, or rather, live out the next year and a half, changing
cells and cellmates several times.

The carpeted paths muffled the sound of our footsteps. The cleanliness
was worthy of a model hospital. Evidently, the prisoners on maintenance duty
were making an effort. The guards prevented encounters with other prisoners
by clicking their fingers or tongues.

My cell, No. 263, was on the upper level of the top floor. It had an area
of over thirty square feet. The ceiling was high. Across from the door with a
peephole was a barred window with metal blinds. Through the slits in these
blinds, you could only look straight ahead or up. I could see the roof of the
opposite wing of the prison, and above it, a piece of the sky. Beneath the window was a radiator. The outer wall was about three feet thick. This prison had
been built to last. In the door, there was a meal flap, with a call button beside
it. Ranged along the side walls were two metal cots, two night stands and two
stools. In the corner were a toilet and basin. The cots were fitted out with cotton mattresses and pillows. I would have been glad of a room like this after I
finished flight school. Such accommodation would have been an unattainable
dream for many Soviet people. I looked around and read the prisoner rules.
Feeling out the walls, I discovered several hollow places. Two years before, a
colleague of mine had told me how he had installed microphones in train
carriages and theaters. After that, microphones in prison walls could hardly
come as a surprise.

I sat on my cot and began to consider the day's events. It was clear that all the operation's participants were now in prison. But was it really? Where were my wife and daughters? Here, or out in the free world? I had to pretend that I didn't suspect anyone and not get too cocky with the KGB agents. Even if my wife was free, that didn't necessarily mean that she had cooperated in order to get me free. It might have simply been her way of getting back at me for the divorce. Or they could have deceived her, saying that her husband wasn't worthy of freedom, that he had deserved the most severe punishment. They could have even told her not to be upset, that they would find her a more worthy husband. There was hardly a shortage of decent Russian men.

But all this would become clear fairly soon. For the moment, I had to get used to my new environment and wait for news. How, in this new world, was I supposed to get information about what was going on beyond the walls? How could I communicate with my neighbors? There were so many questions, and now I came to think of it, sleep wouldn't be a bad thing either. The night before I had slept only two hours, and the day had been tense. I was alone in my cell, no one could disturb me. I went to sleep immediately. In fact, I have always been an excellent sleeper. Once I am asleep, neither light, nor sound, nor music, nor temperature, nor an unfamiliar place can disturb me. After two or three in the morning, I become more sensitive, and I never wake up much later than five. It was as if the prison, and later, the camp timetables were tailor-made for me.

The next morning, I awoke before the wake-up call. I washed. The flap opened and I was given my ration of bread, a packet of sugar (half an ounce), and tea. As I had eaten almost nothing for twenty-four hours, I tucked into my breakfast with gusto. After a little while, a guard brought me sheets, a blanket, and a towel. For me this was totally unexpected. I had been preparing myself to sleep in my clothes on a bare mattress. I sat on my cot, waiting to be called for questioning, which I doubted would make much difference. With my knowledge of Soviet lawlessness, I understood my fate would be decided not by the trial, but by the KGB, based on the political situation in the USSR and abroad. I imagine the KGB had already scripted the whole trial beforehand, including our sentences.

The flap opened again. "Prepare to leave your cell," a guard commanded, almost in a whisper. In a few minutes the door opened. I walked along the corridor, holding my hands behind my back. The guard walked behind me, indicating in a quiet voice where I should turn. Here was the investigator's office.

Ryabchuk greeted me, indicated a chair next to a small table, and sat behind his desk. On the desk were a typewriter, a table lamp, and stacks of papers. In his office were a sofa, a safe, a bookshelf, and a coat hanger. Behind the investigator's back, or rather, above his head, was a portrait of Felix Dzerzhinsky – if my memory doesn't deceive me. His portrait was the eternal kind. It wouldn't need to be changed, like that of his successors or superiors.

Ryabchuk approached me, holding out the June 15 issue of *Evening Leningrad*. "Read here," he said, poking the paper with a finger.

On June 15 of this year, a group of criminals, attempting to hijack a passenger flight, was detained at Smolny airport. An investigation is underway.

Now they wouldn't be able to have a closed trial. This was the first published information. A few weeks later, they would start giving me newspapers, and when they wouldn't give me the newspaper, it meant good news for us.

Next, Ryabchuk acquainted me with the Criminal Code of the RSFSR (Russian Soviet Federative Socialist Republic[1]). I read article 64a, "On Treason," twice, with great attention. Flicking through the code, I got to article 83 and asked a naive question:

"Why can't you charge us under article 83, where the maximum term is three years?"

"If you had tried to leave the country in order to eat pancakes with your mother-in-law, then we'd have given you article 83," the investigator answered, taking the Code from me. He was obviously anxious to stop me from asking further questions.

It was possible that in those days people did cross the border in search of food. Now, when shelves are empty throughout the Soviet Union, such refugees could certainly appear.

---

[1]   Russian Soviet Federative Socialist Republic was the name of the largest Soviet Union republic in central Russia.

That day, I held the Criminal Code of the RSFSR in my hands for the first time. Its contents are, I believe, essential knowledge for any Soviet person. Seventy percent of the empire's population could easily be condemned for violating its articles. And although this statistic is just a rough estimate, I think it is probably too low. A significant part of the Soviet population has been through prison and labor camps. And I am not even taking into account the periods of mass terror and Stalin's purges. I mean everyday crimes. Many Soviet citizens find it difficult, if not impossible, to live on their salaries. The situation of pensioners, disabled people, and students is worse still. These factors have led to a high rate of crime – but not only these factors. Government officials at the highest levels set an example of total lawlessness.

Criminal codes of behavior and prison slang have spread throughout the Soviet Union and have even infiltrated the Soviet Army. Former convicts brought hazing practices to the army, which in turn divided the ranks into an alternative hierarchy.

There is an additional mass of people who regularly commit crimes against society, without formally violating the Criminal Code. I mean the numberless bureaucrats who stunt the country's growth, and the so-called "scientific institutions," which have never done anything for science or the economy, but continue to swallow funds from the budget. It is not for nothing that the Soviet Union is sometimes referred to as the "big zone," in contrast to the "small zones" of the prison camps. There's an old joke that goes like this: An Armenian radio station is asked, "Which is the wealthiest country in the world?" The radio station answers, "The Soviet Union, of course. Everyone steals and steals, and yet no one has managed to steal all the country's wealth." And so, in only seventy years, the country has perverted its ideals by making criminals of its citizens.

At that time, there wasn't any talk of the rule of law. The principle of "bring me a man, and I'll find a crime" was, for the organs, a valuable supplement to the Criminal Code.

I asked the investigator about my wife and children. He answered that they were well, that they were being held in the same building as me, and had asked him to pass on the message that I was not to worry about them.

Was Ryabchuk lying or not? At that point, I didn't rule out the possibility that they were at home.

Later, I learned that he had lied about my wife's health. An emergency doctor had been called to treat her. I learned that my elder daughter, Liza, actually had spent time in prison, while Yuliya had been taken to a home for children of incarcerated parents.

We began to discuss the third version of Operation Wedding in detail. As I have already described our plan and preparations for the hijacking at Smolny airport, I will not repeat myself here. Ryabchuk took all of this down, typing with two fingers.

Lunchtime came around. The guard took me back to my cell. Lunch consisted of two hot dishes. At this prison, the monthly cost of feeding one prisoner was nineteen rubles. (At transit prisons, the monthly cost was eleven rubles.)

After lunch, I rested for a while. We were not allowed to sleep during the day. Only those who had already faced trial could get away with it. For some reason, I felt an urge to sing revolutionary songs. While I waited to be called, I paced up and down my cell, humming the melodies of the 1920s and '30s. But that day I wasn't called again. In the following days, there would be interrogations before and after lunch; later, only in the morning; and ultimately, they would happen only on odd days.

The next day, I began doing morning calisthenics – a habit from the army, which I have maintained to this day. Our breakfast was always bread, sugar, and tea. For dinner, we were given an ample portion of oatmeal. From boiled, unrefined oats and old newspapers, we glued together toilet seats for our own personal use – an important detail which attests to at least some level of civilization in Soviet prisons.

The meal hatch opened. "Prepare to leave your cell." Another interrogation. Now they were asking questions about the Leningrad Zionist Organization and its members. I had never been interested in the Organization and my answers were limited to "I don't know," "I don't know him," "I haven't heard that" – which was the absolute truth. Even when the conversation turned to Butman and the Korenblits, I didn't know whether they were members of the committee or not.

During that interrogation, it became clear that members of the Organization had been arrested as well. For me, this was not unexpected. Now, the questions and answers revolved around my relationship with Hillel, Misha, and

Lev, our preparations for the first and second versions of the hijacking, and their ultimate refusal to participate in the operation.

There is an interesting point, especially for those who went through the second Leningrad, Riga, and Kishenev trials.

I asked the investigator, "Did you leave us alone on purpose, in order to link all the members of the Organization with our hijacking attempt?"

"You accelerated our actions by two months."

That is, we would have ended up in prison in August 1970 even if our group had given up on the hijacking. The example of Hillel and Misha is a powerful piece of evidence. What they did or didn't know about our preparations had no significance to the KGB. Despite their refusal to participate in Operation Wedding, they were still sentenced under article 64a. Because the KGB needed a "big case," they charged Hillel and Misha (two Zionist Organization members) with treason, when they were actually guilty of failure to report.

The rest of the organization's members, when they were arrested that August, might have received the same sentences even without the hijacking attempt. Perhaps they would have been given harsher sentences. Without the operation, the international outrage would have been less.

Later, I learned that a major role in alerting the West to the position of Soviet Jews – mass arrests, our reasons for wanting to hijack a plane – was played by the open letters of Viktor Boguslavsky and Hillel Shur. They gave these letters to foreign correspondents, and their contents became known to the whole world. This first slap in the face was dealt to the KGB around June 20, and no fake articles in the Soviet press could drown out the reaction in the West, and among Russian Jews, to the mass arrests in Leningrad, Moscow, Kishenev, and Riga. Perhaps even then the KGB had begun to doubt the rightness of their intentions. These letters cost Viktor Boguslavsky and Hillel Shur their freedom.

It would be naive to think that the KGB could tolerate the existence of an underground organization which conducted secret classes in Hebrew and Jewish history, while simultaneously sending collective letters and telegrams to the UN and Israel. The name of the organization alone – Zionist – in the eyes of Israel-haters and antisemites, was enough to condemn it under article 70 for anti-Soviet activity. Official propaganda of the 1960s and '70s beat into the heads of Soviet citizens the idea that Zionism was a dire enemy of socialism, that Israel was the frontline of imperialism, and other antisemitic nonsense. These seeds of hatred often fell on fertile soil and bore fruit in an environment of black hundredists[2] and neo-Nazis.

Even now, despite glasnost and perestroika, or perhaps because of them, the fewest changes of all have occurred in Soviet policy on Israel and Zionism.

I haven't even begun to talk about the Brezhnev era, but in the first years of Gorbachev's tenure, Jews have been criminally charged for resurrecting Jewish culture, language, and traditions, without being part of any Zionist organization.

Before the end of the interrogation, Ryabchuk informed me that the bottles of cognac and other spirits in my backpack had been destroyed. He smiled significantly as he said this. How could a Russian summon the will to destroy bottles of alcohol?

At the ensuing interrogations, all three versions of Operation Wedding were discussed. And of course, there was talk of the USSR's attitude to minorities, of politics in the Middle East, of antisemitism, and so on. I will describe some conversations or fragments of conversations.

One episode from the investigation revealed the KGB's desire to make the Zionist Organization seem like the initiator of our operation. Ryabchuk asked, "Mark Yulievich, perhaps it wasn't you who proposed the hijacking to Butman? Perhaps it was the committee that suggested you conduct Operation Wedding? Think carefully."

"I presented the idea to Butman when I was not only unaware of the organization's existence, but could not imagine that such an organization might exist. The idea occurred to me long before my conversation with Butman."

Disregarding my answer, Ryabchuk tried once more to push me in the direction of this false version. Later, I arrived at the conclusion that the KGB not only wanted to lay responsibility on the Organization but had also come up with a plan about me, which I will describe later on.

When the conversation turned to the USSR's policy on minorities, I tried to prove that the various ethnic populations of the USSR did not enjoy equal rights. If the separate republics were subjected to a program of russification,

---

2   Black hundreds were a loose association of ultra-nationalist groups in Russia that carried out pogroms against Jews and revolutionaries and were most active in the early years of the twentieth century.

you can imagine what happened to the nations that didn't have their own territory. In each Soviet republic (and even in other countries), there were Russian schools and Russian theaters, often empty. But in no Russian city could you find a Ukrainian, Uzbek, Armenian, or any other institution of the kind.

The question arises: who was I trying to convince? The KGB investigator? Why? Did I think the KGB was ignorant of how things really were? Did I think they were unaware that these policies had nothing in common with internationalism and socialism? They were conducting very ordinary imperial politics, spending tens of millions of rubles on it, and each KGB officer understood and approved this. Of course, if he was even interested.

In the first place, although I did not consider myself a Soviet citizen, I could not cut all ties with my former homeland. Even now, after more than eleven years in Israel, I am interested in Russia's future, because the future of many nations depends on it. Perhaps the future of the whole world.

In the second place, I think the KGB listened to hundreds of different opinions which, even if couldn't change official policy, could certainly influence personal opinion.

Ryabchuk either answered with the usual canned responses or was silent. There was no point expecting anything better from him. But all I said was recorded and perhaps even read in intellectual circles of the KGB.

The KGB of our time is nothing like the Cheka of the Revolutionary or Civil War period, where the ranks were mostly made up of half-literate sailors and manual laborers. Now the KGB has its own scientific organizations and secret objects. Most KGB employees have a higher education. I have a feeling that the KGB's recommendations play a significant role in the development of government policy.

You might be thinking, "He thinks he's so great because he's a former air force major. But there are thousands of them in the USSR." The fact is that many Soviet officers have defected to the West!

Just as they say, "Constant dripping wears away the stone."

About two months after my arrest, seeing that Ryabchuk was impenetrable to my criticism of the USSR's policy on minorities, I threw him the following challenge: "Let everyone go who wants to go, and then you can eat each other. I don't care."

During the war, more than five million soldiers and officers from the Red Army ended up in German prisoner-of-war camps. This number was larger than the entire army had been before the war. Nearly one million Soviet citizens served the Germans as police, in death squads, in General Vlasov's liberation army, and so on. These numbers led to changes in the Russian Empire – to a strengthening of its attributes. But the fate of the empire as a whole is well known. In 1917, the Bolsheviks saved it from disintegration. But Stalin, hiding behind revolutionary slogans, restored and expanded the empire.

Now, as I write these lines, the people of the Baltic, the Caucasus, Ukraine, and Central Asia are beginning to decide the fate of the Russian Empire.

When I attested, drawing examples from my own life, that Jews were being subjected to discrimination and forced assimilation, and denied the opportunity to study their own language and history, Ryabchuk simply ignored me. He argued that the Jewish Autonomous province provided all possible opportunities for the development of national culture. When I replied that only 10 percent of the population there was actually Jewish and that the province was a fiction, that it was totally empty of Hebrew schools and Jewish theaters, Ryabchuk remained silent and looked at me as if I was some kind of Zionist mouthpiece. He remained silent when I contended that a multinational state should give minority communities the opportunity to open their own schools and theaters in any city, as the Russians had been doing in other republics. Indeed, the USA was a prime example of such a system, where nationality has no significance to the state, where all citizens become Americans and enjoy identical rights to national self-expression.

"I don't want to be Russian, just as I don't want to be English or French," I told him. "For me, it's either equality for all nations like in the USA, or life in a Jewish state. I cannot and will not continue to live in the USSR."

Two weeks after my arrest, I returned to my cell from interrogation and discovered that I had a new cellmate. We made each other's acquaintance. Anvar was twenty-five, tall, from Kazakhstan. He looked more Japanese than Kazakh, a fact that had been useful to him in his brilliant career as a con artist.

I imagine that every first meeting between cellmates begins with the what, where, and how of their respective cases. By the way, our case was No. 15.

We discussed the basics of each other's cases. During the conversation, Anvar asked me an unexpected question, "Who gave you away?" This question caught me totally unawares.

"Probably my wife," I blurted out. After two weeks of solitary confinement, I must have forgotten to be cautious.

And although I immediately engaged my safety catch and added, "maybe Mikhail Korenblit," I didn't really believe that. In any case, my whole answer had already been recorded by the KGB. I had entered a game with them, in which I would be punished for my lapse. The KGB would lead me to the brink of a family tragedy. But I should have known what was coming, since I made the first move. It was my own fault.

To return to my cellmate. Anvar was the son of the Alma-Ata Regional Committee Communist Party Secretary. One of his uncles was deputy prosecutor of Kazakhstan. The other was director of a large state-owned farm and a Hero of Soviet Labor. When Anvar arrived in Leningrad, he was admitted to the university, while simultaneously starting a job at Lenfilm. Aside from his salary, he received eight hundred rubles from his father and uncle nearly every month (more than eight average salaries at that time). But that wasn't enough to maintain his lifestyle. He allowed himself private flights from Lvov in the west to Khabarovsk in the east, not forgetting to pass through the capital, of course. He had mistresses in all the cities he visited, probably hotel employees or stewardesses. The expenses he racked up went far beyond his legal budget, which made up only a small part of his "earnings." The poor kid was forced into con-artistry, where his talents as an actor and his Japanese features came in handy.

An investigation was underway, and as new episodes of his eventful life were unearthed, Anvar would tell me new stories. His constant lack of money had given him endless opportunities for criminal activity. I will reproduce three of his stories here.

Every so often, some of Anvar's countrymen would travel from Central Asia to Leningrad. They would buy up large quantities of goods that were scarce in Kazakhstan, and resell them there at several times the original price. After learning the train schedule, Anvar began making visits to the station, in order to "accidentally" make the acquaintance of two or three newly arrived passengers. With tears in his eyes, he would ask them for news from home, invite them to a restaurant, and offer them his help.

One time, his countrymen asked him to help them find five hundred women's wool blend scarves. At that time in Leningrad, there was a new, popular store called Synthetics. Its huge windows overlooked Nevsky Prospect and enabled any passerby to inspect the whole store from outside.

Anvar set a time for the group to meet near the store. On the eve of their meeting, he took several childrens' mattresses, wrapped them in scarves which he had prepared in advance, folded them in half and packed them professionally, on top of one another. Half an hour before the scheduled meeting, he arrived at the store. After placing his bundles on a bench inside, Anvar waited on the street for his countrymen. The Kazakhs drove up in a taxi. Anvar took their money – fifteen rubles per scarf, plus a hundred rubles for the saleswoman. Back home, they would sell the scarves for fifty rubles a piece. Anvar went inside the store while his victims waited by their taxi, watching through the window as he went from various departments to the registers and back again. He had paper receipts in his hands. After ten minutes of pacing back and forth, Anvar emerged from the shop with his pre-prepared parcels. In such situations, the countrymen would usually tear back the wrapping, see the folded "scarves," pack them into the trunk of the taxi and, tasting the fantastic profits they were about to make, offer Anvar a tip for his services. After pocketing 7,600 rubles, Anvar would humbly refuse to take money from his compatriots. Instead, he would promise to meet them later at the station, as they set off for the distant motherland. But actually, he would never see them again (until the trial).

Anvar conducted a similar operation at a refrigerator warehouse. He would first put his own photograph on the employee-of-the-week board. Then, he would show his compatriots around his place of "employment." Finally, he would take their money, photograph them, and vanish through the back entrance.

Sometimes, Anvar would work his magic at Beriozka foreign currency stores. Dressed in an elegant foreign-made suit and fashionable colored glasses, he would saunter into the Kiev branch, for example. Looking around, he would choose a victim, approach her, and in broken Russian with a smattering of Japanese words (he knew about a hundred), offer his assistance. The victim, very anxious to buy a fur coat, never knew the difference between dollars and yen. She would delightedly hand over several thousand rubles in exchange for Japanese currency and skip off to choose a coat, little realizing that the money was hardly enough to buy a few packs of cigarettes. Meanwhile, our "hero" would get in a taxi and shoot off to his Kiev mistress.

What finally got Anvar in trouble was a carpet, which he had promised to procure for yet another compatriot. He took a large sum of money from the client, walked into the rug store, and slipped out the back door. The difference was that this countryman, a well-respected artist, was buying the rug for himself, rather than for resale. Resale or speculation is punishable by law in the USSR. And so, this artist went to the police, told them what had happened, and described Anvar's appearance. Our "hero" was arrested some days later. He was tried for fraud. His relatives rolled in from Kazakhstan, and Anvar was given a four-year sentence. In the USSR, anything less than five years is considered child's play. His Kazakh victims were present at the trial, and cried out with rage, "Give him to us! We'll tear him to pieces!"

Anvar was sent to a labor camp near Leningrad and managed to have a pretty good time there. The prisoners with short sentences were taken to work night shifts at a factory or building site. At the factory they had access to provisions from the outside. At the building site, they drank with the guards and even fraternized with girls from the neighboring factory.

Sometimes prisoners would have to drag their drunk guards home, carrying their weapons. There was no point running away, as they would risk a longer sentence than the few years remaining to them.

Anvar had counted on being released in two years, and the time was already approaching. But then his con jobs with gold, currency, and drugs came to light. The MVD transferred his case to the KGB, and now Anvar was being investigated by more serious organs.

I spent two months with Anvar. Then he was transferred to Kazakhstan, thanks to his powerful relatives.

"I'll be given eight or ten years there, instead of being shot, and I'll serve five years like a khan near Alma-Ata. I'll get anything I want. Best of all, I'll be out of Russia." That is what Anvar managed to tell me before leaving for his homeland, Kazakhstan.

On July 5, 1970, my meal flap swung open as always. This time, I was led along an unfamiliar corridor to an unfamiliar office. It belonged to the Leningrad director of the KGB division attached to the Soviet council of ministers. At the head of a group of officers sat Lieutenant Nosyrev. All of them were staring at me. It was the first time, in my forty-three years of life in Russia, that I had met a lieutenant general.

Nearly ten years later, on Israel's independence day, I was introduced to Chief of Staff, Lieutenant General Rafael (Raful) Eitan, and we drank a glass of cognac together in honor of the country's independence, to liberation and to freedom itself.

But in 1970, I was doubly unfree, and made to sit at a separate little table in Nosyrev's office. Behind a screen at my back was a recording device or microphone – such that, together with the table, I was moved back and forth in front of the screen, in an attempt to regulate the recording quality. Our conversation did not touch on the hijacking itself. Rather, we discussed the factors which had led me to take such a step. I said nothing new, repeated what I had told the investigator. Toward the end of the conversation, the general concluded, "Yes, you have been well deceived by enemy propaganda. But you will be tried in a Soviet court. We have managed to do something for your family. Take him away."

From this conversation, I concluded that they were not expecting me to conform on matters of principle, as Ryabchuk had already warned me about the possible death penalty. They even made a recording just in case. But it would have been impossible to bend my answers to their advantage, even if they had cut and pasted.

It was almost clear to me that my family would not be tried. This conclusion intensified my suspicions.

On June 20, Ryabchuk informed me that my wife and daughters had been freed. I met this piece of news with mixed feelings. While pretending to be overjoyed, I could not get rid of the thought that this was either my reward for the hijacking, or my wife's reward for cooperating with the KGB. If it was for the hijacking, then time would tell who would pay. But if not? I would have to consider the situation more closely.

After returning to my cell, I decided to ask the investigator about the possibility of registering a marriage with Alya. Even before the operation, we had agreed to register in Sweden or Israel. I thought that this step would make my wife's situation more straightforward, and to some extent extinguish the KGB's suspicions that I might know something. Ryabchuk answered that marriage was possible only after the trial and, of course, only with the agreement of Alevtina Ivanovna.

At the end of August they took Anvar away, but this did not, unfortunately, result in my being left alone. Unfortunately, because most criminals are incapable of reading or keeping silent for any stretch of time and could even be on assignment for the KGB.

So it was that, returning from interrogation one day, I found Sasha Voronin in my cell. A sickly twenty-three year old, Sasha introduced himself as a student black marketeer. He generally talked about the moral degradation prevalent among students and constantly asked me to wrestle with him. I doubt he had ever done much sport in his life. Exhausted by sexual delinquency, thin and pale, Sasha ended up on his back without much effort from me. A few days later, he would be spoiling for another fight.

There is no way Sasha could have ended up in KGB prison for black market trading, especially a month before his release from labor camp. He was always trying to get something delivered to someone, and this was obviously his assignment.

One day, the guards came in, and announced a search of the cell, which they did fairly often. This time, however, they took us into the neighboring, empty cell. They stripped us of our clothes and shoes, alleging that they were taking everything for checks. So we wouldn't have to stand barefoot on the cement floor, the guards brought in two stools, and suggested that we stand on them. For five whole minutes, Sasha and I stood there in our birthday suits while the guards came in and out, stealing hurried glances at the two "statues." Then they brought us our clothes. Once we were back in our cell, I wondered whether the guards, after theoretical training in "how to recognize a Jew," had been taking this opportunity to practice. After all, Jews don't always have semitic facial features, but brit milah (circumcision) was an almost universal custom.

I don't remember the names of all my cellmates, nor do I remember the order in which they came, or which cells we shared. The KGB used a number of them for their own ends, without any scruple.

They began to let us read books in our cell. I think it's important to note that the prison library, full of literature confiscated from "enemies of the people," would have been the envy of any bibliophile. You can only imagine what the KGB agents' personal libraries must have been like.

A nurse also appeared. She did periodic rounds of the cells. Generally, my drug-addicted cellmates would ask her for pills – of any kind – which they would promptly swallow.

On one occasion, I was visited by a delegation from the prosecutor's office. They oohed and ahed over the three versions of the hijacking, and concluded that the third version was totally achievable. Ryabchuk, however, did not agree with this conclusion. He was convinced that we would have been shot down by the anti-aircraft cannon which were primed to shoot down any stray plane. Where he had got hold of such nonsense, I didn't know, and he wouldn't tell.

A twenty-year-old Estonian kid was my next cellmate. He had been arrested for an attempt to cross the border and tried – though "convicted" might be more accurate – under article 83. In a few days, he was sentenced to two years in prison. The kid said he had worked as a chauffeur, but his snow white hands looked like they had never held a wrench. He couldn't even sweep the floor. This weak-willed kid tore up his sheet and braided a rope to hang himself from. I had to call the guards, or else I might have have slept through the suicide attempt. The guards confiscated his rope and took him to another cell.

At the next interrogation, the conversation turned to Israel's political system. Ryabchuk reprimanded me for wanting to live in a supposedly fascist state. There was no point arguing over which government was closer to fascism – the USSR's or Israel's – and I answered that when a country's existence is under threat, politics fall into the background. Once the government was stronger, the Jewish people would decide which system was best for them. Ryabchuk had probably seen the film *Ordinary Fascism*, and I daresay that once glasnost began, he found out about the secret part of the Ribbentrop-Molotov pact, about the alliance signed in blood.

A book called *Italian Fascism* had come out in the USSR, from which any reader might infer that Italian workers lived better and had more freedom than their fellow proletarians in the USSR.

The conversation turned to my family's release from prison. I didn't believe in the humanity of the Soviet judicial system, nor did I believe in the KGB's humanity, but now that I was in the game, I had to keep playing.

"Yes," I said, "you treated my family with humanity. But their guilt was insignificant. They were following me blindly. Mary Hanoch, for instance, could really use some humanity. She's pregnant."

"I will find out about her health and her pregnancy," Ryabchuk promised and changed topics. "Did you know that the secret services in Israel and Germany have the same name?"

"No, I didn't know that. What's the significance of a name? It's more important what they do."

"In Nazi Germany and Israel, they are both called the SS – the security service. Don't you know what Shin Bet means?"

"No, I don't know," I replied, while lamenting how ignorant I was of these things.

Much later, I would learn that the Soviet army was infiltrated by a net of KGB operatives, rather than by army counter-intelligence, as I had thought before.

Ryabchuk gave me an hour-long lecture on secret services in the West, including Israel's. He promised to give me a book to read, but either forgot or decided not to give it to me, and I didn't remind him. The topic was deeply uninteresting to me.

Now that I was playing with the KGB, I avoided taking out detective novels from the library. I imagined that they made a note of which books their prisoners read, and made appropriate conclusions. I read a history of ancient Rome, *The History of the Russian State*, multiple works by Jack London and Romain Rolland, *Brehm's Animal Life*, and so on. My cellmates usually took out detective novels, and I often read over their shoulders to learn the KGB's methods of working.

I have never read more in my life than during my time in Leningrad prison. I don't remember the name of the author or the title of the book, but a quote from one Russian traveler has stuck with me, and since coming to Israel, I have become convinced of its accuracy. Back then, during the tsarist era, there were still English and French colonies in the Middle East. (Israel didn't exist, so you couldn't accuse the author of bias.) He characterized the Arab mentality thus: "An Arab will kiss your boots, but when you turn around he'll stab you in the back." The recent incident with one Israeli settler is a vivid example of this. He was sitting with three Arabs, eating apples and chatting. They took a photo together. But when the settler turned around, he was literally stabbed in the back.

The next interrogation came around, if you could call it an interrogation. After we had talked through the minute details of Operation Wedding, the discussion turned to various aspects of interior and international politics. I talked the most, as the investigator's official point of view was clear. As we were discussing the Jewish question, I accused the organs of destroying the Jewish Antifascist Committee as well as the Jewish intelligentsia. To which Ryabchuk replied with a counterattack. "But you executed White Army officers."

At this, Ryabchuk blushed slightly, obviously realizing that he had gone too far. But I think that, by making me answer for the actions of all Jews, he was just being honest.

"When I accused you, Captain Ryabchuk, I meant the 'organs' from the Cheka to the KGB, of which you are currently an employee. I did not accuse the Russian nation. You, on the other hand, accused the whole Jewish nation. White officers were executed during the Civil War, but there were also thousands of White officers (to be precise, 165,113 former tsarist officers) serving in the Red Army. There was a white terror and a red terror. There was cruelty on both sides, and what war could be without cruelty? The Jewish Antifascist Committee and the Jewish intelligentsia were destroyed during peacetime. They weren't fighting against Soviet power and did much to encourage the West to help the Red Army in its fight against Nazi Germany."

Ryabchuk said nothing.

Now, in our time of perestroika and glasnost, you can't surprise anyone by accusing the Jews. These days, there are neo-Nazis and antisemites on all levels of society, from caretakers to famous writers, from an illiterate member of the Pamyat Society to academician Igor Shafarevich. They all accuse the Jews of all imaginable and unimaginable crimes: from the killing of Christ to the killing of the Imperial family; from the liquidation of White Army officers to the liquidation of the kulaks (wealthy peasant farmers); from the famine of 1929–30 to the economic crisis of the present; from the destruction of churches to the earthquake in Armenia.

Lazar Kaganovich, the last Jew in the Politburo, was removed from his post in 1956. Without defending Stalin's comrade in arms, I feel it necessary to state one fact. In the war years, from 1941 to 1945, Kaganovich managed the country's railroads under the most difficult possible circumstances, and with great success. Currently, in peacetime, when the automotive and air transport have also received their fair share of development, and a Russian is in charge, the railroads have never been in worse shape. This has a disastrous effect on all parts of the economy. But who would think to blame the Russian nation?

The spirit of the pre-Revolutionary judophobe Purishkevich is still alive. Later, when I quoted Purishkevich in a letter from prison camp, the letter was confiscated for defamation of Soviet reality.

The Jewish question is a litmus test for any country's attitude toward minorities and indicates a society's cultural level. The surge of antisemitism in Russia is an indicator of a slave mentality, a national inferiority complex. When Churchill was asked about antisemitism in England, he answered that the English did not consider themselves stupider than the Jews and for that reason antisemitism was foreign to the English.

Many Russians, from Alla Pugacheva to Mikhail Gorbachev, emphasize that the Jews are an intelligent nation. That kind of logic suggests that there are intelligent nations and stupid nations. I have a different opinion. I think that in each nation, there are intelligent people and stupid people. Culture, education, civilization, politics, economics are all another matter. Perhaps these factors characterize a nation more accurately.

The UN resolution which condemned Zionism as a form of racism has given antisemites the opportunity of hiding their judophobia behind a mask of official policy. After all, the USSR signed or voted for the resolution. The Russian Empire's antisemites will not leave Jews alone, even when there are only a few thousand of them, as in Poland.

A little more about the Leningrad KGB prison. When I could and would not live any longer in a society of liars, thieves, and antisemites, the prison served as a temporary alternative. That is, until I left for Israel, it was preferable to life in the "big zone."[3] By 1970, there was no more torture, no more night interrogations. They didn't even beat us for fun, or for tradition's sake. Satisfied with my status as a Soviet prisoner, I started saying "Long live Soviet prison!" to my cellmate before we went to sleep, instead of "Good night."

Far from enforcing the principle, "He who does not work shall not eat," the KGB gave us tolerable food, without long lines, and even delivered it to our doors. We were taken for walks in isolated pens with a net ceiling; they took us to the bathhouse and changed our linen – and here again the service was better than what the average Soviet citizen could expect in the "big zone." It was real Communism, with reasonably limited demands, put into practice by the KGB. Of course, the party high-ups practiced a different kind of Communism, with private distributors, sanatoriums, hunting lodges in national parks (where saunas were also brothels), trips abroad to the decadent West.

A few people might say that I'm embellishing the reality of prison life. Of course, there are individual deficiencies and temporary difficulties, but

---

[3]   Russian slang term meaning any territory of the Soviet state except prisons and concentration camps.

we had got used to all of these in the "big zone." Freedom of movement was limited, but on the other hand, there was complete freedom of speech. When they saw that someone was reading too much, they would change the light bulb to twenty-five watts. But then that would make it easier to sleep, and they would be forced to change it back to two hundred watts.

The cold cell walls made the hair on my head grow thinner, but on the other hand, thick hair began to grow on my back, protecting my lungs from chill. As there were no clocks in the cell and few sunny days in Leningrad, we had to tell the time based on openings and closings of the meal flap.

A few words about my cellmates. Some of them were given specific assignments by the KGB, some of them were chosen without any consideration of their talents and abilities. I have already managed to forget some of their names, and I certainly can't remember the order they came in and the numbers of the cells we were confined to. But I doubt it matters if I confuse Petya for Vanya and vice versa. In any case, I won't add anything to their criminal records.

My new cellmate was Anatoliy Mokrousov, who had come under investigation for trying to transport a young man called Marius over the Finnish border.

After the war, Marius's parents had moved to the USSR from France to build socialism and took their son with them. Marius could never manage to feel at home in Russia, and once he had grown up and was working as a chauffeur, he made several attempts to get aboard foreign ships and return to France. His attempts always ended in arrest. Marius made yet another attempt in the town of Vyborg, where he met Mokrousov – who had both a motor boat and a pass that would enable him to leave Soviet waters. After several rounds of vodka, Anatoliy agreed to take Marius to the Finnish border for a large sum of money. Anatoliy alleged that he put Marius ashore near the border zone and indicated where he should go. But Marius, exiting the country in a place where the border line was curved, managed to end up in the USSR again and fell into the hands of the border police. I never heard what happened to them next.

At the end of September, Ryabchuk met me with a newspaper in his hand, came up to my table with his familiar smile, and held out the front page of *Pravda*.

"My congratulations on the good news. Nasser has died."

I looked at the portrait of the president of Egypt in a black frame, read the article about his death, and replied, "Good news, but we don't know who will be next. But why are you smiling, Vitaliy Nikolayevich? Nasser was a Hero of the Soviet Union and a friend of this country. He was the one who said that Israel was a cancerous tumor on Arab land, and that the Arabs would destroy it. The Soviet administration didn't even protest. Is that what you call the politics of a socialist state?"

"How do you know what Nasser said only at official meetings?" Ryabchuk answered with another question.

"Nasser's announcement was in the Soviet press, and the Soviet government never contradicted him publicly," I responded. "But that's not the only thing. Egypt will betray you sooner or later, regardless of your amoral support."

Ryabchuk continued to smile, but he was probably thinking the following: "Strength breaks straws. There are more than a hundred million people in the Arab countries that took part in the war. We have given them new weapons and trainers, while you folks in Israel have a population of less than three million and are without oil. Israel isn't even visible on the world map, while the Arabs have about seven million square miles of land. That's the formula of our alliance – or, you could say, our interests."

Of course, I couldn't have known then about Sadat and his program of expelling Soviet military experts from Egypt. But I felt intuitively that there couldn't be a firm alliance between the Arabs and Russia. The USSR had already formed such "eternal friendships" with Nazi Germany and China. Politics is built on interests, and Russia's alliances were always changing because its interests were always changing. What is more, Russia usually placed its bets on size and quantity rather than quality and fairness. This tendency was established in the tsarist era. The desire to occupy as much land as possible without having the necessary resources to sustain it exhausted Russia's economy, cost many people their lives, and impoverished the Empire's population.

Once as I returned from the investigator to my cell, I was met by yet another cellmate. We introduced ourselves. Max was a professional thief and drug addict. He was about thirty-five or thirty-seven years old, fifteen of which he had spent in prisons and labor camps. He had smuggled in – or had been allowed to smuggle in – eighty grams of hashish. Max Fyodorovich suggested I try the drug, arguing that it would give me much more pleasure than cognac and women. I argued, in turn, against drugs and thievery. I tried to convince Max that a person could work and live honestly in Leningrad, start a family.

It was, as they say, "a monkey's work." Max replied that he had only ever lived decently in the camps, that whenever he was released from camp, he would be anxious to return after two months. He only had to commit a minor theft to end up back on the bench. Now he was in KGB prison. I don't remember the legend he told me, something to do with a murder in camp. He might have beheaded his brigadier with an axe at the lumber yard. As far as family was concerned, Max's reasoning was solid. As a drug addict he couldn't have children. They could be born addicted, deformed, or retarded. Until his hashish finished, Max slept for most of the day (or got high). Then he started to fall apart and had to beg the nurse for tablets. He loved poetry, and sometimes wrote himself. He had a notebook full of poems.

Back to the investigator's office. Ryabchuk gave me a book on the CIA and, after flicking through a few documents, began chatting to a friend on the phone, supposedly making preparations for a fishing trip, but the conversation had more to do with cognac and snacks than about fishing equipment. Sometimes Ryabchuk would look over at me, to see how I was reacting, but I pretended to be immersed in the contents of my book.

Ryabchuk hung up. "We were just planning a little fishing trip. I like a bit of fishing now and then. Actually, I was looking at your photos recently, Mark Yulievich, and it seems like you were keen on fishing as well, and even hunting," Ryabchuk continued his playacting.

"I was never that fond of fishing, hunting even less so. I shot some partridges and snipe in Siberia, but nothing serious. It was just a way of coping with the monotony of garrison life," I replied, coolly indifferent to Ryabchuk's theatrical enthusiasm. "If I was given the opportunity to fish now, I wouldn't go. It's cold and rainy outside, while here it's warm, bright, and there are good books."

They transferred me to another cell, maybe five or six cells away from No. 193, where Lenin was imprisoned before the Revolution. They must have been cleaning the cell as we walked past, because I managed to catch a glimpse of the table with a jug and cup on it, a neatly made bed, and a memorial plaque.

I met my new cellmate, whose name I don't remember. Let's call him Vasiliy Ivanovich, although I'm certain he wasn't a Vasiliy. But anyway, this

Vasya, a man of about forty, introduced himself to me as the former head of the supply division for the October Railroad. I think this was a legend he had made up. If he had introduced himself as the minister of transport, I would have "believed" him just the same. Not because I didn't believe that a division head or a minister was capable of theft, but I didn't believe Vasya, whose face had "convict" written all over it. Perhaps he had done most of his thieving on the railroads, hence the title.

Vasya told me about his exploits and maneuvers, from tin roofing material and building materials to icons, currency, and gold. His band of robbers had toured beyond Leningrad to Ukraine. Disguised as road workers and highway planners, they ransacked graveyards, breaking into family mausoleums in search of medals, rings, gold teeth, and other valuables. Armed with fake documents, the band cooperated with local governments in search of gold-filled tombs. They even dreamed of finding the tomb of Queen Tamara in Georgia.

This was how I opened a new world for myself, the world of *The Gulag Archipelago*. Vasya, a representative of this new world, expressed regret that we hadn't met sooner. Then we could have bought a plane instead of trying to hijack one. Apparently, fifty to sixty thousand rubles wasn't a problem for Vasya.

"Then you'd have flown off into the blue on your own plane, and the guys who sold it to you would have been drinking for months after. It's sad we didn't meet earlier," lamented Vasya. One of the thousand Ostap Benders of the great socialist land.

Vasya smoked one cigarette after another day and night, and coughed endlessly. Perhaps it was some KGB assignment, or perhaps it was simply from worry. He alleged that all his offenses were punishable by death. My efforts to reduce his daily ration of nicotine did not bring the desired results. And then I made a mistake. I wrote an official request to the prison director to either put me in a cell by myself or together with a non-smoker. The director answered that he would fulfil my request at the first opportunity. Literally the next day, Vasya was exchanged for Pyotr Ikonnikov. Pyotr was a former gang leader and the most disgusting person I have ever had to share a cell with. He immediately began to do tasks for the KGB, obviously making money by selling drugs. Where Vasya had smoked ordinary cigarettes, Pyotr rolled his own makhorka cigarettes the size of a finger.

Ikonnikov was allowed to have playing cards, a razor, a needle, and a wristwatch in the cell. He would stick the needle in his veins and get high, or pretend to get high, while watching my reaction. I had nothing to say to him other than, "Idiot."

Pyotr tried to convince me to play cards, as the KGB knew I had once liked to play Preference. And though I could refuse to play, I couldn't stop him from smoking. I had no right to. The best I could do was get him to smoke out the window. One day, while smoking at the window, Pyotr lost consciousness and collapsed. He was physically strong, but obviously his drug-ravaged body had given out. I dragged him on to his cot and splashed his face with water. When he regained consciousness and opened his eyes, he murmured, "I bet you poisoned me."

"I'm not capable of that," I replied, "but I'd shoot an animal like you with pleasure."

Ten minutes later this KGB pawn was already rolling another cigarette. Later, in the camps, I learned about the despicable things he'd done to other inmates, and that before becoming my cellmate he had smoked only a few cigarettes per day. It's not surprising that he lost consciousness and fell short of the KGB's hopes. The KGB hadn't considered that I was a smoker for fourteen years in my youth, then spent the next eleven years cleansing my body of that rubbish and making myself stronger.

During my time in Leningrad prison, both in my cell and in the yard, I would run four or five miles a day. If I had kept going for 2,500 miles on even terrain, I could have run to Jerusalem.

In November 1970, two Lithuanians, a father and son called Brazinskas hijacked a Soviet plane with firearms and forced the crew to fly to Turkey. In the process, a stewardess was killed and both pilots were wounded. Ryabchuk showed me the article about this in the newspaper, and said, "Bad luck for you. Now you'll be judged more harshly." He said this in the tone people use for expressing sympathy to the relatives of a dead person.

Our position was made worse by the UN resolution against air piracy, which responded to multiple Cuban hijackings and hijackings of passenger liners by Arab terrorists.

The investigation had finished, and I was taken to the investigator's office more and more rarely. When we did meet, it was not to discuss the details of my case so much as miscellaneous topics. We even went as far as "anti-Soviet" jokes, the sharpest and most truthful genre of national folklore. Ryabchuk reminded me of one of the last jokes I had told at work: "An Armenian radio station is asked, 'What will happen in the Sahara desert after the advent of socialism?' 'There won't be enough sand.'"

Here, we're obviously talking about Russian-style socialism.

The KGB had recorded this joke, but it didn't fall under any article of the Criminal Code. In Stalin's time, you could have been arrested and sentenced for a joke like that alone. But in the period of "stagnation," in the years of "humanism," I only got a smile – moreover, a smile which agreed with the contents of the joke.

We talked about glasnost, although we didn't use that term and spoke rather of lies and concealment of facts. When I made the accusation, "You don't even publish news about plane crashes and natural disasters," Ryabchuk answered, "Why frighten the people?"

"In the West they publish everything and people fly all the same, unafraid, although they know accidents happen," I pressed. "On the other hand, when a passenger plane crashed in Chita in front of a crowd of people, the airport ticket counters were deserted for two days afterwards.

"Of course it's your business, Vitaliy Nikolayevich, what to make public and what to keep secret. All I'm asking is to let us go, those of us who want to leave the Soviet Union, and then I don't care if you eat each other!" I exploded for the second time ever during the investigation. The first explosion had occurred during a discussion of who should be considered the aggressor in the Middle East. This was during the first days of the investigation, and I was embarrassed for my loss of cool.

Perhaps they were even right about glasnost. There are many people out there who prefer to hear a pleasant lie than the bitter truth. Every nation has its characteristic features. I am no specialist in this complicated matter, but considering I had spent my whole life among Russians, I was able to express one of their important characteristics ("eat each other") in a few words. I think Edik Kuznetsov got it right during the trial:

> I think that the typical structure of Russian political culture can be called despotic. There is little room for movement as a despot, given the standards were set by Ivan the Terrible and Peter the Great. I consider Soviet power to be a legal heir of these two Russian leaders, both ideal in different ways.

8 The Trials

1970–1972

Judgement day was drawing closer, and I had to come up with a plan for my appearance in court. I decided to use the trial as an opportunity to discuss the reasons that had led me to conceive the hijacking. I decided not to touch on any other questions of internal or external politics, except for the question of minorities and the question of Israel.

Once it became clear to me that we would not be charged under article 83 of the RSFSR Criminal Code, I stopped worrying what the lengths of our sentences would be. I even thought that the longer they were, the more noise would be made, and the fiercer the fight for aliyah and for our freedom would become. Ryabchuk had made hints and even spoken about the death penalty, but I had never taken his threats seriously.

Before the trial, I had to become acquainted with my case materials. There were forty-two volumes for two different court cases. Ryabchuk kept a schedule for this and regularly noted which volumes I had examined. I didn't bother looking at all the volumes, as I was certain that the KGB had already decided our sentence in advance. If it had been in my power to expedite the process of waiting for the trial, and the trial itself, I would have done it. Only then would the results of our operation come to light.

Before the trial I met with my lawyer, Pevsner. This meeting and the lawyer himself were totally useless as far as the trial was concerned. His only achievement was to legally rob my family, though our property had already been confiscated.

The First Leningrad Trial, or as it is still called, "The Airplane Trial," began on December 15, 1970.

I decided that I had to look decent, even in prison. As the Russian song "Varyag" goes: "The last parade is upon us..." I asked for a tie, but they wouldn't give me one. Even at the Nuremberg trials, the accused had been allowed to wear ties. I tried to convince Ryabchuk, but it was useless. "It isn't allowed," was the most common answer among Soviet bosses, and not only in camps and prisons. On the other hand, I was given a large piece of paper for the first time, to aid my preparations for the trial. I wrote down a few words, and drew a few geometric figures. Ryabchuk looked at the paper in surprise. "Is that all?"

He was obviously hankering to know what I would say at the trial.

No one, however, could stop me from looking like a man of conviction, from holding my head up high. In fact, I think I managed to do just that, judging by what Yosef Mendelevich says:

> Mark Dymshits, energetic and fit, had scarcely stepped out of the first police van, when a joyful cacophony of greetings filled the air. Our crowd was immediately broken up, and the vans were driven around to the entrance. (*Operation Wedding*, p. 136)

And again:

> Mark was the first to be questioned. He spoke proudly and stubbornly, with a kind of inner resentment. His speech was very convincing, and I thought that even the young communists who had been allowed into the room on special permission could not have failed to feel the rightness and sincerity of his words. (*Operation Wedding*, p. 138)

My resentment was for their system, of which the trial was a part, a system which discredited socialism and internationalism, a system which trampled on justice and human rights. The KGB's whole system of compulsion and duress was intended to make us, and all Soviet Jews, afraid. We had to spoil the KGB's plans.

Accompanied by a special convoy, each of us in a separate police van, we were taken to the Leningrad city court. The column of vans was headed and tailed by the police. At the entrance to the court building on the Fontanka stood groups of police and KGB officers. The entrance to the court building was closely guarded. Only our closest relatives were allowed into Courtroom No. 48, where our trial was to take place. From the police vans, we were led down corridors and up staircases lined with police and MVD soldiers. They led us into the courtroom and sat us on the defendants' bench, behind a barrier. Once the MVD soldiers had flanked us on either side, they began to fill the gallery, which had seats for about three hundred people. In a short time, all the seats were occupied. This "theatrical production under the direction of the KGB" had far more willing audience members than there were seats, and so representatives from the high Party ranks changed places almost every day. Three or four rows were set aside for employees of the "competent organs." Their neatness and similarity to one another made them instantly recognizable. Most numerous of all were representatives of regional and Leningrad society. According to the script, they were meant to assail us with cries against us and our families, and at the end of the "show," would greet the sentence with applause. This would demonstrate the patriotism of the working class and their unanimous approval of our well-deserved punishment. They and their predecessors had gained significant experience of demanding the death penalty for "enemies of the people."

But those people on whose reactions we were counting were outside the courthouse, and mostly outside the Russian Empire.

The first piece of good news had already reached us: Jews had begun to leave. Now the trial would intensify the general furor which had begun after our arrests. We didn't have long to wait.

Nine o'clock on December 15, 1970. The street was cold and dark, while the courthouse was warm and the lights were bright.

"The court is in session!"

Here are the main roles and their actors:

Presiding judge: Chairman of the Leningrad City Court, N. A. Yermakov
Member judges: People's assessors P. D. Rusalinov and M. L. Ivanov
Secretary: K. I. Likhomanov
State prosecutor: Leningrad prosecutor S. E. Solovyev
Assistant to the state prosecutor: Leningrad senior assistant prosecutor I. V. Katykova
Plaintiff: V. A. Mednanogov, representative of Aeroflot

There were eleven of us accused. The twelfth, Wolf Zalmanson, would be tried later before a military tribunal, as a military serviceman, and would be sentenced to ten years of imprisonment.

There were guards and audience for "crowd scenes." The script was developed at Leningrad KGB headquarters under the supervision of the

Communist Party Regional Committee (and Tolstikov personally), before being approved in Moscow.

After the show trial, we hoped that "theater critics" from Washington, London, Paris, Jerusalem, Rome, Madrid, and other cities would catch on.

The presiding judge read the charges. We were all being charged under articles 15-64a, and 15-93.1 of the RSFSR Criminal Code (attempted treason and attempt grand theft – of an airplane – respectively), both of which carried maximum sentences of death. None of the other articles had any significance, as the sentences they carried were swallowed up by these two articles.

After all the formalities were over, I made the following plea: "I do not consider myself guilty of the charges made, though I do not deny the facts of the case."

Next, each of my fellows made his or her plea.

Then, the court began to question the accused one by one. I was the first to be questioned. I spoke of the motives which had driven me to leave the USSR for Israel: antisemitism in the USSR, the USSR's foreign policy in the Middle East, the USSR's internal policy on ethnic minorities. I supported each of these points with evidence I have already discussed.

I had a collection of newspaper and magazine articles about Soviet foreign policy in the Middle East, dating from 1947. It formed a separate volume in my case materials. As the official party line moved back and forth, so did the official attitude to the articles, some of which could be considered anti-Soviet.

Next, I spoke about each of the different escape plans.

The Aeroflot representative asked, "What do you intend to do in Israel?"

I answered, "I would work as a civilian pilot, or perhaps as a chauffeur or even a tractor driver."

"Perhaps you would be asked to bomb peaceful Arab settlements," he continued.

"Do you think that only the Soviet army bombs military objects, while everyone else bombs women, children, and the elderly?"

The prosecutor asked, "You were born in the USSR. The Soviet Union is your motherland. Did you want to betray your motherland?"

"Yes, the Soviet Union was my motherland. But after the events of 1967, for the reasons I have already discussed, I ceased to consider her my motherland. She became worse than a stepmother to me." Here, the audience booed. "A man, unlike an animal, does not have to consider the burrow or nest where he was born his motherland," I continued. "I like the definition of motherland given by Elsa Triolet: 'A country is your motherland when you need her, and when she needs you.'"

There were no further questions.

My fellow accused and the witnesses were questioned over the course of the next few days.

On December 22, the court began to hear the speeches of our defense attorneys. It was pitiful to see the valid arguments of the defense run up against the KGB's plan. But this was just an element of so-called "socialist law."

As there have now been two volumes published on anti-Jewish trials in the USSR (1969–1971), I will not dwell on the court proceedings in detail.

As for the prosecutor's assertion that I behaved provocatively in court, I don't think that has any relation to the truth. In the first place, I dealt with only a handful of issues, assuming that the rest were internal KGB matters. If they wanted to live in a George Orwell novel, I wasn't going to stop them, but I believed they shouldn't stop others from seeking freedom. In the second place, I would have expressed myself more stridently had it not been for the "game" I had begun with the KGB. What I didn't know then was that the KGB had taken control of the game insofar as my wife was concerned. Later, I learned what their methods of work had been.

When Sylva Zalmanson took the stand, she declared that she was a Zionist and that she had been trying to obtain the necessary documents to travel to Israel since 1963, with no success. Sylva told the court how she had used her typewriter to copy and distribute Jewish materials, and how she had first told Kuznetsov, as well as other acquaintances in Riga, about the escape plan.

Yosef Mendelevich explained that he had grown up in a family that valued Jewish traditions and that he had always been interested in the history and fate of the Jewish nation. He said that he and his family had long been convinced that their spiritual and historic motherland was Israel. He had applied to the Migration Service three times for permission to leave and had been refused all three times. Colonel Kayi had told Mendelevich that he could "rot here, and forget Israel!" In response to the question of why he wanted to escape, Yosef replied, "I had one goal, and that was to get to Israel." In response to the question of what he would do there for a living, he replied, "The material side is not of great interest to me. But I am convinced that Israel is the only place where I can live."

Eduard Kuznetsov spoke in detail of the circumstances which had preceded his attempt to leave the USSR illegally: his childhood and youth, his first seven years in prison, his vain efforts to obtain an exit visa for Israel. Edik declared that we were being tried under the wrong articles, that neither the USSR nor its prestige had played any role in our actions and intentions. "I decided to flee the country only in response to the egregious violation of my human rights," he said. "It was an act of desperation." Edik rejected the charge of theft, as we had been convinced that the plane would have been returned to its state of origin. "The idea of 'motherland' does not occupy first place in my hierarchy of values. The first place is occupied by freedom. This is why I am drawn to Israel. For me, it represents both motherland and freedom." Edik's testimony was interrupted by the prosecutor many times. He had to answer a lot of questions.

Israel Zalmanson's testimony centered on his desire to live in Israel. His family had received entry visas to Israel but had not been allowed to leave the USSR. Other than flight, he saw no other way to get to Israel.

Aleksey Murzhenko spoke of his unsuccessful attempts to build a life after his release from prison camp. This was his main reason for wanting to leave the USSR. Aleksey drew attention to the fact that his charges placed a great deal of emphasis on his past criminal record, despite the fact that he had not engaged in anti-Soviet activity since his release.

Yuriy Fyodorov had refused to testify during the preliminary investigation. He testified in court that, judging from previous experience, whenever he had given evidence on the most insignificant points, he had been made to look like a threat to the whole Soviet power structure. "Besides, I have a fundamental distrust of this organization (the KGB). There is too much blood on their hands." Yura voiced his disagreement with the KGB's choice of articles 64 and 93 and refused to acknowledge his guilt. It would be possible, he argued, to consider article 83 – illegal border crossing – but as there was no article in the Criminal Code on airplane hijacking, some analogous article would have to be used, i.e., on automobile hijacking.

The prosecutor asked Fyodorov an interesting question. "Did you know that you were included in the group in order to mask their criminal intent, in order to conceal the group's Jewish makeup?"

Fyodorov answered, "I don't understand what you mean."

"You knew that there would be only Jews in the group?"

"Yes, I knew."

"You knew and yet you agreed to participate?"

"Only Butman talked about hiding the group's Jewishness," answered Fyodorov. "But among us there was no talk of concealment."

Anatoliy Altman spoke too of his reasons for wanting to leave the USSR. As a child, Anatoliy and his family had attended synagogue and an amateur Jewish theater. Then, the family moved to an area where there were no Jews. It was then that he first felt a hostile attitude to him personally, and to Jews in general. The family moved to Chernovitsy, where both synagogue and Jewish theater had been closed. This fact made a deep impression on Anatoliy, and his interest in Judaism, in Jewish history and philosophy, grew even more intense. More and more, he understood that he could only live in Israel, but in both Odessa and Riga, Anatoliy was refused exit visas.

Arye Hanoch described his upbringing in a Jewish family. He had gradually reached the conclusion that the future of the Jewish people lay only in Israel. In 1966, he had been refused an exit visa. He had written letters to various institutions, including the UN, all without result. Then, Arye understood that he would have to act illegally. Arye answered many questions from the prosecution.

In Mendel Bodnya's testimony, he described how his family had been separated in 1944. He had remained with his father, but where his mother and brother had disappeared to, he did not know until the 1950s, when he discovered that they had ended up in Israel. He applied for multiple exit visas, and his requests were multiply refused. For this reason, as soon as he learned of our operation, he immediately joined in, hoping to reunite with his mother.

Boris Penson gave an account of his life and of his desire to live in Israel. In 1964, he had been sentenced to five years on a false conviction. In 1967, he had been prematurely released and since then had worked as a designer.

I have already mentioned that lawyers in political cases play only a token role and are unable to influence the KGB's plans. This is how Lesko, Altman's defense attorney, began his speech: "We defenders join our voices to the outrage of all Soviet people."

The defense asked the court to replace articles 64, 93, and 70, but the lawyers understood that all their arguments and demands would remain suspended in mid-air. After all, they hadn't been hired to change the finale of this show trial.

The plaintiff, Mednanogov, took the stage. He had donned all his medals, honors, and ribbons. He began reading his speech from a piece of paper, which would have been easy to put together from compiled newspaper articles of the period – articles which stoked up hatred toward Jews and Israel, hiding antisemitism under a guise of anti-Zionism. Mednanogov concluded his speech by demanding the death penalty for all the operation's participants.

On December 23, the presiding judge declared the deliberations concluded and gave each of the accused the opportunity to make a concluding speech.

I began by saying that each of the accused thought the proposed punishments too harsh, and that I personally considered the prosecutor's demands excessively cruel:

> You miscalculate if you think that by executing us, you will strike fear into the hearts of future escapees. On the contrary, they will hijack planes, not with clubs and brass knuckles, but with automatic rifles. They will have nothing to lose. I understand what fighting is, and I know that for you, this kind of severity is only meant as a deterrent.
>
> The representative of Aeroflot spoke supposedly in the name of all pilots. It is a pity that his colleagues from the human resource department, to whom I applied in vain for so many years, are not sitting here in the courtroom now. Only they, before the autumn of 1969, had the power to stop me from attempting to hijack a plane.
>
> We, the accused, are all different in personality. Some of us met each other only on the final day of our operation. And even so, it is encouraging that here, in court, we have not lost our humanity, and have not begun to bite each other like spiders in a jar. I thank the court for the humanity it has shown to my wife and daughters. I ask the court to treat me with fairness and humanity.
>
> And I would like to say, in conclusion, that I firmly believe a day will come when I and my family will live in Israel.

In this concluding speech, my thanks to the court for their humane treatment of my family was part of the game I was playing with the KGB, as after my meeting with General Nasyrev, it had become clear to me that they would not be charged.

Sylva Zalmanson expressed her shock at the sentences demanded by the prosecutor, especially the death penalty. "I am convinced that according to law, the people who have illegally contravened our right to live where we want should be brought to justice." Sylva added that our dream to live in Israel could not compare to our fear of the pain that we could be subjected to. She concluded in Hebrew and Russian, "If I forget you, Jerusalem, May my right hand wither away" (Psalms 137:5).

Yosef Mendelevich acknowledged that his actions had been unlawful. "I acknowledge that I deserve punishment, and I ask the court to treat my comrades with magnanimity."

Eduard Kuznetsov concluded his speech by requesting lenience for Sylva and fairness for himself.

I will not reproduce the last words of each of the accused. They have all been printed already. Only a few words from Anatoliy Altman's speech:

> Your Honors, I ask you to save the lives of Kuznetsov and Dymshits, and to award Sylva Zalmanson, the only woman among us, with a minimum sentence.

And from Arye Hanoch:

> I ask the court only that lenience be shown toward Sylva Zalmanson, and mercy toward Kuznetsov and Dymshits.

On December 24, 1970, after all our crimes and their corresponding articles were listed, our sentences were read in the name of Russian Soviet Federative Socialist Republic. The so-called collegium of judges read the sentences that had been fixed by the KGB long before our trial:

1. Mark Yulievich Dymshits: sentenced to death with confiscation of personal property
2. Eduard Samuilovich Kuznetsov: sentenced to death without confiscation of personal property, in the absence of such

3. Yosef Mozusovich Mendelevich: sentenced to fifteen years of imprisonment without confiscation of personal property, in the absence of such

4. Sylva Iosifovich Zalmanson: sentenced to ten years of imprisonment without confiscation of personal property, in the absence of such

5. Israel Iosifovich Zalmanson: sentenced to eight years of imprisonment without confiscation of personal property, in the absence of such

6. Anatoliy Adolfovich Altman: sentenced to twelve years of imprisonment without confiscation of personal property, in the absence of such

7. Leib Girshevich Hanoch: sentenced to thirteen years of imprisonment without confiscation of personal property, in the absence of such

8. Yuriy Pavlovich Fyodorov: sentenced to fifteen years of imprisonment without confiscation of personal property, in the absence of such

9. Aleksey Grigorievich Murzhenko: sentenced to fourteen years of imprisonment without confiscation of personal property, in the absence of such

10. Boris Solomonovich Penson: sentenced to ten years of imprisonment with confiscation of personal property

11. Mendel Abramovich Bodnya: sentenced to four years of imprisonment without confiscation of personal property, in the absence of such

Before the court session was declared closed, the presiding judge explained our right to appeal.

A noteworthy detail, which gives a sense of Soviet society's moral and cultural level: After the sentences were read, the "audience" broke into applause. This piece of barbarity overshadowed the cruelty of the sentences themselves. Not to mention the fact that this was all happening in the cultural center of the Russian Empire.

I can imagine myself executing some Nazi criminal or Arab terrorist, that is, I can imagine shooting such a person myself without any pangs of consciousness. But I couldn't bring myself to applaud if one of those murderers was sentenced to death in open court. Even if we acknowledge that the whole script of the show trial written by the KGB was amoral, this finishing detail was doubly amoral.

It is one thing if the government bodies act amorally (we had all become used to their political murders, kidnappings, conspiracies, and coups). But it is another matter to get ordinary people involved and to degrade them in such a way. And then people wonder where the cruelty and low morale in society come from!

Now, twenty years after those events, from the comfort of my own home, the applause of a few hundred extras seems insignificant when compared to what "enemies of the people" were subjected to over the course of many years. When millions of people were slaughtered to the applause of millions more; when the death penalty was demanded in the press and at demonstrations, long before trials would begin.

But on December 24, 1970, the audience's applause filled me with a powerless rage, which was cooled by the unexpected click of handcuffs around my wrists.

Some of our family members stood up on their benches, shouting words of support: "We're with you!" "Israel is with you!" "Everything will be all right!" "All Jews are with you!" and so on. They were met from all sides with spite, abuse, and threats. But from time to time, other reactions to the trial could be heard. Boris Penson's mother was in the courtroom at that time and overheard an elderly communist party activist asking his neighbor, "Was it really worth cooking up this trial?" It had obviously become clear, at least to a few people, that the organizers of the trial would be its real victims.

The police wagons pulled up and we were taken back to prison, except that Edik and I were now given special cells for those who had been sentenced to death. There were several such cells in the KGB prison. They were all close to Lenin's former cell. I imagine that if Lenin hadn't died in 1924, he might have had the opportunity to do time under Stalin for treason or anti-Soviet activity. Or else he would have been shot by the very organs he created. Perhaps they thought that proximity to Vladimir Ilich's cell would make it easier for his spirit to visit those of us who were bound for the "next world." It was the same world promised to us by the Internationale ("we will build our new world…"). Each successive leader of the so-called Soviet Union promised a new world to us working people.

I forget now whether the cell number was 195 or 196. All objects in the cell were attached to the floor. The radiator and toilet were encased in wood. Even my spoon and bowl were given to me only during mealtimes. The peephole in the door opened constantly. Everyone was anxious that we didn't deny them the pleasure of carrying out our sentences.

Silence. I sat on my bed. I had to think over the situation calmly. I couldn't get it into my head that they could condemn me to death for an attempt – not even for an attempt but for an *intention*, as the attempt was to have been made in Priozersk. I couldn't believe it, all the more so because I was an optimist. They were trying to frighten us, trying to drive us to our knees, to make us repent. On the other hand, the organs had liquidated more than a few people for nothing, dreamt up fantastical charges.

The following thoughts began to go through my head:

All right, suppose they change the death penalty for fifteen years in prison. I'm already forty-three. Even if I get out of labor camp alive at fifty-eight, I'll probably be a helpless cripple.

Snap out of it, optimist! Weren't you counting on an international fight for aliyah and our early release? Yes, I was, but I wasn't expecting the death penalty. I wasn't expecting their twisted logic. I guess I should have been.

When God wants to punish someone, he deprives them of reason. The KGB chose the least reasonable solution. They made decisions based on interests of the moment, on the principle that "where there is brawn, you don't need brains."

But that's what you think, Mark. What about the KGB?

Who can guarantee that the KGB won't follow through on their (in your opinion, stupid) original plan? The West never spends much time dwelling on the cruelty of the Soviet regime. I've known them to close their eyes to it entirely. The West couldn't even make the USSR adhere to the Declaration of Human Rights.

What's your problem, Mark? Didn't you know what kind of monster you were playing with?

I knew. I weighed up the pros and cons. I made my own decisions.

So, keep playing, Mark. It's a good thing Stalin's not in charge anymore, or they'd have finished you off at the aerodrome and said that you were Anglo-American spies and agents of international Zionism.

Why shouldn't the KGB threaten you with death? They'll use any strategy, and you, Mark, agreed to play by their rules. The end justifies the means. You think it's amoral? Yes. But you're playing with an amoral regime. Would you have dared to hijack a plane in a democratic country? Of course not. You would have bought tickets and flown to Israel. It was they who made you fight fire with fire. What if you're just the same as them? What if you've also got the cruelty bug?

I could have, but not entirely. I haven't lost my sense of fairness like they have, and in any case I wouldn't have dealt with the situation like they have. But, okay. That's enough for today. The deed is done. Everything's clearer in the morning. Death or fifteen years in the camps – it's not like one's much better than the other. Though fifteen years doesn't mean I'll have to serve the whole sentence, whereas death is death, and that's it. But now it's time for bed. Life goes on.

The night after the sentencing, my sleep was full of dreams. In my first ever technicolor, widescreen dream, I floated above the clouds in the company of biblical heroes.

In the morning, I did my morning calisthenics, and life returned to the ordinary prison routine, Except that the peephole in the door opened with greater regularity, I wasn't allowed to go for walks, and I had to shave under the observation of three guards.

Time went by slowly on death row. As I wasn't allowed to read, I had ample time to dwell on past events. I understood how high the price of failure would be, that is, if we failed to mobilize the West and the international Jewish community.

Before June 15, we had been afraid of early arrests and closed trials. The KGB met us halfway by arresting us at the aerodrome and making the event public knowledge. This meant that the world knew about us – and indeed, the first pieces of news about protests in the West and the emigration of hundreds, or maybe thousands of Soviet Jews had begun to seep through. This meant that, until the trial, everything had been going well.

Next, the KGB had had a choice to make between article 83 with short prison terms, or No. 64 with long prison terms and even execution. If the KGB had chosen article 83, and given us prison terms of up to three years, they would have made themselves look humane in the world's eyes. After serving our short sentences, we would have gone off to Israel without causing a fuss, but without a fuss there would have been no large-scale aliyah. They would have given exit visas to a few thousand Jews, and everything would have gone quiet for a few years.

But the KGB acted in a cruel and bloody way, without considering how the West and the Jewish community would react. It may have been an unexpected blow for us, but for the common cause of aliyah, this way was better. My logic may sound cynical, but we were dealing with a whole hoard of cynics. If the KGB was going to act against state interests, how could we – those who wanted to leave the USSR – fail to rejoice in our enemies' mistakes? We were traveling along parallel tracks toward totally different goals. We had begun to approach our goal. I wasn't sure about the KGB. I had to wait and see, but this time, in total isolation without even newspapers or a cellmate.

Of course, even this situation had its pluses. I had no one to stop me from thinking and "looking over life," as they say in Odessa. My best years were behind me, youth had flown by, aviation was just a memory. My wife and daughters were free. I'd been counting on ten or twelve years. They'd given me the firing squad instead. That's how it was.

What are you going to do, Mark? Do you think you can change anything?

No. I couldn't even attempt an escape without help from the outside.

But you can refuse to believe that the sentence will be carried out. And you'd be justified for doing so.

If they gave me fifteen years instead of the firing squad, I'd be able to learn the results of our operation, and there might be some hope of early release as a result of Western intervention or a prisoner swap. The West must have a fund of Soviet spies and left-wing terrorists for exchange. Israel might even have captive Soviet soldiers who had been serving in Arab countries. In short, I shouldn't lose hope.

December 26 was an ordinary Leningrad winter day, short and gray. Through a crack in the blinds I got a glimpse of the leaden sky. Individual snowflakes fell against the panes. Pigeons cooed on the window ledges. Then, the meal hatch swung open and a guard instructed, "Prepare to leave your cell."

In a few minutes' time, I was led to the legal visit room. There, I met a cheerful Mr. Pevsner, who, without waiting for me to sit down, told me, "You have to make an appeal in cassation to the RSFSR Supreme Court, now."

A thought flashed through my brain that something unusual, out of the ordinary, was going on.

"What's the rush? I still have five days," I muttered, with the exaggerated gloominess of a man battered by circumstances.

"You have to make an immediate appeal in cassation. All your comrades are writing theirs already. I'll come up with the text myself while you're here. I have to leave for Moscow later today," Pevsner continued.

His agitation made clear the urgency of the situation.

"But don't say that I repent my actions!" I insisted.

"All right, I'll get it all down how it should be."

It suddenly occurred to me that they might overturn the death penalty. I even wanted to show off a bit, refuse to sign the cassation. Whether I wrote it or not, whether I signed it or not, it would make no difference if they were acting from a script.

I had to stop myself: *Mark, don't get cocky. If you're going to play, don't play the fool. Pretend that you're pleasantly surprised by this new state of affairs.*

I didn't know then that on December 23, 1970, a Spanish court had sentenced three Basque nationalists to death for murdering policemen. On December 26, Franco reversed the sentence. Some people think that this "humane act" on the part of a fascist dictator decided our fate as well. I think that it only accelerated the KGB's inevitable decision to commute my and Edik's death sentences to fifteen years, and shorten the prison terms of some of our comrades.

Another thing I didn't know was that many governments, the Socialist International, the Pope, and several Communist parties worldwide had spoken out against the severity of our sentences.

Nor did I know that hundreds of Soviet Jews had begun to write collective letters and telegrams to the general secretary of the Communist Party of the USSR, the chairman of the of the Supreme Soviet Presidium, the prosecutor general of the USSR, the United Nations, and so on. The academician Andrey Sakharov had sent an open letter to President Nixon of the USA and to Chairman Podgorny.

Below are some excerpts from the letters and telegrams:

> We are shocked by the inhumane sentences handed down by the Leningrad court. We demand its immediate reversal and free passage for all Jews who wish to emigrate to Israel…
>
> We are disgusted by the bloodthirstiness of the judges. We demand not mercy, but justice for the accused. We decry the senseless murder of human beings, whose only offense was an insurmountable desire to live in their own country, a desire which

could not be satisfied legally. We call upon all honest people to stop this murder!...

A sentence has been passed not only upon the eleven accused, but morally upon all of us, upon our children, upon all Jews who hope to live in Israel. The sentence had only one goal: to frighten us and make us abandon our intentions. No one has ever succeeded in using violence, repression, or threats to make the Jews abandon their dream of returning to the Land of Israel. They will not succeed this time.

On December 30, 1970, a group of democratic intellectuals and Soviet citizens "deeply troubled and shocked by the wave of severity set in motion by the death sentences passed in Burgos and Leningrad," sent a letter to Chairman Podgorny. They petitioned him to spare the lives of the condemned.

These pieces of good news would take some time to reach our cells. But, some noise had begun; emigration had begun. The KGB's strategic plan had begun to fail, after their tactical success at the stage of arrest.

On December 29, 1970, in Moscow, at the headquarters of the Supreme Court of the RSFSR, the Supreme Soviet Judicial Council began to examine the appeals in cassation of the accused and their legal counsels. About ten "members of the public" were present in the courtroom, among whom were relatives of some of the accused as well as the academician Sakharov.

The court session continued on December 30, beginning at nine thirty in the morning. Prosecutor Pokhlebkin gave a ten-minute speech, in which he argued for my and Kuznetsov's sentences to be commuted, considering they had never actually committed a crime and the death penalty was an exceptional measure in the USSR. It seems likely that the KGB and the rest of the key players in the Leningrad show trial first learned of this from Pokhlebkin's speech.

Then, the judges left for deliberation, and at eleven o'clock, the Supreme Court of the RSFSR announced its decision. The changes in our punishments were as follows:

1. Kuznetsov and I had our death penalties commuted to fifteen years of imprisonment.
2. Mendelevich had his prison term shortened to twelve years.
3. Hanoch and Altman had their prison terms shortened to ten years.

The rest of the sentences remained unchanged.

On December 31, accompanied by three guards, I was taken to the office of the prison director, Major Kruglov, who informed me that my sentence had been commuted and handed me a telegram from my lawyer. Kruglov proceeded to say that Kuznetsov had also had his death sentence commuted to fifteen years, and wished me a happy new year. "You will have to remain in your current cell for a few more days," he continued, "as today is a holiday, and we are currently unable to move you to a new cell."

For the first time, I spent New Year's Eve not only in isolation, but in an isolation cell. It was an ordinary night in prison. I spent another week in the silence of death row. There was no cigarette smoke, no criminal chat.

They put me back on the ordinary prison routine. They started giving me newspapers and returned my spoon, bowl, and teapot. I lay on my bed and read. Then ten minutes of calisthenics, and back to my reading. After the trial, they didn't even stop me from sleeping during the day.

The first week of 1971 went by in this manner.

I was transferred to another cell and put together with the film actor Andrey Naymushin. His idol was Casanova. He was thirty-five, tall – over six foot – his shoulders a mile wide. In short, he was a fine male specimen from head to toe, but with the physiognomy of a classic bad guy. In the 1970 film *White Sun of the Desert*, Naymushin played the role of the main villain's assistant.

Until the age of thirty, he had absolutely no relations with women, saving his juices for later. I don't remember what ultimately inspired him to act, but in the five years which followed, he had his way with six hundred women between the ages of fifteen and sixty in single and group "combat." He even managed in a single evening to sleep with a young girl, her mother, and the mother's younger sister. He was a strolling player, in all senses of the word.

Naymushin did not, however, end up in prison for sexual promiscuity. Between his meetings with women he somehow also managed to squeeze in some money manipulation. He dealt with currency and underground concerts. One of his friends came under suspicion for espionage. This last point attracted the interest of the KGB.

All Naymushin's stories were exclusively concerned with sex. It seemed to me as if he drew sexual pleasure from telling stories about his sexual exploits. I had never met such a debauched person before and would never again encounter anyone like him. He told many stories, both funny and unpleasant. I will recall a few of the fifty or so he told me.

Here's one unpleasant story, in brief: with an intimate circle of young Leningrad actors, he spent an evening drinking cognac and watching a male sheepdog copulate with a young actress, who was mistress of the apartment.

Here are two of the tamer episodes in his five-year epic:

One evening at a party, Naymushin met a woman of his own age. After the dancing was over, he ran to the store to grab some drinks and snacks, before accompanying his new friend home. She lived in a communal apartment, but did not share a room – good living conditions by Soviet standards at that time. After a late dinner, the time came for Naymushin's principle activity – emulating, and even outstripping, Casanova. However, his chosen heroine continually repeated "no," and tried to make him leave. But the modern incarnation of Casanova pursued his goal with more intensity than the USSR had tried to outstrip the USA in meat and wool production. Naymushin evidently knew that Casanova had become impotent at forty-five, and since he only began at thirty himself, our contemporary must have felt extra pressure to meet his quota. For this reason, he ignored the woman's protests. She gave up her last line of defense with the words "I've been categorically forbidden." But, as they say in Russia, "a drunk is led by his penis," and Naymushin had an important historical precedent. Now, in the time of glasnost, he might have ended up in the Guinness Book of World Records.

When Naymushin awoke early the next morning and made preparations to exceed quota, he discovered the woman's cold and lifeless body. After turning on the light and becoming convinced that she was dead, he called the police and an ambulance. They arrived, confirmed the young woman's death, and began an investigation. Only a week later, Naymushin recalled the details of their conversation, and most importantly, her words about being "forbidden." Through doctors, the investigation concluded that the woman had been undergoing a course of treatment and was taking medication, but that she had been categorically forbidden to engage in intimate relations until the end of treatment. Though Naymushin was released, he ended up in police records – not as Casanova (yet), but as an urban Don Juan – after bragging to the investigator about his exploits.

Of course, this death not only did not stop but did not even slow the pace of his activity. Naymushin went through "girlfriends" without remembering their faces or names, but on the level of quantity, he kept a strict count.

Everything was going well, until Naymushin ended up in front of the same investigator a couple of months later. "You don't think you're going to escape criminal charges this time? We should really castrate you, but unfortunately there isn't an article for that in the Criminal Code," was how the investigator began his speech, rubbing his hands together with pleasure at the thought of bringing this sexual disturber of the peace to justice. Although at that time, the sexual revolution was only just beginning to penetrate our underdeveloped socialist country. No one had ever heard of AIDS.

To skip ahead a bit, it must be said that the investigator got excited too soon. Our hero was to continue his frenzied activity among the fair sex, at least within the boundaries of the USSR. Only the KGB could stop him in the end. Perhaps forever, perhaps only for a while.

The reason for this second investigation was the following incident: One evening, Naymushin wandered into a youth club, where he quickly chose his next victim – a girl who was studying at a vocational college. They got themselves revved up on spirits at the bar and had a bit of a dance before going back to her room in the college dormitory.

Without turning on the lights, they went into the room – which had two beds and two nightstands in it – and immediately got to work. After all, Naymushin had to meet quota. The room was in half darkness.

According to his count, this girl was the three hundredth, that is, an important milestone. Considering his extensive experience with the fair sex, our hero could generally make room for a bit of research. He liked to examine the facial expression of his partner at the moment of climax. When Naymushin flicked on the bedside lamp, the girl opened her eyes and shrieked wildly. Then her eyes rolled back in her head, and she fell silent. The image of the recent corpse swam once more before our hero's eyes. As he expressed it, "It was just the same. I broke out in a cold sweat, and couldn't say a word. It occurred to me that I wouldn't be able to avoid prison this time. I wanted to run, but then she began to move, opened her eyes, and shrieked again in horror. Her gaze was fixed on the corner by the door. I turned over and saw a hanged man. The kid had tied a rope to the air vent and kicked the chair away."

Naymushin continued, "Then it was the police again, another investigation. It turned out that the room's second inhabitant slept around, and this kid was really in love with her. He had obviously read too many nineteenth-century novels and believed in pure feelings, and this was the result.

I'm not likely to end up that way. I only read movie scripts and true crime. I don't have time to fool around like our ancestors did. I'm a practical man."

I somehow doubt that Naymushin's excessive sexual desire was a sign of mental illness – what they call satyriasis. For him, it was probably a kind of sport.

One time, he was even forced to run from the field of battle. Somehow, he managed to come into contact with a female nymphomaniac. His back, lips, and neck were so bloody with scratch and bite wounds that he needed a week's rest before resuming his frenzied activity.

Naymushin could talk about his exploits for hours. Sometimes he would forget what he had already told me and start repeating himself. In such cases I would stop him and, after thinking for a moment, he would launch on some new story. Toward the end of our cohabitation, his stories started to get on my nerves. He could never read for long and was tormented by boredom. A day or two before I was transferred to a different cell, Naymushin told me two addresses where, according to him, "I would get first-class, Paris-level service." I thanked him for his trouble (perhaps it was the KGB's trouble) and said that in fourteen years' time I'd be lucky to remember my home address, or where Paris was.

It so happened that in fourteen years, my home address was in Israel, and I had visited Paris as a tourist. But I would not arrive in Israel until eight years after that conversation.

Meanwhile, outside the prison walls, the effects of our attempted hijacking were continuing to be felt. Jews were starting to leave the USSR, the fight against antisemitic policies had already begun, and hack writers like Evseev continued to publish lies about Operation Wedding and the judicial farce that followed. However, for all the articles decrying international Zionism, imperialism, the US military industrial complex, Western propaganda, and so on, you could see that the "evil empire" was feeling the push. Here are a few excerpts from articles of the period:

> We must not ignore the fact that in several Western countries there are individuals who, following the sentences handed down by the Leningrad city court – to criminals, for heinous crimes – have decided to stir up anti-Soviet mayhem. (*Pravda*, with reporting by TASS, January 1, 1971)

Among other blatant lies, V. Borisov and A. Fedoseyev wrote:

> Yet another wave of anti-Soviet agitation and hooliganism, set in
> motion by Zionist circles and the government of Israel, has arisen
> following the Leningrad trial of Dymshits and others. Israeli
> prime minister Golda Meir was quick to make an inflammetory
> statement over Israeli radio, which was immediately picked up
> by the bourgeois propaganda media. The radio station *Svoboda*
> [freedom] has now joined its voice to the multi-part chorus of
> anti-Soviet rhetoric. (*Izvestiya*, January 1, 1971)

A. Aleksandrov's blatantly false article in the weekly magazine *Beyond
the Border*, entitled "Zionism: an anti-Soviet weapon of aggression,"
reads like a satire of Soviet realities. Especially now, in 1989. Forgive me
for quoting heavily from this article, but it gives an excellent idea of the
dishonesty of Soviet propaganda, especially with regard to the Jewish
question.

> International Zionist organizations, which control the capitalist
> media in the United States and Western Europe, are fanning the
> flames of a fierce anti-Soviet campaign. They are supporting a
> gang of criminals who recently attempted to hijack an airplane,
> kill members of the crew, and escape Soviet justice overseas.
> The Zionists are exploiting the fact that some of these criminals
> were Jews to libel the Soviet people and mire the Soviet state in
> scandal.
>   Zionist leaders are literally maddened by the fact that all
> Soviet citizens, no matter what nationality they belong to, live in
> peace and friendship, enjoy equal rights, and are protected by a
> constitution. For this very reason, Zionists are using these crim-
> inals as a pretext for launching a malicious chauvinist campaign.
> (*Za Rubezom* [*Beyond the Border*], January 8–14, 1971, 8)

The campaign against Russia's chauvinist policies, against discrimination, for
free passage to Israel, and for our freedom, had begun in earnest. What we

had been hoping for during the conception of Operation Wedding was now coming into being. Now, we could sigh with relief. We could smile.

The KGB's vision had ended with the trial. They didn't even anticipate how the progressive world would react to their harsh sentences. It's a good thing they didn't choose article No. 83. The harsh sentences played a bigger role than the operation itself in mobilizing the international community, and the Jewish community.

During the propaganda campaign that followed, the KGB got everything mixed up, blaming Zionism, imperialism, the West. They only forgot to blame themselves, their principles of imprisoning, banning, terrorizing, oppressing, lying.

As if it wasn't the KGB who led us to the aerodrome. As if it wasn't the KGB who planned the bloody show trial, in order to frighten all Soviet Jews. As they say, "If you sow a wind, you'll reap a storm." This storm blew open the borders of the empire. Aliyah began.

It was pleasant for us to reap the first fruits of victory on a large scale. But in our personal lives, nothing had changed.

Our group (like other groups) came through the trial without any casualties. The military tribunal sentenced Wolf Zalmanson to ten years. The West had spoken. At our trial, he would have been given a longer sentence as a member of the military.

There were still the trials in Riga and Kishenev to be heard. The second Leningrad trial, at which Hillel Butman was sentenced to ten years' imprisonment, was postponed to May 1971. He and Misha Korenblit were charged under article 64 for treason.

At the later trials, the KGB heeded the lessons of the first trial, and kept their cruelty and bloodthirstiness under control.

As for us, we had to while away the time in prisons and labor camps. As an optimist, I hoped for early release. Hope is a great strength. You must never lose it, but you also need to be prepared for the worst.

Time went by in a fairly uniform way. I could leave my cell only for walks, baths, and haircuts. One day, they led me down an almost forgotten corridor to my investigator's office. I thought I would never have to see Ryabchuk again after the trial, but here he was with his sly smile and familiar voice.

"Good morning, Mark Yulievich! Do sit down. How are you feeling?"

"Fine, thank you. Are you short on work at the moment?"

"We always have enough work. Interesting work. Perhaps you would like to work for us, Mark Yulievich? Colonel Dymshits! How does that sound?"

"For some reason I didn't think there were Jews in the KGB. You must have kicked them all out while the Doctors' Plot was going on."

"No, why do you say that? There are Jews working here. In other departments. No investigators. They were too fond of protecting their own people from deserved punishment. But anyway, Mark Yulievich, what do you want to hang around in a prison camp for, when you could be swimming in the Black Sea as early as May?"

"In the first place, Vitaliy Nikolayevich, I want to see what life in a prison camp is like. I've never been to one. I've always had to observe from the sidelines. In the second place, I've already done my fair share of swimming in the Black Sea. I want to swim in the Mediterranean Sea."

"Well, whatever you say, Mark Yulievich, it was just a suggestion." Ryabchuk became more serious, and continued, "Perhaps you have questions for me?"

"I do. Where are the camps for political prisoners?"

"There aren't special camps for political prisoners in the USSR. You will probably end up in a correctional labor camp in Mordovia," here he lowered his voice to a whisper, "but you could also be sent to a psychiatric hospital. If you end up in Mordovia, it's not that far from Moscow."

"I have two more questions. I asked you to find out about marriage registration. Have you learned anything?"

"Yes, I have spoken to Alevtina Ivanovna. She isn't against it. I imagine it will be possible to register your marriage in the spring."

"Another question. When will they send me to camp?"

"Why the rush? The time will come when you'll remember our institution fondly. In any case, you won't be sent before May. Perhaps there's a request you'd like to make?"

"No."

"Perhaps you'd like to end up in the same camp as one of your comrades?"

"I don't know any of them that well. But since we're the same age, and both served in the army, I suppose I'd like to be with Wolf Zalmanson."

"I won't see you again. I wish you good health!"

"Thank you."

Ryabchuk summoned the guard, and I returned to my cell. I began to ana-
lyze our conversation. Had his offer been real, or was it a trap? If it was real,
then on what grounds?

But then they did have grounds. I had been a Party member, and not for
the sake of my career, like most of them. Albeit for a short time, and without
results, I had worked for them. They hadn't said anything about it, but it was
probably in my file. I believed that socialism was ideal for a just society. I had
never stolen a single ruble from the state, despite living in a society where the
majority take all they can get. I served in the army and worked with a good
conscience. What more could you want?!

I had approached the operation like a maniac or a fundamentalist. At the
end, I was 95 percent certain we would be arrested. But the KGB also knew
we had seen them. What they didn't know is what we were counting on in the
case of arrest. Our decision to fight to the end suited them perfectly. We were
also united by a common principle: "The end justifies the means." True, for
them this principle was the rule, and for us the exception – considering the
lawless world we found ourselves in. But due to my whole track record, I can
understand why they might have wanted to offer me a job.

What about my dissenting positions on ethnic minorities and Israel, not
to mention antisemitism? I reckon the pragmatists at the KGB consider dis-
sent to be an emotion. So when a Soviet person has to choose between fifteen
years in prison and a job with the KGB, he would be mad not to choose
the second option. And then the whole business with the airplane becomes
nothing more than provocation.

But what if the KGB's offer was a trap? What were they planning to do
next?

If I agreed to work for them, they would immediately demand some form of
payment: either condemning the operation, repenting my actions, or appear-
ing at a press conference. Then my actions would look less like provocation
than delusion or ordinary human weakness and fear in the face of a fifteen-year
prison term. After all, there were those who had changed sides when threatened
with much lighter sentences. In return for the press conference, they would
give me some kind of insignificant medal, "for friendship between nations,"
and then it would be easy to push my car off a cliff – a well-worn path.

Those were the ideas that presented themselves to me following my conversation with Ryabchuk. I haven't described them in any particular detail,

but at the time, I spent hours contemplating the KGB's potential actions. I was even afraid that the KGB could cook up a newspaper article saying that I was working for them, or "reward" me for uncovering a "Zionist plot," and I wouldn't even have the opportunity to contradict their lies. If they let me live, that is.

After all these considerations, I came to the following conclusion. I had agreed to "play" with the KGB as a member of a group, in the face of great risk. In the game we were playing, our group had begun to take the victory. However, my personal game with the KGB – surrounding my wife's possible cooperation with them – was still in progress. But that was enough for me. I didn't want to play anymore games with an organization like theirs, or else I ran the risk of cooperating with or provoking them. It was really the role of other government departments, that is, professionals, to deal with them.

After the RSFSR Supreme Soviet handed down its final sentence, I was allowed to correspond with my family, and one package of groceries (ten pounds) per month. I didn't know then that the sausage, cheese, and other groceries I received in those packages came at the expense of a great sacrifice for my family. Their diet came to consist primarily of vegetables. Later, in order to visit me, Alya would give (rather, sell) blood. Her health got so bad that the doctors marveled that she was still alive. My wife and daughters hid their true situation from me, while I received reassuring letters and imagined that half of my confiscated money had been returned to them, since it was my wife's property. That is what ought to have happened by law.

On May 10, 1971, I was taken to the visiting room. Alya was there with a bouquet of flowers, as well as the city clerk, two witnesses, and, of course, a couple of prison guards. In a matter of minutes, they registered our marriage for the second time – on our joint (forty-fourth) birthday. In honor of the occasion, the guards were lenient, and let my wife give me a bar of chocolate. And so, twenty-two years later, we were married again, albeit without a party or champagne. My first wife became my second wife.

Between May 11 and 12, 1971, the so-called "second" Leningrad trial took place. I, along with many others, were called to act as witnesses. The accused were a group of Jews, members of the Leningrad Zionist organization. They were all facing charges for "anti-Soviet" activity. Hillel Butman and Mikhail Korenblit were additionally charged under article 64 for their participation in the initial plans for Operation Wedding. Although the Zionist Organization had refused to participate, there was nothing they could do to change the KGB's plan, considering the KGB's determination to link all the show trials with the plane hijacking.

On May 20, 1971, the collegium of judges handed down the following sentences:

1. Hillel Israilevich Butman: sentenced to ten years of imprisonment without confiscation of personal property, in the absence of such
2. Mikhail Semenovich Korenblit: sentenced to seven years of imprisonment without confiscation of personal property, in the absence of such
3. Lassal Samoylovich Kaminsky: sentenced to five years of imprisonment
4. Lev Naumovich Yagman: sentenced to five years of imprisonment
5. Vladimir Osherovich Mogilever: sentenced to four years of imprisonment
6. Solomon Girshevich Drezner: sentenced to three years of imprisonment
7. Lev Lvovich Korenblit: sentenced to three years of imprisonment
8. Viktor Noyevich Boguslavsky: sentenced to three years of imprisonment
9. Viktor Iosifovich Stilbans: sentenced to one year of imprisonment

The Court of Cassation left the verdicts of the Leningrad city court unchanged.

Once more, there was an increase in the number of telegrams, letters and messages to various government and judicial organs. Here is one of them, addressed to Chairman Podgorny of the Supreme Soviet of the USSR. A copy was sent to USSR Prosecutor General Rudenko.

> We demand you to reverse the sentences imposed on Butman and others. You must pass judgement on those who in violation of the constitution, deprived the accused of the ability to freely study their native language and the history of their nation, as well as preventing their free passage to their historical motherland, the State of Israel.
>
> Signed by Riva Moyzes, daughter of a fallen soldier, and Mark Moyzes, former inmate of Dachau concentration camp.

But the Soviet press launched yet another campaign of lies, abuse, and disinformation.

On May 24, 1971, the Riga trial began. All four accused were accused of anti-Soviet activity. On May 26, the Supreme Soviet of the Latvian SSR heeded the public outcry in response to the previous two trials and issued a surprisingly light sentence. One must also consider Latvia's position within the Russian Empire and its relationship with so-called Soviet power. The prison sentences were as follows:

1. Boris Meyerovich Maftser: sentenced to one year of imprisonment
2. Ruth Isaakovna Aleksandrovich: sentenced to one year of imprisonment
3. Mikhail Zelikovich Shepshelovich: sentenced to one year of imprisonment
4. Arkadiy Abramovich Shpilberg: sentenced to three years of imprisonment

Political news agency special correspondents B. Antonov and V. Katin wrote in *Literaturnaya gazeta*:

> The trials of criminal elements in Leningrad and Riga have led to an unmasking of Zionist circles and their reactionary nature. The accused were made to answer for the crimes of international Zionism. (On July 7, 1971)

The newspapers' false propaganda shone a bright light on the supposedly non-existent "Jewish question," intensified antisemitism among Soviet people, disfigured the public image of Israel, and distorted the essence of Zionism.

On the other hand, the same false propaganda opened the eyes of Soviet Jews to the world they were living in and showed the West what it could never have understood in the 1930s. Perhaps our trials helped the world's progressives understand the true meaning of US president Ronald Reagan's words when he called the Russian Empire an "evil empire."

Another effect of the antisemitic campaigns and anti-Jewish trials, of the baseless slander of Zionism and Israel, has been the creation of a huge antisemitic language base. In the first five years of perestroika and glasnost, all the chauvinist goblins have come out of the woodwork spouting antisemitic slurs from this earlier period of propaganda.

This force for evil in Russian society, supported by various forces within the KGB and the Party, is preventing Russia from normalizing relations with Israel, as well putting Soviet Jews in a position of mortal danger.

Out of all the victims of the two Leningrad trials, I had the good fortune to share a cell for two weeks only with Viktor Boguslavsky. We spent most of our time reading, and talked little. Viktor made architectural sketches of buildings and a plan of several apartments. I tried doing some drawings myself. You could spend years with a cellmate like Viktor. We didn't get in each other's way.

Izvestiya published an article by I. Orlov, entitled, "What are they so worried about in Washington?" The article discussed the US State Department's concern following our trials, while at the same time propagating yet another lie: "Many political prisoners are languishing in US prisons. A wave of political trials is mounting in various parts of the country." The article was written on the principle that only a thief cries, "Stop, thief!"

Where are they now, these hacks from the yellow press? Are they enjoying their retirement? Or showering praises on the American way of life?

On June 21, 1971, at the Kishenev headquarters of the Supreme Court of the Moldavian Soviet Socialist Republic, a group of Jews was tried for "anti-Soviet activity." On June 30, the supreme court collegium announced the following sentences:

1. David Iserovich Chernoglaz: sentenced to five years of imprisonment
2. Anatoliy Moiseevich Goldfeld: sentenced to four years of imprisonment
3. Hillel Zalmanovich Shur: sentenced to two years of imprisonment
4. Aleksandr Zeylikovich Halperin: sentenced to two years and six months of imprisonment
5. Arkadiy Saulovich Voloshin: sentenced to two years of imprisonment
6. Semyon Abramovich Levit: sentenced to two years of imprisonment
7. Lazar Abramovich Trakhtenberg: sentenced to two years of imprisonment

8. Hari Yakovlevich Kizhner: sentenced to two years of imprisonment
9. David Yakovlevich Rabinovich: sentenced to one year of imprisonment

In addition to this, the Moldavian Supreme Court decided to add to the national budget by demanding that each of the accused pay a fine of eighty-six rubles and seventy-two kopecks.

In his letter to the Presidium of the Supreme Soviet of the USSR, Hillel Shur revealed the arbitrariness of the KGB's actions. Shur had a gastrointestinal illness, and when it worsened after his arrest he was denied medicine for ten days. His investigator, Kulikov, told him, "Give us your testimony and you'll feel better straight away."

Intimidation was constantly used during the process of investigation. Kulikov threatened Hillel with having to choose between a maximum prison term in Svalbard or being sent to a psychiatric hospital. They arrested his younger sister as blackmail. When news surfaced of the hijacking of a Soviet passenger plane and the murder of a stewardess (in October 1970), the investigator informed Hillel that this was the doing of Lithuanian Jews, and all of them would now have to pay the price.

Intimidation of this kind had been practiced before the earlier trials as well.

Since I was a witness at the Kishenev trial, and the trip to Kishenev was fairly interesting, I will describe it here in brief.

I was given no advance warning of our trip to Kishenev. When they loaded us into a minibus, converted into a police wagon on the KGB's orders, and began to drive us through Leningrad, I realized – from what I could see through the air vent – that we must be going to the airport. Our minibus drove right up to the plane, where it was met by a black Volga. When the KGB agents came out of the car, the flight crew approached them, and I was able to hear part of their conversation. The KGB agents told them the details of our case in brief. The pilots talked a bit about their "problems": "Because of them (that is, us), we have to have weapons with us all the time. Now we're taken to the shooting range for target practice. We have to clean our pistols after every session. Mandatory baggage control has been introduced, and you have to show your passport before you can buy a plane ticket."

In sum, we had created additional work and inconvenience for them.

They sent a few of us as witnesses to the Kishenev trial. I only knew Hillel Butman, Lev Korenblit, and Solomon Drezner, whom I saw after we had boarded the plane. We were all placed in different compartments and were accompanied by a large group of KGB agents, headed by Colonel Barkov. I had a KGB agent on either side of me and an additional beefy guy sitting off to one side. I was not handcuffed.

The whole flight turned into one big argument accompanied by the hum of the engines. An argument about the same worn-out issues I've already discussed. I will quote an excerpt from the conversation, which went beyond the worn-out issues. The two KGB agents sitting on either side of me changed places with one another, and my new neighbor, dressed in civilian clothes, began the following speech:

"Mark Yulievich, you have cooked up this whole porridge and now you've got to help us eat it. The Jews don't feel at home in the USSR. They are literally packing their bags. You should give a speech before the Jewish community, say that you've made a huge mistake, that you realize that now. Tell them that the Soviet Union is their motherland, and they should stay here. If you do this, you won't have to go to prison camp, and you can be home in a month."

My interlocutor introduced himself, but I don't remember his name.

I replied, "I don't owe you anything. It's not my fault that Soviet Jews are leaving. So I won't be the one telling them to unpack their suitcases. I have been sentenced to fifteen years, and now I must serve my sentence in prison, and not at home, as you are suggesting."

"Just make sure you won't regret your answer later. You know you'll have to serve your sentence in the company of common criminals. In transit prison they can have knives."

"I've already shared a cell with recidivists, so I have some experience."

"So you should understand what kind of people they are. They can cut a man's throat over a packet of tea."

"There are all sorts of people in prison, just as there are all sorts of people everywhere. A year before my arrest, a young man cut his own mother's throat in the Moskovsky district of Leningrad, because she refused to give him money to buy vodka. There are enough amoral people everywhere."

On that note, our conversation in the plane ended. That night, we were taken to the Kishenev prison. They housed us in a room with graffitied walls, and massive doors with padlocks on them. Darkness reigned. It could have been a prison, or a fortress, or even a monastery.

We were searched. Though I had almost nothing in my backpack, the search continued for five minutes.

"It's late already. You won't get to wash. Maybe another time," the elderly guard muttered, and led me to a cell with two bunk beds. The two bottom bunks were already occupied. I undressed, clambered up to the top bunk, and immediately fell asleep. In the morning I had a chance to examine my cellmates, two young disturbers of the peace. They spent whole days using bits of broken glass to scrape the hair off their bodies. Sometimes they would jump from bunk to bunk, evidently hoping to emulate their distant ancestors, to spite evolution. We were given well-used books, but the kids' intellect only sufficed to look at the pictures.

I had no food with me. For five rubles, you could buy fresh vegetables from the prison store, but I didn't have any money either.

At this prison, the monthly ration of food for each prisoner cost eleven rubles. By buying up end bits from the local abattoir, they managed to feed us tolerably enough. Every day, we were given a thick borshch with pieces of pork skin floating in it. These were covered in bristles, and would have been very useful for making paint brushes. We also got good quality bread and a lot of sprats. The abundance of sprats was the prison's direct response to prisoner requests.

Somewhere close by, behind the prison's high wall, music was constantly blaring. It was either a club or a dance hall, and it seduced the youth of Kishenev prison. The prison yard was located right next to the wall. If a construction crane drove up from the other side, it would have been easy to escape in foggy or rainy conditions. Theoretically, I had never considered the possibility of escape. Practically, I knew I would need help from the outside. But the main problem was to figure out what to do next. Usually, those who managed to escape were caught in a month or two, not to mention those who were caught on the first day, in the first bar they had stumbled into.

I knew none of the guys facing judgment at the Kishenev trial. I had been brought here in order to give an account of Operation Wedding. It was the KGB's opinion that the story alone would link this trial to the operation, and make the "anti-Soviet" actions of the Kishenev group appear weightier.

After the trial was over, the KGB made no haste in returning us to Leningrad. We were handed over to the MVD and sent by railroad, in prison carriages. This was my first acquaintance with a Stolypin carriage (special railroad carriages for prisoner transportation).[1] Our first stop was in Odessa. On the edge of the station, we were packed into police vans like sardines into a can. Even in my one-seater "bottle" for highly dangerous criminals, I had to make room for an additional prisoner. Packaged in this way, we were made to sit from early morning until three in the afternoon under the beating sun. They didn't even move the police vans into the shade. This was a calculated form of humiliation. In general, the Odessa prison was famous for its lawlessness, its humiliation of prisoners, its filth, more than any other prison I have had fortune to pass through.

At three in the afternoon, they started the unloading process, which was accompanied by howls, groans, shrieks, and obscenities. We were each put in a box of forty by thirty inches with a small bench opposite the door. In the door, six inches from the floor, were three openings of about an inch in diameter. These were for air circulation. I was initially placed in such a box alone, but after ten to fifteen minutes, two more men were brought in. My immediate neighbor on the bench was a seven-foot giant with the face of a bandit. A sinewy sixty-five-year-old man squatted opposite us, who demonstratively coughed blood into the palm of his hand, before examining it and wiping his hands with a dirty rag. He silently gazed at me while repeating the procedure, as if to warn me about what might be awaiting me at prison camp. Safe to say that his actions failed to arouse any compassion or sympathy in me.

The giant and I got to chatting. He was a gang leader, thirty-seven years old. He had begun thieving at fifteen, never worked anywhere, been tried several times, and done time in multiple prisons and camps.

I won't even attempt to reproduce his lexis: prison slang dotted with swear words, or the other way around – since the ratio was one to one. But I will convey the sense of what he told me in a few lines.

"It's a pity you didn't manage to hijack the plane. You should have hijacked the whole Kremlin ship of fools with that stinking goat Lenka (he was referring to Brezhnev) at the helm, flown it to the Bermuda triangle, and crashed the hell out of it."

---

[1]   These special carriages were introduced in the Russian empire in the middle of the nineteenth century by a minister named Stolypin. Before that, prisoners and convicts were transported thousands of kilometers by foot and by horse.

"Khrushchev was all right, though," I tried to squeeze in a word of praise for Brezhnev's predecessor.

"Are you serious? Have you seen his stupid face? You'd need three days to cover it in shit. He only needed to oink his pig's nose and they gave him the leadership. He's got an ear of corn instead of a dick, that's why he made us plant corn at the North Pole. He's better off on a pig farm screwing Katka Furtseva[2] than running the country."

"But you did time under Stalin too," I managed to interject with difficulty.

"So what? You're comparing a dick with a finger. Stalin was the boss, he was just what we needed. He kept a firm hold on us drifters. I've done time under all the leaders, and it's fine by me. You can only live like a human being in prison. Here in Odessa, everyone knows me. I'll have everything I want: money, vodka, cards, and broads."

How many lost souls populate the Gulag archipelago of our great Russian Empire? In other transit prisons I've met people from eighteen to seventy years of age, from hardy young men to women with children and a blind old man who killed his wife.

In an hour or so, my two cellmates were taken away. The giant wished me all the best, and I likewise. The old man departed in silence.

In the corridor there was noise, cries of abuse, knocking, and howls of men being beaten. It was difficult to distinguish the prisoners' obscene language from that of the guards. Fortunately, I had been given nothing to eat or drink all day, which meant I didn't have to ask for the toilet. This was the main cause of conflict between prisoners and guards.

I wasn't allowed to sit in pleasant solitude for long. After ten minutes, they shoved a couple of kids into my cell. We introduced ourselves. One was eighteen, the other was nineteen. Both were so thin and pale, I could hardly believe they had spent only four months in prison. They had been respectively sentenced to eight and ten years and were being transferred to camp. Before arrest, they had been in their last year of technical college. One Saturday, the pair had gone for a walk in the park. They had scraped together a bit of money to buy a bottle of cheap wine. It wasn't much, but… And suddenly there was a piece of good luck. One of them saw his uncle. The three of

---

[2]   A former dairy worker who became minister of culture under the Khrushchev government.

them went to a cafe, found a table. The uncle ordered a bottle of vodka and a snack. They drank together, and it still seemed insufficient. The kids asked the uncle to order another bottle, but the latter stubbornly refused. He even tried explaining to the kids that they shouldn't drink anymore. The kids took the uncle outside to settle matters. They beat him up so badly that he was taken to hospital on the brink of death with several broken ribs. That's filial gratitude for you.

The kids had a bread roll and butter with them. They offered me a piece, before each lighting a cigarette. Tobacco smoke filled the box. But what could you do… there wasn't a separate smoking room, or a window. As long as they didn't pass out. Not only was there no calling for help, there wasn't even water. In the end, they were fine.

Towards evening, we were taken to the ablutions block. After washing, I was taken to a cell occupied by four other inmates, ages twenty to fifty, about ten years apart. There were two bunks in the cell, with nothing to cover the uneven planks. Between the door and the bunks was a table, behind which all the inhabitants of the cell were sitting.

As things tend to go in such "cultural" institutions, we introduced ourselves. They already knew something about me from the papers, but as they didn't believe the papers, they asked me to tell the true story of the airplane epic. My story totally bewitched them. It was clear that they would have agreed to participate in a similar operation.

I had only just finished my story when the meal flap swung open, and five bowls of watery wheat porridge landed on our table. At this point, all four of them untied their bundles and white bread, butter, sugar, cucumbers, and tomatoes also appeared. Each of them offered me some of what he had, and this wasn't in payment for my story, so much as a sign of respect for my defiance of the regime.

I had no provisions myself. Since my army days, I have had a habit of keeping my hands free. Such a habit was useful in transit prison, as it meant I had nothing that could be stolen and could sleep soundly.

Lights out was called. There were five of us and only four beds. I called one of the guards. In a few minutes he came back with a few planks, and threw them on the floor between the bunks. All four cellmates started insisting that I sleep on one of their bunks. I tried to refuse, but they proudly insisted that I take the bunk of the youngest among them.

The next day, towards evening, I was taken back to transit prison. All of us prisoners were searched and handed over to our escort. The soldiers in our escort threw themselves upon my nearly empty backpack like jackals. It was the first time I had encountered such marauders. They pocketed everything, from pens, to papers, to socks. I called the officer in command, and asked him, "Is this what you teach them in theory classes?" The first lieutenant made the thieves return everything they had taken.

Though I considered my Soviet citizenship a matter of form, I was ashamed for these soldiers. I remembered my army years as the best years of my life in the USSR.

Butman and I were taken to the train in a single police wagon. The next transit prison was Kaluga. I had never been to Kaluga before, so I had no concept of what the town was like, but the prison… After Odessa, the Kaluga prison seemed like a hotel for prisoners. Cleanliness, quiet, order. Alone in my cell, I enjoyed the silence.

Once, during my years as an officer, I had to spend a night in a hotel at Buy railway station. The most notable feature of this hotel was its abundance of bed bugs, dirty sheets, and kerosene lamps. My cell in Kaluga was better in all respects than the ten-man dormitories at the hotel in Buy.

There used to be all sorts of "model" institutions in the USSR: factories, collective farms, schools, and so on. I have a feeling that the Kaluga prison was a model prison, the kind you could show to foreigners. It's a pity they didn't let me stay there for at least a month. We were gathered up quickly the following morning, and our journey continued.

Earlier, I described how I had celebrated New Year's Eve, 1945, between two train carriages on the way to Leningrad. Back then, in the town of Kalinin, I had been able to use the few minutes of stopping time to buy a ticket and get a seat in the warmth of the coupé.

Now, as a prisoner, I was traveling to Kalinin – that is, to the Kalinin prison – in more comfortable circumstances. It's true that they squeezed twenty prisoners into one coupé carriage, but that was better than standing in the freezing cold in nothing but a worn-out greatcoat. As they say in Russia, "it may be cramped, but there's no ill will."

I met all my fellow passengers, among whom was a group of Georgians, and among them was a Georgian Jew. Mikhalashvili had been sentenced to eight years for theft, had now served half of his sentence, and was being transferred to another camp. They had obviously decided he'd had enough Georgian sunshine and were moving him closer to the polar bears. Hillel and I started trying to convince him to throw everything else aside and emigrate to Israel at the end of his sentence. We did this with no particular delusions. As they say, "A hunchback stands up straight in his coffin." But we felt sorry for his children. His eldest son had just finished university, the younger son had just been admitted, and his daughter had finished ninth grade. Here is an excerpt of our conversation about emigration to Israel:

"No, I can't. My younger son still has to finish university. What will he do there without higher education?"

"In the time it will take you to serve out the rest of your sentence, he'll finish university."

"I guess you're right. I should go! But my daughter also has to go to university."

"Well, you might get arrested again. And then while you're doing your time, she'll have a chance to go to university too."

"Yes, you're right. I really should go! But what will I do there without money? I would have to earn some first, and then go."

"But while you're trying to earn money, you'll get arrested again."

"Yes, that's true. I should go as soon as possible. But I need to think about it first."

We parted ways in Kalinin. Perhaps his children are still trying to solve the problem of emigration, worrying about their own children's education. How many Jews perished in Hitler's Germany and Khomeini's Iran from similar indecision and shortsightedness? How many more may perish in the Russian Empire, or at best, get stuck there forever?

And so, we arrived at Kalinin prison. I was given a strange cell of the corridor type, which was divided into two floors by an artificial ceiling, according to Khrushchev-era standards. It contained two beds. On one of them sat an elderly man by the name of Shevchenko. He was tall and thick set with an intelligent face. He spoke a pure Russian without a single swear word – a rarity at that time, especially in prison. When he was younger, he had spent twenty years in prison for so-called Ukrainian nationalism. In 1956, he was rehabilitated, and had worked in Leningrad as head engineer at a vitamin factory.

However, the KGB refused to leave him alone. For some reason, the organs were irritated by the portrait of Taras Grigorievich Shevchenko, which hung in the engineer's apartment. The KGB explained to him that such a large portrait had no place hanging in a private apartment. Shevchenko made an impolite answer. But because they couldn't arrest him for the portrait, they had to cook up a criminal case, connected to the opening of a new factory. He had to listen to his investigator repeat the familiar words: "Bring me a man, and I'll find a crime." And this wasn't in the age of Beriya, but in 1971. They sentenced him to three years, and when I met him he had been in prison for six months from the time of his arrest.

His adult children were in Moscow petitioning for his release, and he was hoping to be released in the near future. Shevchenko assured me that twenty years of prison camp had destroyed his health to the point where he was unlikely even to survive three years. Back then he had been on the brink of death; livor mortis had even begun to break out on his skin. But by some miracle he made it through and survived. I spent two days with him before we bid each other farewell. He remained in Kalinin, in anticipation of release, while I was transferred onward to Leningrad.

A notable feature of my departure from Kalinin was that, after we had been let out of the police wagons and were marching to the train, accompanied by an escort with dogs, two young women walked at the front of our group. One was carrying an infant. The other was pregnant.

It was the time of summer holidays, and the platform was crowded with people, who cast glances at our group as it stood by the prison carriage – not only of pity, but of interest. They were obviously used to such scenes. Or perhaps they were thinking: "There but for the grace of God…" Or even: "We've had to go through that. Let others have their turn." After all, many Russians are subjected to similar trials. There is even an old saying: "A man can't get through life without doing time." Or: "The sooner you're in, the sooner you're out."

We arrived in Leningrad that night. The police vans delivered us to Kresty prison. After the usual admission procedures had finished, they began distributing us amongst available cells. My guard opened a door and pushed me forward. The door slammed behind me. I stood there in half darkness, frozen to the spot, and began to examine my new place of residence. Almost immediately over the threshold a huge puddle of water began, which seemed to cover the whole floor. It was just as well that I hadn't moved, as another step would have had me up to my ankles in water. The cell was large, about a hundred square feet. A basement. The small window with thick bars instead of glass was divided in half by the level of the earth. As I looked at the window, a large rat ran along the windowsill and sprang outside. There were bunks under the window, the whole width of the room, on which five or six people were sleeping. One of them in a padded jacket sat up, looked at me, and lay back down on his bunk. I had a fantasy – perhaps a justified one – that he was one of our fellow passengers from June 8, when we had flown to Priozersk on reconnaissance. At least, I was certain that he was a KGB agent. Two benches, one long and one short, stood along the side wall. Having sized up the situation, I made a bridge of these two benches and climbed up onto one of the bunks. After frightening yet another rat, I put my emaciated backpack under my head and immediately fell asleep.

The next morning, I was awoken by noise. Some inmates were being taken away for transit, others were being admitted. The meal flaps banged open, the guards shouted. I sat up on my bunk and looked down at the floor. It was still dotted with small puddles, but you could at least walk around without getting your feet wet. Where did the water go? There was no drainage pipe visible. Maybe the rats came here to drink, or the else the water evaporated out the open window.

A key rattled in the enormous lock. The door opened and two young men came in. One of them, Asian-looking, struck up a conversation with me. He said he was from Kyrgyzstan and was in for disorderly conduct and knife crime. After we had become acquainted with each other's cases, our conversation took the following turn:

"Why are the Zhyds (Yids) leaving the Soviet Union? Was it really so bad for them here?"

"First of all, not Zhyds, but Jews. I don't call Kyrgyz people 'flatbreads' or 'donkeys.' Terminology like that has been made up by people who want to spread hate among the people of the world. Who want to 'divide and conquer' like the colonizers of the past."

"Ok," the kid agreed, "but Jews live better than many other people."

"You have your own republic, you studied at your own school in your own native language, you have your own theater, and so on. Jews don't have any of that here. Their material position is better because they don't drink away their wages."

"And they steal more," the kid interjected.

"I don't know if they steal more or less," I answered. "But in any case, there are many people who grab anything that isn't bolted in place and don't think about the consequences. Jews don't do that. Jews don't receive any extra salary for being a minority nation, and don't even get discounts like local minorities in the various republics. In brief, I would say that you have a motherland, and the Jews also want to have their own motherland. Their own home. That's why they're leaving for Israel. We also wanted to leave for Israel."

Our conversation was interrupted by the guard, who barked right in my ear, "Anyone who hasn't had their head shaved should get ready to be shaved!" He shouted this, pointing at my full head of hair.

"This is what I look like in my mug shots, with hair. You should ask someone first, or the KGB will shave off more than your hair," I replied, and noticed that I had begun to talk back to the authorities in their own language.

The guard went off to ask someone. When he came back in a few days, he said that I didn't have to shave, and that I should get ready for transit.

Soon, another police van delivered us to the Leningrad KGB prison.

Once more, the perfect order of the "Big House": quiet, cleanliness, books, letters from my wife and daughters. A prison idyll. "Long live Soviet prison!"

It so happened that before being sent to camp, I was made to bear witness at yet another trial. On August 10, 1971, Boris Azernikov was arrested in Leningrad. He was a member of the Leningrad Zionist Organization, and would have participated in the first version of our operation, but after the committee disassociated themselves with us, he also decided not to participate. Boris was called to bear witness at the Leningrad trials, while he was still at liberty. In late June 1971, he had submitted documents to the Migration Service in order to obtain an exit visa to Israel. This was to decide his fate.

Azernikov's trial took place on October 6–7, 1971, at Leningrad municipal court. The court handed down a judgment, according to which Boris was sentenced to three years and six months. After this trial, there was no further reason to keep me in Leningrad.

9 The Camps

1972–1979

On the evening of October 14, Hillel Butman, Misha Korenblit, and I were taken into transit. The weather was foul. It was as if we were inside a lead-colored box, dotted only occasionally with white snowflakes. At that time, the weather had not yet begun to dictate my mood and sense of well-being. We were not being made to walk tens of miles in a column of other prisoners with chains on our legs. Our time in prison coincided with an age of technological progress. We were driven around in police wagons and conveyed in heated train carriages to our final destinations.

I had first met Butman about two years ago. The two of us began to plan the operation; then Misha Korenblit joined us. Now all three of us, sharing a three-man compartment in the same prison carriage, were being sent to some far-off camp. The cogs we had set turning continued to turn, and more and more people, organizations, statesmen, and politicians were being drawn into the motion. You could say that the flywheel was spinning. My mood was positive, and I was optimistic about the future.

Our Stolypin carriage was packed to the gills, but the three of us had more space than we knew what to do with. It was almost like a regular train compartment. In fact, the atmosphere in the carriage as a whole was cheerful. In one of the compartments, among fifteen other prisoners, was a quartet from the Baltic states. They had started a massive fight in a café with some officers, for which they were being sent into exile. In the compartment for repeat offenders – called stripeys, because of their striped uniforms – rode a gypsy with a guitar who gave wonderful renditions of old romances. Two compartments were full of women prisoners. A choir of these "gals" sang the hit list of dirty prison songs.

This semi-professional musical group on wheels gave such a concert that all the guards gathered in the corridor of the carriage. Their officer in command handed the guitar back and forth between the compartments, regulating the order of performance.

We made it to Yaroslavl with our spirits high. After a short stay in Yaroslavl transit prison, we were quickly transferred to the town of Gorky. Gorky prison was more like a factory for prisoner sorting. We spent three days walking in the prison yard under the watchful eye of surveillance cameras before setting off again for Ruzayevka. Hillel, Misha, and I were once more given a three-man compartment. The further east we traveled, the shabbier we prisoners began to look, as did the towns and villages we saw floating by through the window in the corridor.

Our escort soldiers managed to turn everything to their own material advantage. They would sell tea or vodka to the prisoners at twice or three times the usual price, delivered letters, traded tea for personal belongings, and even organized a local sex trade. A young lady from one of the women's compartments would be taken to the toilet. There, a suspension system would be made out of belts, just like a parachute harness. Then, male convicts would be let in one by one, as if they were going to relieve themselves. The cost of one session was ten rubles, half to the girl, half to the soldiers. Almost all the soldiers in our escort (MVD troops) could have easily been convicted of some crime or other. From fraternizing with criminals, they became criminals themselves.

Ruzayevka is a hub station in Mordovia – an autonomous republic, which was home to the most developed penal camp system in the European part of the USSR. After going through sorting at Ruzayevka transit prison, we three were taken to a large cell, which was so spacious that we decided to have a wrestling competition. After that, a guest came to call on us, wearing the MVD uniform and an academician's badge. He spoke with us for two hours, asking numerous questions about Operation Wedding. He was so anxious to know everything that he began to praise my open gaze and criticize Misha for hiding his eyes behind dark glasses. To this day, I am certain that he wasn't a transit orderly at all, but a KGB agent – despite his MVD uniform and armband.

The next day, we were sent onward to Potma railway station. In the next compartment, a group of so-called "Chinese spies" were applying themselves to the study of Russian swear words.

From Potma we were returned to Ruzayevka. From the station, the three of us were led over the railway tracks on a wide bridge toward the city. My backpack was nearly empty. Misha had a full backpack and a suitcase. With the same amount of luggage, my family and I had moved house during my time in the army. I helped Hillel carry his large suitcase, and after one hundred yards, I began to feel a sharp pain in my chest. I swore in Hillel's direction, swung the suitcase on to my shoulder, and kept going. Butman had decided to take his winter clothes and shoes with him, considering what we all knew about life in the camps. But the suitcase also contained something truly valuable: a smoked sausage. Later, Hillel divided it into three equal parts. That sausage would constitute an essential supplement to the meager rations we would receive in Saransk.

We were taken to the regional police headquarters. We waited. Our escort started fussing around, going in and out of various rooms, leaving us alone for several minutes at a time. It occurred to me that they might be provoking us to escape. But where were we supposed to go, in an unfamiliar city with no money, without friends? If they caught us, they would probably shoot us for "resisting authority." Or perhaps one of the other people sitting in the room was watching us. After some time, we were placed in a cold, beaten-up police wagon. Frosty air blew in on us from the many holes and cracks. Wherever they were taking us, it certainly wasn't to any of the camps. My head spun with thoughts of a possible prisoner exchange or extradition. Maybe we were about to be sent to Israel?

We drove into the center of town and stopped outside a two-story building. We were led along the first floor corridor, which was lined with prison cells on one side. We climbed to the second floor of this strange prison in an unknown city. They opened a door with a peep hole and meal hatch, but the room itself looked more like a normal room. It was spotlessly clean, and the newly painted floor shone with a coat of varnish. Three cots were made up with clean linen.

As a result of the strange events of the last few days, I now potentially owed Hillel and Misha twenty-six bottles of cognac. We had made a bet on the likelihood of being released before January 1974. I had placed my bet on 1973, if only because I was convinced that it would be better for our cause if the KGB held us for longer and the fight for our release continued. "The worse for us, the better for everyone."

The director of this strange prison came in to our cell. A strange captain of advanced age, who had most likely served under Budenny, pronounced the long-forgotten, "Greetings, comrades!"

We returned his salutation with surprise.

"You are currently imprisoned in the town of Saransk. On the first floor of this building is the MVD prison. Here, on the second floor, is the KGB investigative isolation cell. I expect that you will enjoy your time here. We have a library, should you want to borrow books. Are there any questions?"

"Not yet."

"Then I will bid you farewell, comrades! If any questions arise, I will be happy to assist you."

During the two months we spent in Saransk prison, we would see this strange "comrade" only one more time. KGB agents were the real bosses.

The food at Saransk prison was disgusting in quantity as well as in quality. Meals were prepared by inmates, who stole most of the ingredients for personal consumption. Only when the reserves had been eaten and we prisoners began to starve, did the Saransk KGB begin paying attention to our daily ration. They would talk to us, at the beginning. Once they had become convinced of our immunity to brainwashing, they stopped talking to us. Among ourselves, we started calling them "the kindergarten teachers" (ironically). Once they brought some in-house Jews to talk to us, to convince us how good things were for them in "our Soviet land," under the warm sun of "internationalism." But we had rejected such lies long ago, and the brainwashing bounced right off us like a pea bounces off a wall. We would have had more luck convincing them of the opposite.

After over a month in Saransk, we could still detect no signs that we would be transferred onward, to camp.

"Hey you, KGB bureaucrats!" I felt like shouting. "The faster you trade in your Jewish goods, the better it will be for everyone! First of all, you've got to swap Sylva Zalmanson for Angela Davis, and then you can swap the rest of us. Have you really forgotten how peasants used to be exchanged? Let's pray to God we have crop failure, then you'll be trading Jews for wheat. The average Jew weighs 175 pounds, so let's have 175 pounds of grain from Uncle Sam. Hey, KGB, should I really be telling you this?"

This was how I imagined the near future, as I lay on my cot suffering acute pain from the salt deposits in my hip joints. Hillel gave me a massage, and the pain became more bearable. Later, however, I must have eroded the crystal deposits in my hips from intensive walking, and caused them to concentrate in my feet. That is, although the pain in my hips died down, it intensified in my feet.

I had yet another activity at that time. I wrote the whole text of our sentences on a piece of white fabric. Then, I sewed this large piece of fabric, covered in minute writing, into the lining of my coat. However, my labor was not destined to survive. Later, at the camp, there was a fire in the storage building which held our personal belongings, although the storage building was probably plundered before the fire. Perhaps one of the "authorities" ended up wearing my coat, without having a single suspicion of its secret compartment.

A KGB colonel arrived from Moscow. At least, he introduced himself as a colonel. If someone outside of prison had asked me who he was, I would have said he was a professor or a diplomat. I don't remember his name and patronymic, but it hardly matters. At that level, they never give you their real name.

I once witnessed – at a family party, in the presence of visitors from Eastern Europe – how a man introduced himself under a false name, the name of a celebrity, in order to have his photo taken with the foreigners. But I digress.

So, this colonel spoke to each of us individually for an hour and a half. At the beginning of our conversation, he inquired about my health. Then, he calmly listened to my thoughts about the Jewish question and the USSR's Middle East policy. He listened calmly without arguing. Then, the colonel asked me a question:.

"In your opinion, how many Jews live in the USSR?"

"According to the 1970 census, 2,150,000," I answered.

"Yes, that is true," he allowed. "But that is just the census. We have counted 3,000,000 Jews. Our information is more precise. Many Jews are registered under other nationalities. There are mixed marriages. What do you think, Mark Yulievich, how many of them have left the USSR?"

"I haven't conducted a survey of Soviet Jews, but I think that if they were free to leave, 50 percent would do so. Let them go, as Poland did in 1968."

"We can't do that, let alone ask them to leave. Jews have more significance here than in Poland."

Then, the colonel held out a piece of paper. "Read this carefully and sign it," he said.

"While I'm a prisoner, I won't sign any pieces of paper," I answered the colonel, without even looking at the text. On this note, our meeting ended.

Judging by what Misha Korenblit later told me, the paper contained an offer to cooperate with the KGB, with the promise of a reward – for Misha, a doctor, reward was in the form of an important position in the Israeli Health Ministry. Misha signed the paper, but made no secret of it around the camp. I imagine they might have offered me something connected to aviation.

Toward the end of January, Hillel received a visit from his wife, Eva. Hillel was allowed to meet with Eva for two hours and to receive from her a suitcase of provisions. Misha also had a visit from his friend Polina and a suitcase of provisions. The night before, I had gotten angry with Hillel and Misha for their loud nighttime conversation and laughter, so was unable to take part in their feast. However, it was encouraging to hear Eva and Polina's news of the mass aliyah. Operation Wedding, the show trials, and the reactions of the world's progressives were bearing fruit.

A few days later, we were taken into transit.

A narrow-gauge railway ran from the transit prison in Potma deep into the country. Camps of various security levels dotted the railway line: minimum, maximum, supermaximum camps for foreigners, camps for women, camps for adolescents.

Our recidivist fellow group members Murzhenko and Fyodorov ended up in a supermaximum security camp. Butman, Korenblit, and I were assigned to a maximum security facility. Officially, there were no camps especially for political prisoners in the USSR, just as there was officially no prostitution or drug addiction in the USSR. However, there were several camps for those who had been convicted of political offenses.

The mini Stolypin carriages distributed us prisoners throughout the system of Mordovian camps known as Dubravlag. Dubravlag was an essential part of the Gulag archipelago.

We were led out of the train carriage. Three-foot-high snowdrifts surrounded us. The temperature outside was -20 or -30°C. Pretty cold, considering I was wearing my autumn coat and ordinary shoes. Only my Siberian conditioning helped me keep a brave face. We were loaded into a police van together with Lev Yagman, who was returning to his own camp. He had arrived in Mordovia a year earlier than the rest of us, and had managed to get a sense of the camp system. We drove along a forest road, if you can call potholes and furrows a road. We were jolted to and fro so violently that if we hadn't grabbed hold of the benches in time, our heads would have gone through the roof.

Hillel and Lev were the first to arrive at their destinations, Camp No. 19. Misha and I had to gyrate for another ten miles before arriving at our camps. Misha was assigned to the big zone of Camp No. 17, and I to the small zone of the same camp. The two camps were divided by about three hundred yards. My camp was officially known as ZhKh-389/17. Its neighboring settlement was the town of Ozerny.

As I walked from the police van to the guard post, one of the prisoners caught sight of me from the front porch of the manufacturing building. A second later, a little group of people were already waving to me, all of them dressed in gray hats, gray padded jackets, and gray trousers. It was difficult to make out their faces, especially as I had yet to learn which of my associates had also been assigned to this camp. At the guard' post, I had my head shaved, and was given a prison uniform to wear. After feeding me a hot meal, the guards led me to a residential barracks intended to house eighty people. All the prisoners were out at work. The orderly indicated which cots were available, and because of my experience of dormitory life, I chose the third cot from the stove.

When the other prisoners returned from the work zone, a group of Jews came up to me, and we got to know each other. Mendelevich was the only one I knew. Several Jews from the Kishenev trial were also being held at this camp: Shur, Trakhtenberg. Shimon Grilius had been sentenced in 1969 for so-called anti-Soviet activity. Even before their arrest, the group had made connection with the Moscow Zionist movement.

Right there in the barracks, at the communal table, which the others had made free for us, we celebrated our meeting, and for the first time in my life I made Shabbat. Yosef lit a candle and read a prayer. We exchanged information, and I discovered the reason we had been held in Saransk for an extra month. It turned out that our fellows from the Leningrad and Kishenev trials, who were already incarcerated in the camps, had sent an open letter to world leaders and the international Jewish community. On December 24, 1971, the first anniversary of the sentencing in the first Leningrad trial, they had announced a hunger strike, demanding free passage to Israel for all Soviet Jews. They had also asked for Israeli citizenship, for their Soviet citizenship to be repealed, for Sylva Zalmanson to be released, and for the other cases to be reexamined. They had asked to be transferred to a camp for foreign prisoners and for representatives of the International Red Cross to be present.

The small zone of Camp No. 17 was Mordovia's smallest camp, both in territory and in number of inmates. The whole camp was heated by wood stoves. I was immediately assigned to prepare firewood for both the residential and work zones.

I began work the next day. My partner was a Latvian who had been convicted for cooperating with the Nazis during the war. He was sentenced to something from fifteen to twenty-five years. A sinewy man from peasant stock, he had kept his physical strength even at an advanced age. We had to prepare a minimum of 20.73 cubic feet of firewood per shift. The logs were thick in diameter, and anywhere from thirteen to sixteen feet in length. What's more, we worked with a hand saw, an axe. Just over the prison fence, the guards were buzzing away with a petrol-fueled chainsaw. Either they had stolen the camp's chainsaw, or a decision had been made that the labor of two prisoners was cheaper than mechanization. I could immediately tell the Latvian was cooperating with the administration. He had evidently been told to wear me out during the first few days, while I was still weak from prison. And in those first few days, he did an excellent job. After prison, where I scarcely ever went outside, and did no physical labor, I was suddenly spending whole days working in the frosty air. It was enough to knock me off my feet. After work, I returned to the barracks exhausted, lay on my cot, and fell asleep instantly. But this situation didn't last for long. In a few weeks, I started feeling more myself, caught my breath, and started taking my revenge on the Latvian. "Come on, come on and work. You can smoke later. First you need to meet quota," I taunted him.

Once the KGB realized that I had regained my strength, and preparing firewood had become less a torment than half work, half sport, they immediately transferred me to the sewing workshop, where I sewed tarpaulin mittens.

Soon, I received the first letter from my family. They were preparing to come and visit me. I awaited their arrival with impatience. Then a new problem arose. It was one thing to correspond by mail, and another thing to actually meet my wife in person, considering my continued suspicions of betrayal. We might have to spend one to three whole days in a room together. According to prison rules, the administration – and in the case of political camps, the KGB – decided whether or not to grant visiting rights, and if so, for how many days. We were allowed one personal meeting and two general meetings per year, the latter of which could last from one to three hours.

Initially, an absurd idea occurred to me that I would strangle my wife in revenge for her betrayal. But after suppressing my emotions, I began to consider the matter rationally, asking myself the following questions:

Are you 100 percent certain that she betrayed you?

No!

Are you really prepared to murder the mother of your children?

No!

Even if she did cooperate with the KGB and did betray you and your comrades in order to save us from harsher punishment? Even if you knew that for a fact? Would you still be prepared to kill her?

No!

If you kill your wife, it's as certain as 2x2=4 that they'd shoot you. What would happen to your daughters? Do you want to make orphans of them?

No!

If you've answered 'No!' to all these questions, then you must get rid of these murderous thoughts!1 Will you, Mark, be able to play your conjugal role, casting suspicions aside?

I have to.

Once again, that "have to." Some people use the services of prostitutes. You have the opportunity to go to bed with your wife of twenty years. You haven't been in bed with a woman for a long time. You haven't even thought about it. Your head was occupied by other problems. Now, your physical instincts will help you overcome your feeling of alienation. Also, remember not to talk about the past, and not ask any questions.

In a few days' time, I was summoned and told that I would be allowed a two day visit. During the first day, I would be taken out to work, but the second day fell on a weekend.

---

1   I could easily have omitted all mention of these murderous thoughts, but I am still unable to forget them. They torment me to this day. As a product of the Soviet system, I was unable to escape the inborn tendency to see enemies everywhere. In our present age of perestroika and glasnost, the Soviet tendency to blame someone else for every problem has become particularly obvious. Soviet people are always ready to grab each other by the throat.

No sooner had we been taken to the visit building, after an exhaustive search, than Alya, in the presence of the guards, started talking about petitioning for clemency. This came as a surprise, and made me anxious. I lost no time in replying that there could be no discussion of such a petition, since I had only just begun my sentence. People usually started petitioning after serving half their sentences.

We were given two rooms to ourselves. Alya and I talked late into the night. For the first time, I suggested that she and my daughters apply for Israeli visas. Alya replied that she wouldn't leave me alone in Russia.

"Then let the girls go. They will have a better life, and I will be able to serve my sentence without worrying about them."

Alya said that they would discuss that question all together, and send me their decision in a letter.

Two days flew by almost without my noticing. Now the next personal visit wouldn't be for another year. That is, I would have to wait until early 1973, if I didn't get in trouble for some minor infraction, or get on the KGB's nerves.

Until then, it was back to the usual grind. In March and April 1972, I had three memorable dreams. I wouldn't have paid them any attention, had I not heard that Shimon Grilius interpreted dreams. And although I had never believed in psychics or fortune telling, I was curious what Shimon would say.

What did he say? Shimon's interpretations of all three dreams were soon justified by real events. I will give a brief account of their contents. In the first dream, I stood on the roof of a camp building and gazed into the distance. There wasn't a cloud in the sky. And suddenly, black clouds appeared, lightning flashed, and flames engulfed the camp and its surroundings. It was a vivid dream. Shimon explained that there would be a great fire and a crop failure that year. And so it was. A peat bog and its surrounds caught fire in Moscow province. There were crop failures.

In the second dream, I found myself sitting at a round table in a luxurious room with antique furniture, and conversing with Chairman Podgorny of the Presidium of Supreme Soviet of the USSR, persuading him to let us all emigrate to Israel. He initially refused, but then agreed on the condition that I send him some stock cubes from Israel. Shimon repeated his prediction about the crop failures.

In the third dream, I observed an airport from the cockpit of an An-2. Arab MiG planes were parked below me. Suddenly, a whole host of Israeli tanks appeared in clouds of dust and began crushing the planes. I could even hear the scrape of metal. Shimon said that Israel would soon launch a military operation against an Arab country. In a few days, that is exactly what happened.

I wasn't fated to sew mittens in the small zone for long. In May I was taken into transit, if you can call a ten-minute walk "transit." I put on my backpack and, accompanied by a guard and two soldiers with machine guns, arrived at the big zone of Camp No. 17. At this zone, I met Aaron Shpilberg, Arkadiy Voloshin, and Lassal Kaminsky. I was already acquainted with Lev and Misha Korenblit.

This camp boasted a much larger area than its smaller counterpart. It had a large mess hall, a solitary confinement cell for both zones of Camp No. 17, and a bathhouse. The big zone held over three hundred prisoners, who were accommodated in high-density barracks, with less than seven square feet per capita. You could only squeeze between the bunks on one side.

In the big zone, we became unwilling blood donors to a mass of mosquitoes. And despite taking rolled up newspapers to bed with us – and swatting the mosquitoes to the point where the white walls became spotted with red and black – we always woke up with bites all over our bodies.

Like most of my fellow prisoners, I spent my work hours sewing mittens. A smaller group of prisoners worked on the construction of a large workshop. Later, the camp was turned into a women's camp, at which point the last male inmates went on strike against the humiliations to which they had been subjected by the administration, ransacked the new workshop, and threw their sewing machines into the toilet hole.

At this camp, I began to study Hebrew again with my very first teacher, Lev Korenblit.

On one of my first days, I was called up by my unit commander, a young lieutenant, and offered the chance of doing community work: publishing the camp's news bulletin or joining an amateur theater group. In local slang, this was called making a bitch of oneself; I didn't even take the commander's offer seriously. Instead, I made a perfectly serious offer of my own: to organize a shooting club, and even serve as its president. After all, I had already received training in rifle and pistol shooting for sport. Due to my serious tone, the unit commander also answered seriously, and with a measure of regret, that unfortunately shooting clubs were not allowed in the camp system. That was the end of our communication.

Of the several hundreds of books in the camp library, were allowed to choose a few for personal use. The *Party Program* from the Twenty-Second Party Congress of 1961 was one of the most popular titles. It was an example of dishonesty on an imperial scale: all their promises to exceed American manufacturing norms per capita, to satisfy the Soviet population with high living standards before 1970, to create a Communist material-technical base, which would ensure material and cultural benefits for the whole population – in short, to build an ideal Communist society before 1980. All these lies had been underlined with a red pencil. Once the prison directors noticed how popular this book had become among prisoners, they removed it from circulation. It was too incriminating of the country's leaders, and their lies.

In June, rumors began to spread of an approaching transfer. Rumors, assumptions, and suspicions were a common occurrence at that time, not only in prisons, but throughout the country.

In the first half of July 1972, I was called to meet with a KGB agent. Our conversation was brief. "We would like to release you.," he told me. "But you must understand that if you refuse to make an appearance before the Soviet Jews, we will be unable to do so, with all the good will in the world."

"I understand."

"If you refuse to speak, your actions will be interpreted as provocation, and you will have to stay in prison."

"I have thirteen years left in my sentence, and I am prepared to serve them to the end."

"You can go now. Good-bye!"

"Good-bye!"

So now I had something to think about. What was this, anyway? Payment for my wife's services? Or payment for the operation – in which case, were they playing cat and mouse with me? Were they preparing to eat me, now that they'd caught me?

But they couldn't be rewarding me for the operation. It had already become clear that our aims and the KGB's were widely different. A mass exodus of Jews from the USSR had already begun, and the KGB and their cronies were already being made to look like cruel tyrants in the eyes of the world. So what does that mean?!

Either my suspicions of my wife were justified, or they were playing with me.

But in fact, I still don't understand what the KGB's plan was, and may never understand.

In a few days, all us prisoners were lined up for inspection. The camp director read the names of all the prisoners who would be transferred to other camps. My name was called. The names of these camps were kept secret, but the director explained that we would be traveling for several days. Then, he informed us what we would be allowed to carry with us, and what we had to pack and send as luggage. Our luggage would be sent in special train carriages.

Only prisoners with shorter sentences remained in Mordovia. The rest of us prepared for departure. We were given dry rations for the journey: bread and canned meat. After being searched carefully, we handed over our luggage, and on July 13, most prisoners were driven to the railway on trucks. Others, including myself, were loaded into police vans.

Our transport echelon consisted of Stolypin carriages, one ordinary carriage for the officers and guards, and three boxcars for luggage.

The weather was hot. The Stolypin carriages were packed full with prisoners. For both of these reasons, the carriages were stuffy, and we were hardly able to breathe. Everyone was dripping with sweat. The train stood at the station for a long time. There were murmurings, shouts, groans. Some lost consciousness; one man died. The prisoners began to rock the carriages with anger, at which point the guards opened the windows in the corridors and poured water on the roofs of the carriages. It became easier to breathe only after the train started moving.

Each compartment accommodated eight prisoners on each of the lower bunks. Five prisoners lay on the middle folding bunks, while only two lay on the upper bunks. These upper bunks were most comfortable of all since there was enough room to spread out, but because of the steamy temperatures near the ceiling, no one was too anxious to occupy them. I could lie there all day without moving. My experience of flying at twenty-three thousand feet without oxygen certainly came in handy.

The further east we traveled, the cooler it became, but the days were still hot. In four days we arrived at our final destination in the town of Chusovoy, a local administrative center. The Ural region greeted us with a beautiful sunrise and a pleasant morning chill. The low mountains of the Ural range were just visible. A row of trucks stood near the station, waiting to receive their load. They had been constructed such that two soldiers with machine guns could stand between the cab and the rear compartment. This compartment, with raised sides, was where we prisoners were made to sit. Our escort was made up of guards, soldiers with machine guns, more soldiers with dogs, and a large group of officers. At the front and rear of our convoy rode policemen in cars and on motorbikes. We drove through the empty streets of the town. There was almost no one on the street. More often, we were met with quick glances from the windows of houses, as if the local population was under curfew.

The one- and two-story buildings were grey from factory smoke, while the factory smokestacks belched out smoke in rainbow colors. There was filth and stink wherever you looked. Nature had given us such a beautiful morning. But the political and economic system had demonstrated how humans could put nature in its place, turn a Ural town into a heap of garbage and scrap metal. Our convoy on the streets of this town looked like an insult to humanity and to nature.

We left the center of town. The air became cleaner, and nature came into its own. After two years in prisons and camps, it was pleasant to see the fields, mountains, and forest. But all this already seemed foreign to me.

In the past, I had loved going out of town to gather mushrooms and berries, or even simply to walk in the woods. My daughters and I could gather a bucket of mushrooms and another of berries (blueberries or raspberries) in a single day. On the Karelian Isthmus I alone could gather two buckets of mushrooms in five hours. But when the forest is easily accessible, and you can sit on a train any weekend morning and be there in half an hour, it doesn't seem so attractive – just like all easily accessible things. Looking at the forest through the window of a Stolypin carriage, or over the side of a prison truck was a different matter.

We drove past unremarkable villages. We drove for more than an hour, although the camp was less than thirty miles from town. The reason for this was the nearly impassable dirt road.

The camp appeared in the distance. Its characteristic fence with watch towers made it possible to spot from many miles away. From the outside, the camps are like twins. We drove closer. I could already see the two rows of barbed wire, followed by a high fence. We already knew that five meters behind the first fence was a second one, and between them was another row of barbed wire, topped with spirals of the same. The fences were also topped with barbed wire, sirens, and a high-voltage cable. Behind the fences were another two rows of barbed wire. At each corner of the camp was a watch tower, and inside the zone were infrared sensors. Between the interior fences and two rows of barbed wire was the forbidden zone, a guarded strip of bare earth. Pickets were positioned around the camp at night, and soldiers with German shepherd dogs patroled the perimeter. Some said there were mines planted between the fences, but I don't know if that wastrue.

We drove up to the gates of Camp VS-389/36. Nearby was the town of Kuchino, where the camp administration lived with their families.

The camp was located in a swampy area, with the characteristic microclimate. Two hundred and thirty prisoners passed through the gates of the camp. There was a screech of steel upon steel, a rattling of keys, a clicking of locks. Now it was anyone's guess how much time each of us would have to spend in this institution.

After a lengthy "*shmon* (search)," we were divided into units and marched to the bathhouse. The bathhouse was on the verge of collapse. Its logs had rotted and warped. The only way to get to the bathhouse was over the swamp, on a path of loose boards. In fact, the camp would have been more suitable for mosquitoes than for people. The mosquitoes had a surplus of fresh food. As the camp had been empty for a long time, it was full of hungry mosquitoes just waiting to throw themselves on our long-anticipated flesh.

After the bathhouse, we were distributed among four sections of two barracks. Double bunks, one nightstand to each pair. At this camp, each prisoner was given a little over seven square feet of living space.

At the mess hall, we were greeted by a hearty dinner made by the guards' wives from who-knows-what ingredients. Then we were put on a traditional camp diet, but the bread was good quality, not the sour clay we had been made to eat in Mordovia.

At this camp, I was part of a group of Jews drawn from various Mordovian camps. Another group of Jews ended up in another Ural camp, VS-389/35. We organized our own eight-person kibbutz of sorts, whose members were: Arye Vudka, Shimon Grilius, myself, Wolf Zalmanson, Yosef Mendelevich, Yakov Suslensky, Asher Frolov, and David (Mahon) Chernoglaz.

To begin with, we were busy cleaning up the territory and creating a store of logs and wooden boards. This kind of work, without quotas, permitted us to gather around a wood chip fire, talk, and drink tea. We prisoners formed small groups like this in both residential and work zones, mixing pleasure with profit.

But I must introduce you to the camp administration. Here they are, in a few lines:

Major Kotov – the camp commandant. A young, pleasant, educated man. A representative of the new generation of prison officials, those who began their careers during the Khrushchev period. If the old Stalin-era rank and file didn't eat him alive, I imagined he would have a great future in camp administration. He was skilled in exploiting the contrasting inclinations and responsibilities of his deputies, and tried to look like a liberal while using repressive means – most likely on KGB orders, rather than in accordance with his own wishes.

Major Fyodorov – deputy commandant. An unremarkable sort of administrator, considering the personalities one met with in the Soviet camp system. He was a malicious man who understood all the details of the camp system and of the inmates' lives. Carrying out tasks that would usually be the province of guards, Fyodorov loved picking on us prisoners. It always made him smile. This smile was the smile of a sadist. In camp No. 35, which had been built on the foundations of a former penal colony for female juvenile offenders, you could still see inscriptions calling for "Death to Fyodorov!" I think that apart from his primary duties, he also formed the link between the camp administration (MVD) and the KGB.

Captain Zhuravkov –political executive. I imagined him as a former company political director, who had been forcibly transferred to the camp system and was waiting patiently for retirement. In the post-Stalin camp system, he was perfectly well suited for work with political prisoners. When Kotov was promoted, Zhuravkov became director of camp No. 36.

Our first serious conflict with the administration, after our arrival in the Urals, surrounded the issue of beards. Many prisoners in Mordovia had grown beards. Management in the Urals, evidently remembering the reforms of Peter I, had decided to resurrect the tradition. After labor strikes and hunger strikes, our fight for the right to wear beards ended with a forced shaving in handcuffs. There was also a period of struggle against breast tags.

This struggle for basic rights, against personal humiliation, took place at a time when work was short in the manufacturing zone. Soon after, all prisoners were needed for construction and repair work, and later for work in the lumberyard.

In August, I was summoned to a meeting with the unit commander. He told me that if I gave up on my idea of emigrating to Israel, I would be released, and I could be home in two months.

"I didn't go to trouble of planning a hijacking attempt in order to give up on Israel," I responded.

"Think carefully before making your answer," he cautioned.

"I have already thought carefully, and there will be no other answer."

On that note, the conversation ended. Of course, the unit commander had been speaking at the behest of the KGB.

In literally a week's time, I received an interesting letter, written in my wife's handwriting. I had a habit of numbering all my letters and sewing them into a folder. I did the same with this letter. The letter, written in a dramatic tone, accused a mysterious "them" of lying. "They" had promised to release me, and yet I was still in prison. A little while later, I went into the shed where our personal belongings were kept, in order to sew a few more letters into my folder. I also wanted to have another read of the previous letter, but it wasn't there! In its place, with the same number, written in the same handwriting, was another letter without any accusations of lying or hysterics.

The question arose: Did my wife write these letters, or had they been faked by KGB specialists? I couldn't answer this question, and at that time was unable to ask my wife.

After we prisoners had finished building the workshop, we began making parts for electric irons. Workplace conflicts surrounding so-called violations of protocol began to arise. Initially, the guards tried to stop us from studying Hebrew and Jewish history. They took in our notes and textbooks for inspection. And though this practice eventually stopped, they continued to hassle us. They prevented us from celebrating Jewish holidays and punished us if we gathered all together in one room, or even if we were found in the wrong section. In short, the administration didn't need a reason to punish us. There was even one time when they stopped us from celebrating Victory Day over Nazi Germany, at the same time as the camp's neo-Nazi contingent was allowed to celebrate Hitler's birthday.

Most conflicts were accompanied on our side by hunger strikes and refusals to work. On the administration's side: they denied us visiting privileges and packages; they put us in solitary confinement; they sent us to the camp's internal prison (Pomeschenie Kamernogo Tipa, PKT) or to an outside prison.

Summer in the Ural region was short. As early as the morning of August 15, we awoke to find a core of ice in the wash basin. True, the wash basin was outside. But night frosts began early.

Before long, my wife and my elder daughter Liza arrived for a general visit. We were given two hours, and our tables stood about ten feet apart. What is more, my table was surrounded by a glass wall. The least diversion from family subject matter, and the visit could be ended abruptly. Two guards and an officer were present in the room and made jottings in their notebooks. I continued to insist on my family's emigration to Israel. Apart from my true conviction that my daughters' lives would be better in Israel after all that had happened, I also surmised that Alya would refuse to emigrate if she really was working for the KGB. We decided to compromise, and wait until April 1973, when Yuliya would turn eighteen. Before then, they were reluctant to leave.

The prisoner population in the camps was varied. About 40 percent had been sentenced for war-era crimes, that is, for cooperation with the Nazis. Many of them had been arrested as they were already approaching retirement age. The other 60 percent had been sentenced for so-called anti-Soviet activity – for nationalist activity in Ukraine, in the Baltic States, and in Armenia. There was a small percentage of ordinary criminals who had committed certain "crimes" on purpose, in order to end up in political camps. There were also a few so-called "defectors" and people who had been accused of espionage. During my whole time in the camps, I never once heard of someone being charged for great-power chauvinism, despite the fact that chauvinism is often an underpinning value for nationalist movements which have a defensive character, or antisemitism.

The Soviet government has been implementing chauvinist and antisemitic policies for decades. Now, during perestroika, the propagandists themselves are (allegedly) surprised by conflicts between minority groups.

A few examples of the types I encountered in labor camp:

Zverev (not his real name, but an entirely appropriate one[2]) was sentenced to twenty-five years. In the early years of the war, he was taken prisoner by the Germans and became a killer. He fought against the partisans, while

---

[2]   Meaning "savage," *zverev* is a Russian epithet.

simultaneously murdering civilians, including Jews. In prison, he loved telling his fellow criminals how he had shot Germans as a Red Army soldier at the beginning of the war, and then shot partisans after changing sides. Zverev blamed the Jews for spreading Christianity throughout Europe, which he said had weakened Europe as a whole, and Russia in particular. He had managed to spend a few weeks in a German prison for stealing meat from the soldiers' mess.

Stroganov was sentenced to fifteen years for treason. Like millions of others, he had been captured by the Germans. At POW camp, he had agreed to work for them, participated in killing operations against the partisans, and retreated to Germany with the rest of the army. After the war ended, he hid in England, where he spent a few months in prison for theft, like Zverev. Then, he travelled to Australia through the Suez Canal. It was paradise (for someone like him) – work a week, play for three. So he "suffered" in far-off Australia, until he learned of the amnesty Russia was offering for people like him. The motherland was calling him, and he believed the government's promises and returned home. He was left alone for a few days. But then he was called to the KGB, where they took down his details, and advised him to find employment as soon as possible. He did so, and quietly worked until retirement age. Then, according to the KGB's plan, he was sentenced to fifteen years for the sins he had already been forgiven under the amnesty, and sent to a labor camp. Here you had to work forty-eight hours per week rather than one week per month, without a pension fund or vacations. Remembering far-off Australia, he spent his spare moments admiring the tops of his native birch trees through the rows of barbed wire that topped the fences.

After serving seven years of his sentence, and exceeding his five-year quota, he died in the camp hospital. From my window, I saw how his corpse was shoved into the back of a truck and taken to the guard post. By this time, they had stopped beating nails into corpses to make sure they were really dead. Prisoners had been known to get ideas from *The Count of Monte Christo*. Stroganov's fate would be a foot tag and a nameless grave in the camp cemetery.

In Mordovia, by the way, farmers with a nose for business would exhume fresh prisoner corpses, and use them for pig feed. We prisoners didn't get to eat the pork. It was destined for the bazaar, where its principal buyers were the camp "admins" and their families. As a result, the camp administration both literally and figuratively ate prisoners.

Chernyakov was sentenced to ten years for treason. A professional teacher until middle age, he had worked in a rural school, barely scraping by. Eventually, he decided to make a bit of extra income and hired himself out as a sailor on a fishing trawler. The trawler, besides catching fish, was assigned to drop off Russian spies in Scandinavia, from whence they could reach the rest of Europe. Chernyakov decided to inform the West of the Soviet fishing industry's (really the KGB's) false actions – he took a piece of paper and described everything in detail, inserted the letter into a bottle, sealed it with a cork, and threw it into the sea. However, the bottle did not manage to swim further than the fishing flotilla. Chernyakov's vigilant comrades caught the bottle, and it ended up on a desk at KGB headquarters. It was hardly difficult to find the perpetrator, based on his handwriting, and the rest was like clockwork.

Levko Lukyanenko had received the death sentence for treason, which had then been commuted to fifteen years. He had founded a small organization in Ukraine that demanded a referendum on Ukraine's independence – in perfect accordance with the USSR's constitution. The KGB immediately stamped them as "bourgeois nationalists," cooked up a show trial for appearances' sake, and packed them off to labor camp.

Akimov, a young man, was sentenced to seven years for anti-Soviet activity, which had expressed itself in a speech against "Soviet-Chinese friendship forever." (Two years later, this "friendship" led to armed conflict on Damansky Island, and the USSR and China were at loggerheads. Akimov, however, continued to rot in prison as an enemy of their "friendship.") He wrote to all possible government agencies, but always received the same response: "You have been correctly convicted." Then, Akimov set fire to the isolation cell. This act of protest cost him three more years. His initial seven years became ten.

Yuriev (a fictional name, as I have forgotten his real one) was sentenced to seven years for so-called anti-Soviet activity. He was a former police captain who had helped to keep the peace during a workers' meeting at Kirov Factory in Leningrad. Yuriev told us a little about the meeting:

Before the work day had ended, the factory courtyard filled up with people. All were eagerly awaiting the arrival of Khrushchev, who was to give a speech. Mr. Khrushchev was late, and knocking off time was fast approaching. The workers rushed to the exit, and many slipped away before management got it into their heads to close the gates. When, at length, the leader of the great power arrived, he was met with an empty courtyard. With his microphone switched on, Khrushchev cursed the Leningrad city administration for their inability to organize a workers' meeting. The result of the meeting was a series of anecdotes about the peasant-leader.

Yuriev was part of an organization whose aim was to revive Leninist principles. The organization's members, without hiding their intentions, wanted to ascend to positions of power and change the country's political order from the top. This was, in fact, the same method used by Gorbachev, before he began his wide-ranging reforms. Yuriev's father, a KGB colonel, approved of his son's views, and said so at the trial.

The Pestov brothers. These half-literate workers had distributed "anti-Soviet" leaflets calling for the living conditions of the "ruling" class to be improved. No, not the party nomenclature, but the working class. Their father was Azeri and their mother was Russian (or perhaps the reverse). The elder brother was sentenced to seven years; the younger, to five. The brothers' half-Muslim heritage obviously had something to do with their opinion on the Jewish question: "Send all the Jews to Israel, then drop an atom bomb on the Jewish state." Later, during the Yom Kippur War, I overheard the elder Pestov saying that he supported the Arab countries – not because of any Soviet interests, but out of Islamic solidarity. As he expressed it, "I want to see the Soviets in a coffin."

Ladyzhensky was sentenced to three years for possession and distribution of anti-Soviet literature. With a PhD in mathematics, and a commensurate knowledge of Russian literature and European art, he was firmly convinced that Western civilization would collapse under the brute force of the Soviet army. Ladyzhensky likened the situation to that of ancient Rome, which had fallen to the barbarians' brute force. It was impossible to shake his convictions. He was ready to be a citizen of the third Rome, but couldn't imagine a world in which humanity was wiped out by an atom bomb – which is what would happen if Russia attacked Western Europe.

Ladyzhensky most probably gave some testimony at the KGB's behest and had his term of exile repealed, after he had served his sentence.

I will make no attempt at describing even a small proportion of the inmates of camp No. 36. There are as many prisoners as there are human fates and worlds. It may sound banal, but you really could write, if not a book, then at least a story about each inmate. But for that you would need to be a writer.

On August 10, 1973, Liza and Yuliya departed for Israel. If it hadn't been for the help of the Jewish community, my daughters wouldn't have been able to pay for their exit documents. It cost five hundred rubles to renounce Soviet citizenship, five or six times the average monthly wage of the period. Alone in a new country, without any family, they experienced many difficulties. They kept their letters calm, however, to avoid upsetting their parents.

On the evening of October 6, 1973, we learned from a Soviet radio broadcast that the Yom Kippur War had begun. Soviet propaganda, using information provided by the Arabs, described the Israeli army's attempts to land on the west bank of the Suez Canal, and cross the Syrian border. These attempts had been rebuffed, and the Egyptian and Syrian armies were making a counter attack, pursuing the Israeli forces. It was clear that this report was false, that Egypt and Syria had launched the attack on Israel. From further information, it became clear that Israel was fighting defensively on two fronts.

Although daily life in the camp didn't change, our thoughts were on the Middle East. The situation was more critical than in the run-up to the Six-Day War, and yet I felt calm in my understanding of the Israeli army's capabilities. I even overestimated them, as evidenced by their decision to break through the middle of the Egyptian front, rather than encircling the Egyptians and their allies on the Sinai Peninsula. Then they could have come out onto the west bank of the Canal and turned north to Port Said, or south to Suez. From there, they could have surrounded the Arab troops from the opposite side of the canal.

That was how we discussed the events of the war and "planned" the subsequent actions of "our" troops. This time, our troops were the Israeli army, not the Soviet army fighting Nazi Germany. This time, our troops were fighting those who wanted to "solve" the Jewish question once and for all.

All the antisemites, from young neo-Nazis to old Nazi POWs, rejoiced at the Arabs' first successes and predicted the demise of the Jewish state. On the third day of the war, Yosef Mendelevich and I were walking along, discussing Israel's situation, when we saw the aforementioned Pestov brothers coming towards us, cheerfully discussing the same topic. "Yosef, smile. Pretend you're happy!" I said, breaking into a smile myself. When the Pestov brothers drew level with us and saw our happy faces, they were taken aback, and opened their mouths in amazement. What could those two Jews be smiling about when Israel is on the verge of disappearance? It was as if they were wondering,

"What has happened? What are those Zhyds (Yids) doing to our Muslim brothers, three thousand miles away?"

One evening, when we were all in barracks preparing for lights out, a broadcast was issued by the state news agency that a Soviet ship had been sunk near the port of Tartus in Syria. The fact that the armed watercraft had been anchored in a war zone, at a naval base, obviously went unmentioned. The reaction of the pro-Arab antisemites to this broadcast was curious. They squealed with pleasure, despite the fact that the ship had been sunk by Israel. Hatred for Soviet power prevailed over their antisemitic feelings. For me this was unexpected. After all, the Nazi sympathizers cooperated with the camp administration, and were in favor, whereas we, who had tried to escape the USSR, were considered enemies.

Some of the administrators openly regretted that Hitler had not managed to solve the Jewish question, and now they had to deal with us.

One day, there was a broadcast on Soviet radio that four Israeli tanks had "seeped into" the west bank of the Suez Canal, and that the Arabs were trying to eliminate them. News like that is worthy of a satirical paper. The word "seeped" alone is a fine specimen of military terminology. False Arab propaganda did so much harm, not only to the Arabs themselves, but to their Soviet protectors and role models.

As always, the great powers didn't let their Middle Eastern allies fight the war to a decisive victory that would ensure lasting peace. Once again, Syria suffered the fewest losses of all, and remained Israel's most extremist neighbor.

After the end of the war, rumors were spread (and confirmed in letters we received) that there were Soviet specialists in Israeli POW camps who had fought on the side of the Arabs. I thought that this would mean a healthy fund for prisoner exchange. But the rumors dried up, and we stayed where we were.

Sylva Zalmanson was released in the autumn of 1974. This pleasant piece of news was accompanied by rumors that she had been exchanged for a Soviet officer.

A few words about camp food. In our zone, it was sufficient in quantity, but the quality of ingredients, nutrient content, and preparation of the food were unsatisfactory. Prisoners in the solitary confinement cells were fed starvation rations – bread and water every second day. This was especially difficult when the temperature was low in winter and there were no sheets or blankets.

If we met manufacturing quotas, we were allowed to buy five rubles' worth of food at the camp shop. Those who did not abuse their rights might be allowed a further two to four rubles' worth. After serving half their sentence, prisoners were allowed to receive one ten-pound box, and two two-pound parcels per year. That was, of course, if you weren't denied parcel privileges for some minor infraction.

Our daily ration was 0.5–0.75 ounces of sugar, an ounce of meat (which included bones and gristle), 0.2 ounces of fat, which looked like industrial lubricant, but was red in color. They often gave us fish so stinky that even the hungry cats didn't want to eat it.

We weren't allowed to have pets in prison camp, although in minimum security camps some people managed to keep animals in secret. Scraps from the mess hall went to fatten up pigs for slaughter. My Leningrad cellmate Anvar, who had spent two years in such camps, told me that the prisoners not only fattened the pigs up, but screwed them as well. And it was true that swinish behavior flourished in the camps.

When we first arrived, there was only one cat in the camp, by the name of Murka. As the zone had been empty for a long time before our arrival, she had become used to hunting rats. At camp No. 36, water pipelines were laid above ground. They were insulated with felt and sawdust and encased in wooden boards on three sides. This heating system served as an ideal habitation for hordes of rats, who even in icy weather traveled along these warm pipes from the mess hall to all the barracks and other buildings. In summer, they made exit holes for themselves, and moved about on the surface, with total disregard for us humans. There were efforts to kill the rats, but they had evidently developed an immunity to poison. Only Murka had the power to keep the burgeoning rat rabble under control.

But the cat had her enemies among the prison administrators. The first sight of them would send Murka running to the basement, though she felt at home among us prisoners. One day, a well-fed male called Vaska arrived from the admins' village, and kittens began to appear. A few years later, the zone had become home to over twenty cats. Every time we went to the mess hall, we would be followed by a whole feline brigade. On particularly lucky days (or weeks), we would be given smelly fish. If even the hungry cats refused to eat it, we would be perfectly within our rights to file a complaint.

One night, the guards conducted a mass killing. They caught all the cats apart from Murka, put them in a sack, and burned them in the stove. A few days later, they killed Murka as well, after which the rats were able to breathe easy.

One time, we had chicken soup for a whole week. The chicken was boiled to the point where you couldn't tell what bit of it you were eating. Only the black spots on preserved bits of skin explained the reason for such a course of "health" food. It's likely that an epidemic at the local poultry farm had enabled collectivized agriculture to give their quota of meat to the state, and resulted in us prisoners being fed on carrion.

The bread was good quality, and there was almost enough of it to go around, thanks to a large percentage of elderly, toothless prisoners.

At camp No. 35, we were given a meat patty for lunch on Sundays. I used to call Sunday "Cutlet Day." These cutlets were made up of about 25 percent meat and 75 percent bread, but the sight of the cutlet alone reminded me of home.

Not long before my release, we were given tomatoes for several days in a row. This "miracle" set off rumors about an imminent amnesty.

It took me a few years after my release to cure my bleeding gums.

Medical care in the camps was unsatisfactory. The camp doctor Petrov openly acknowledged that he was a "Chekist" first, and a doctor second. When Yakov Suslensky began to have problems with his heart, Petrov prescribed him a course of political lectures before giving him any medical assistance.

Medicine was given out without any packaging, such that it was impossible to determine its expiration date. There was a sick bay in the camp with four beds in it, supervised by a convict-orderly. The Mordovian camp system had boasted a prison hospital. Twice a year, a dentist would visit the camp. The dentist in the Urals was a stout, mature woman, who was also an MVD captain. She was skilled at humiliating us prisoners. Once I came to her with a toothache, which she refused to do anything about, citing my bleeding gums as a reason. I had to seek help from a fellow prisoner who used to be a paramedic. There were some rusty dental instruments locked in a cupboard in the sick bay (the dentist brought her own instruments). In the evening, after the guards had done their night rounds, we slipped into the room, and broke the cupboard open. After rubbing my gums and the instruments with iodine, the half-blind paramedic spent a whole hour tugging at my tooth, eventually breaking it and removing the roots in pieces. This "pleasure" cost me only a packet of tea. In future, I gave the paramedic two more opportunities to experiment on my teeth.

When I made a second visit to the lady captain a year later, she advised me to tend to my gums first, before consulting a dentist. She then pointed at a poster with images of fruits and vegetables, blithely suggesting that I add foods to my diet that I had no access to.

In 1975, my health was in such a state that it was difficult to say which part of my body was well. I had the impression that my whole system was poisoned, falling apart. I threw out the pills given to me by the Chekist-doctor. In the mess hall, I was eating from the common pot, so actual poisoning was ruled out. The only solution was self-treatment. Wild chamomile grew on the edges of the camp. I gathered the flowers, made a tea from them, and drank it three times a day. I think it must have had a healing effect on me, as I took no other medicines. In a few days, I started to feel better, but a week later I returned to my previous condition. That was when they sent me to the Ural political camp hospital, which accommodated ten or twelve people. The hospital was fifty yards from camp No. 35 and surrounded by two fences. I spent a week there taking multivitamins, before being returned to camp.

Once, the camp orderly detained Sopelyak, a young man sentenced for nationalist activity in western Ukraine. The orderly, Captain Dovchiy, took him to the orderly room and beat him to a pulp. The next day, there was a huge prisoner strike, in which everyone except the young neo-Nazis and old Nazi sympathizers participated.

The day after that, the MVD and KGB camp supervisors for the Ural region arrived. Our demand was that Captain Dovchiy be dismissed. After investigations were concluded, Kotov announced that there had been no violence against Sopelyak; that the beating was a fabrication intended to provoke. Issuing threats of further punishment, he demanded that we return to work. Simultaneously, the administration started bribing strikers with package deliveries and visits. A number of prisoners returned to work. They began to punish the rest by sending them to external prison, PKT, and solitary confinement.

The strike continued, though the ranks of strikers had significantly thinned. Some were already coming out of solitary, while seven or eight of us, including several Jews, remained on strike. Yosef Mendelevich was arrested two days later. The rest of us were called to meet with Fyodorov, who first cajoled, then threatened us. Some strikers were already being punished for a second time, while I, Wolf Zalmanson, and two other guys, still remained untouched. At this point, a group of strikers who had come out of solitary were returning to work, including Sopelyak himself.

I was summoned once more by Major Fyodorov. With a saccharine smile, he began cajoling me to return to work. An outsider would have thought that either Fyodorov's own fate or the fate of the whole prison labor force depended on me alone. Apart from caring about the outcome of the strike, I was curious to see what they would do with me.

"Citizen commandant, I have told you more than once that I will not go to work."

"I don't want to have to punish you."

"You will have to punish me. You don't have any other choice."

At this point, Fyodorov transformed. His face went purple, and his eyes became narrow and bloodshot. I had never seen him like this. Next, Fyodorov roared out a statement that was evidently prepared for him by the KGB: "Three days in punishment cells! You won't get out of this camp alive! Don't even think of revealing the name of the person who denounced the preparation for the plane hijacking. It will only make things worse."

Although I had been curious to see how this strike would end for me, such a revelation on Fyodorov's part was totally unexpected. It was clear that he spoke in the name, and on the orders of the KGB. After all, camp administrators didn't care about our cases. They were concerned with camp rules and regulations. Political games were the province of the KGB alone.

Fyodorov called a guard, and I was led to the punishment cells. Three days were at my disposal, and I had to think what I would do next. There were four of us to a cell. All the other cells were full of strikers. During the day, we could do nothing but walk and sit. Sleeping was only permitted at night. The days were hot, and the nights were chilly. I could only think over this new situation after nights out, in the moments before sleep.

When the KGB agent had tried to scare me with knives during my flight to Kishenev, I had interpreted his threat as an attempt to "take me with fear." Now I could sense that the KGB had lost all hope of returning me to the bosom of Communism, were experiencing serious fallout from the airplane affair, and might certainly carry out their threat on the person who had got them into this mess. It wasn't as if they were going to blame themselves, or punish themselves for short-sightedness. But it wouldn't cause them much difficulty to do away with me, while I was in their clutches – all the more so in transit.

I felt it imperative to convey a message to Israel about what was going on, through some trustworthy person, especially since my daughters were there, and my wife, in the case of my death, would probably want to be with them. Considering my aforementioned suspicions of Alya, I imagined the following situation: Together with the mass exodus of Jews to Israel, the KGB sends agents not only to Israel, but through Israel to other countries. This was much easier than going through Scandinavia, for instance. You would have to be an idiot not to use the aliyah in this way. The KGB wouldn't miss such an opportunity.

My wife was, of course, totally unfit to be a spy. But she would still have relatives in Leningrad, who in turn had relatives in Yugoslavia. In my imagination, I already saw my wife meeting her beloved sister (blessed be her memory) on Cyprus, through whom my wife would transfer secret information to the "competent organs" in Moscow. That is, I saw my wife in the role of messenger.

Next, I imagined that the messages she was conveying would be used for disinformation. Among other things, the organs would be interested in Western electronics. In this area of technology, they were about ten years behind. The following picture drew itself in my imagination: the KGB would be given maps revealing the locations of radar detectors, radar homing devices, and infrared seekers for missiles, along with an additional device which would permit them, using radio signal, to throw the whole network out of whack at the most crucial moment. And what if this information was somehow transferred from Russia to the Arab countries? A war would begin, and all the technology would malfunction.

In short, I had a fertile imagination. Then a practical question emerged: who would convey my suspicions, as well as the KGB's most recent threat, to Israel? Both Wolf Zalmanson and Yosef Mendelevich had fathers living in Riga. Both had relatives in Israel. I decided to transmit my message through whomever of them was visited first by his father.

After my release from the punishment cells, I returned to work, and camp life regained its normal rhythm. Captain Dovchiy was not fired, but we saw him in the camp less and less frequently, until he disappeared altogether.

In Camp No. 36, only three of us were left of the original kibbutz: Wolf Zalmanson, Yosef Mendelevich, and I. The others had all been released, apart from Arye Vudka and Yakov Suslensky, who had been transferred to Vladimir prison. The three of us made Shabbat and discussed the pressing questions of the moment, but it wasn't the same as it had been when there were eight of us Jews in the zone together. In fact, there were more than eight Jews in the zone. But there had been eight of us in the kibbutz, united by a single cause, a single goal. First two, then three Jews were not members of our kibbutz, and our relations with them varied over time.

It wasn't long before Yakov Suslensky returned from prison, alleging that life in prison was much better than where we were. Yakov managed to convince several prisoners of this, and a struggle for the status of "political prisoner" began. Some of these prisoners were sent immediately to prison, others were put through PKT, before being sent to prison. The three of us decided not to let ourselves be seduced by the advantages of prison life, the additional free time prison inmates were allowed. We decided to stay in camp. In fact, it wasn't long before forced labor was introduced at Vladimir prison too – following the construction of a new cell block.

Major Kotov was soon promoted up the administrative ladder and transferred away from our camp.

Under the Brezhnev government, there was an unusual spurt of enthusiasm for promotions, ranks, and awards. Brezhnev himself set a fine example, decking his broad chest, from collar to waist, in medals of all kinds. I guess the only one he was missing was "for maternal heroism." The whole Soviet power structure at every level was dedicated to showering itself with medals.

Kotov deserved his promotion, after putting the greater part of us in punishment cells and sending a third of camp No. 36's inmates to external prison.

Zhuravkov was a simpler man. The camp system may not have been his calling, but he adapted to it well enough. It was he who took Kotov's place as camp commandant. One day, Zalmanson and I happened to pass by Zhuravkov. He stopped us and asked me, "Dymshits, why do you always look at me with such hatred? If I was at your mercy, I imagine you would shoot me."

As it happened, I considered him to be the safest of all the camp administrators. "No, citizen commandant," I responded, "I feel no personal hatred toward you. Indeed, hate is blinding, and I want to see and learn all I can about your prison system. I certainly wouldn't shoot you. I would probably shave your head, hang a dog tag around your neck, and make you work just like we do. But your time will come." On that note, our short conversation ended.

As I came out of the punishment cells, I learned from Mendelevich that his father would be visiting soon. Deciding that I would use his father to transmit my message to Israel, Yosef and I chose an isolated spot, and I gave him all the information he needed to convey. His father never came, but...

In the spring of 1976, Arye Vudka was unexpectedly returned to camp from prison. He had only a few months left until release. They would not release him into the zone, but rather held him in the isolation cells under quarantine. It was surprising that he had been brought back to camp at all, so soon before his release. He would have the opportunity to collect fresh material on camp life. I was especially curious to meet with Arye, as he might be able to convey my message to Israel himself, getting rid of at least three middlemen. We all knew that Arye wanted to go straight to Israel after release.

On April 28, Yosef began a hunger strike, demanding that Arye be released from solitary confinement, given his term of quarantine had expired, and he was not being punished for anything.

I decided to remain in the shadows in order not to make my desire to meet with Arye too obvious. However, on April 30, the administration asked Wolf and me to use our influence on Mendelevich, to get him to end his strike, which was when we joined him in striking for Arye's release.

On the night of May 2, Arye was released into the zone. In case he was taken into transit the next morning, I immediately met with him and gave him the necessary information to be transmitted to Israel. I will give my interpretation of this episode later on.

Arye stayed in the camp almost until the end of his sentence and worked at the camp workshop. Using his exceptional memory, Arye began to collect information about the camp's prisoners and the conditions in which they lived. This became his principle goal during his remaining time in camp. Soon, Arye was released, and left for Israel.

A short time later, Yosef was sent to PKT for his refusal to work on Saturdays, despite the fact that he met his Saturday quota by distributing it among the other working days. In order to frame Mendelevich, the administration began stealing articles he had made and set aside for submission on

Saturday. It was clear that they had decided to send Yosef to prison, after the humiliation he had been made to face on religious grounds. After a month in PKT, Yosef was released into the zone, but in April or early May he was taken into transit. At the Chusovoy peoples' court, Mendelevich was sentenced to three years of prison and sent to Vladimir.

Now there were only two Jews from the original group, Wolf Zalmanson and myself, left in the camp. We continued to make Shabbat and talk in our free time. Wolf was intensively studying both English and Hebrew. I knew my own linguistic limitations, and got through the first two parts of *Elef milim* with difficulty.

After two more months, I was taken into transit. They loaded me into a police wagon, and shook me up and down the bumpy Ural roads until we got to camp VS-389/35. This zone was larger than the previous, with about the same number of prisoners. It contained a large stone barracks and a large mess hall, and the manufacturing zone boasted a large workshop with lathes for metalworking. I had spent over a year operating a lathe at camp No. 36, and now Anatoliy Altman and I were assigned to work on the same machine in different shifts.

At the end of October, Alya left to join our daughters in Israel. Initially, when she submitted documents to the Migration Service, the KGB insisted that she divorce me in order to be granted an exit visa. When I received her letter, informing of this bizarre demand, I immediately advised her not to agree to divorce under any circumstances. I didn't understand the point of this demand. I would only be able to leave for Israel after my release, at the invitation of my daughters. The KGB certainly wouldn't be able to pretend that my daughters were distant relatives (although at that time they could pretend whatever they liked). Even now, I am not quite certain what the KGB wanted to achieve.

In zone No. 35, I was reunited with Hillel Butman and Anatoliy Altman, whom I hadn't seen since the trial. In a few months' time, Butman was transferred to Vladimir prison, and the two of us case mates were left together.

Soon another Jew arrived at the camp who had an interesting and broken fate for which he was at least as much to blame as the KGB. I will call him Vladik. So, this Vladik had a job somewhere in the MVD. A tall, handsome man with soft, white skin and a soft character, he attracted the attention of the KGB, who found him work discrediting foreign visitors at Soviet hotels. How the KGB uncovered the homosexual tendencies of foreigners, Vladik did not reveal, taught by bitter experience. At the KGB's orders, Vladik would go to bed with his intended victim, and the whole ensuing process would be recorded on video. Then, the KGB would blackmail the victim and attempt to use him for their ends. All that would have been fine, and Vladik would have received his captain's shoulder boards, had the KGB not decided to reveal Vladik's role in the nation's security and his colleagues not decided to make fun of his conscientious efforts to undermine the decadent West.

Vladik decided to take revenge on the KGB while simultaneously improving his material position. He knew some secrets about deals done by Russians in the Middle East. Secrets that could interest the secret services of his clients' nations. Vladik lived beyond his means, was a frequent visitor to restaurants, and was up to his ears in debt. He couldn't mortgage his property, given he had none, but he could sell secrets. He attempted to involve an Iranian student, but the latter refused, fearing a KGB trap. An Egyptian student decided to make some money on Vladik, and gave him up to the organs. Though Vladik said he was sorry, and the secrets hadn't been particularly secret, he too was made to do his five years (less than the minimum).

Israel didn't interest Vladik. I doubt the Soviet Union did either. In fact, he was only interested in obtaining the earliest possible release and returning to the sweet life. For this reason, he had already begun cooperating with the KGB, that is, with the same people who humiliated him and on whom he had wanted to take vengeance.

The rest of us got acquainted with Vladik but became quickly convinced of his uselessness as a person. People like him, as they say, will only come right in the grave.

Things had been tense in camp No. 35 in the weeks before my arrival. The camp's criminal elements had decided to conduct a pogrom. A that time, the camp was dominated by a thief called Hitler. In camp No. 36 was another thief called Eva – Hitler's homosexual "wife." Camp No. 35 contained a large, tight group of Ukrainian nationalists, with whom the Jews were on good terms. These Ukrainians gave the criminals a serious warning, after which they quieted down. Later, a number of them were transferred to other camps or released, and the tension subsided.

By the time I arrived in camp No. 35, life was flowing along calmly and monotonously. There were intense frosts in the winter of 1978–79. At night, the temperature could sink to -45°C. An icy haze hung in the air. Inside, the temperature could get as low as five degrees, partially because the administration was economizing on fuel.

When anyone opened the outer door of the workshop, several sparrows would always manage to fly inside, only to die in a minute or two from the sharp change in temperature. Only after a short strike did the administration agree to light another boiler in the boiler room, which raised the indoor temperature to ten degrees. A large flock of pigeons lived in the attic of the prison mess hall. By the spring of 1979, half of them were dead, and many of those that remained had stumps instead of feet.

10 Freedom
April 1979

One day, Altman was called to the censor's office. When he returned with the letters he had received, he explained that there had been a KGB agent in the censor's office, who said he had participated in the arrest of our group at Smolny airport.

The next day, I was also called to the censor's office, to receive a parcel. Another man was sitting in the room, about thirty-five years old, in civilian clothes. He asked, "Dymshits, do you recognize me?"

Despite having no recollection of this man, I remembered what Tolik had told me, and replied, "You participated in the arrest of our group at Smolny airport in 1970."

"Yes, I was a participant. How are you feeling?"

"Fine, thank you. I've done nearly nine years. I have six to go. How are things with you? I'm guessing you haven't repeated what you did in 1970?"

"No, we wouldn't do that again. We should have just let you go quietly. We made a big mistake."

"I'm guessing a few *papakhas*[1] lost their jobs?"

"A whole lot of things happened."

On that note, our conversation ended. I signed for my parcel and went out.

We were brought lunch at the workshop. It was possible to eat quickly and spend ten or fifteen minutes warming yourself in the April sun. After a frosty winter, it was pleasant to feel the warmth of spring on one's skin. Three-foot snowdrifts lay all around, but water was already dripping from the eaves; icicles were melting.

Anatoliy Altman had a little under a year left in his sentence. I still had six years. There was no hint of significant changes, although I never lost hope.

On April 15, 1979, Altman was taken into transit. Generally, prisoners weren't transferred or sent for "reeducation" in the last year of their sentence.

---

[1]   *Papakha* is a winter fur headdress, worn by colonels and higher-ranking officials.

233

The KGB must have realized that after nine years of prison, there was no point trying to make fools of us or draft us on to their team. While I had been counting on early release before, a combination of optimism, logic (skewed a little to meet Russian standards), and even intuition were now telling me that release was in the offing. When Tolik was taken away, I was the only veteran of the Leningrad and Kishenev trials left at the camp. Though I tried not to display my premonitions openly, I was internally prepared for something good to happen.

Among many prisoners, even among the best of them, there was a sense of envy toward Jews and their position in the camps. We had Israel to aim for. People were waiting for us there. We received letters from different countries, where people were thinking about us and exhibited concern for our fate. What did the Ukrainians, Lithuanians, Armenians, and other prisoners have to look forward to at that time? New difficulties, new exiles, new convictions. Considering what awaited them, it was more difficult for them in prison than it was for us. Envy (although not green envy) was a natural feeling under the circumstances, which our fellow prisoners did not always want to hide. For this reason, it was hardly worth demonstrating one's hopes of early release.

What if they told me they would release me now, but wouldn't let me go to Israel for another year or two? In that case, I thought it would be better to spend that time in camp. I felt estranged, not only from a system perverted by all-consuming lies, but from a country populated with thugs at all levels of power. This was why I didn't want to remain on Russian territory, outside of camp fences and prison walls (and I got what I wanted). My feeling was not so much one of hate, as of contempt.

For clarity's sake, I will provide the following example: I have visited Europe as a tourist but have never been to Germany, and would never want to go. My reason tells me that Germany is now inhabited by a new generation, that almost all those who brought catastrophe upon the Jewish people are dead. But pure feeling makes me stay away. If I was a politician, then reason would have conquered feeling. But as an ordinary citizen, I can't do violence to my feelings by subordinating them to reason.

I harbor similar feelings toward the Russian Empire. I understand that most people in Russia are not guilty of the state's antisemitic or anti-Israel policies. Nonetheless, even twenty years after the trial and applause in the courtroom, I wouldn't set foot there. The official attitude toward Sakharov under perestroika only strengthens my feelings.

My optimism was justified this time, and my intuition did not deceive me. April 24 was an ordinary working day. I was working on the lathe, cutting out details in metal, when a guard approached me, and informed me that I had been summoned by the camp commandant, Captain Pimenov. Right there in the workshop, on the second floor, in the office of the head of manufacturing, I met with Pimenov – a corpulent man of forty with a triple chin and a friendly face. Smiling mysteriously, he handed me two telegrams. Telegrams were usually distributed by the censor, but this time the camp director himself had come to the work zone in order to give me some good news. One telegram was from Wolf Zalmanson. The other was from Altman, Butman, Penson, and Hanoch. Both telegrams revealed that their writers were released and would soon be departing for the motherland.

I don't know what Pimenov was smiling about, but as for me, after the news of a mass aliyah and my daughters' emigration to Israel, I was truly glad for my liberated comrades and felt that freedom must be close for the rest of us.

Bodnya, after a four-year sentence, and Israel Zalmanson, after eight years, were already free and in Israel. Now only five of us were left in the camp system: Kuznetsov, Mendelevich, Murzhenko, Fyodorov, and me.

After receiving the telegrams and conveying their content to some of my fellow prisoners – those with whom we (Jews) maintained good relations – I invited them to celebrate the release of our five friends during the lunch break. According to prison custom, I brewed a pot of strong tea, and we wished them a swift journey to their motherland.

I continued working at the lathe after lunch. About an hour and a half before the end of the working day, the head of the workshop approached me and told me to finish up what I was doing, as I would need to fill out some forms. It became clear to me that something unusual was going on. That is, when I was transferred to camp No. 35 from camp No. 36, I did not have to do any paperwork. But I asked no questions and tried to remain calm. I returned to the residential zone together with the other prisoners, went to dinner, and after dinner sat on my bed by the nightstand, reading a newspaper.

There were two hours remaining until lights out when a guard approached me and told me to prepare for transit. I gathered my things, gave a packet of tea to my remaining friends, and asked them to celebrate May 14, Israel's Independence Day. I said my goodbyes and followed the guard to the checkpoint, where my personal belongings were inspected. I was allowed to take my electric razor, handkerchiefs, ball-point pens, and gloves. The orderly explained that all my other things would be sent to my new address. Of course, I received nothing. They stole all my letters, family photographs, notes, albums of Israeli cards and stamps, underwear, and so on. My escort arrived an hour later – an officer and three soldiers with machine guns.

So here I was in a police van, setting out on the bumpy road to freedom. We drove up to the railway station and stopped fifty yards away from the tracks. Ten paces away from me, the ordinary escort commander spoke to a group of officers, quietly, so that I would not hear. Then a major, the commander of the officers' escort, signed a piece of paper, obviously checking me against my description in the inventory of state property. I awaited the train, surrounded by four officers, while the major walked back and forth, conversing intermittently with a KGB agent who stood a little way off. At last, the train approached. My guards and I shared an ordinary passenger compartment. I lay on the middle bunk, while my guards sat below. The major had a compartment to himself. The train had only just left the station when my escort, divided into two shifts, began making trips to the restaurant car. I fell asleep to the noise of their drunken conversations.

The next morning, we arrived in Perm. I was taken to the local prison in a police wagon. The prison doctor asked me several questions, the most serious of which was "Are you infected with syphilis?" after which I was taken to an ordinary cell. Before there was time to inspect my new surroundings, I received the command to prepare for transit.

Under a new escort, I was taken to Perm airport. A major and two sergeants, armed with pistols, sat on either side of me in an ordinary passenger Tu-124 aircraft. I spent the whole journey from Perm to Moscow in handcuffs. When I explained to the major that I wouldn't jump out of the plane if he removed my handcuffs, he answered, "That's just protocol, and we must not violate instructions."

I was dressed in my camp uniform: grey hat with earflaps, padded jacket with a sewn-on number, high leather boots. The other passengers cast furtive glances at the "highly dangerous criminal" in their midst. It is rare for prisoners to be transported by plane. The flight lasted about two and a half hours.

It was already late April, and the country below us was covered in a thick blanket of snow. At Moscow airport – rather, at the plane itself – I was met by a group of KGB agents, who conveyed me to Lifortovo KGB prison. At this point, I was almost entirely certain that freedom was fast approaching. There could be no other reason for transfer to Lifortovo.

I was taken to a cell whose other inhabitant was an ordinary criminal. He had been serving time in a camp, but the KGB had opened a new case against him to do with currency fraud. As there was no reading material, we talked for almost the whole day. I said nothing to him of my impending release. When the major visited our cell on April 26 and wrote down my clothing and shoe sizes, my cellmate immediately concluded that I would be released soon.

"Perhaps," I said. "Almost" is full of possibilities. They could take me to the airport, then something could go wrong, and I would be back at camp. Even in Wonderland, you can't be 100 percent certain of anything.

On April 27, 1979, I was taken to the prison commandant's office. In a large room, with a portrait of yet another supreme leader on the wall over the colonel's desk, sat two imposing officials in enormous armchairs. One of them stood up and in a calm, quiet voice, holding a document in front of him, informed me that by order of the Presidium of the Supreme Soviet of the USSR, I had been stripped of Soviet citizenship and must leave the USSR in the space of two hours.

If it had been within my power, I wouldn't have waited two minutes.

"Do you have any questions or requests?" the colonel asked. "Perhaps you would like to make a formal declaration of some kind?"

"I only have one request. I would like my belongings from camp, and the money in my camp account, to be sent to my wife's sister in Leningrad."

The colonel made a note, and only said, "Good." Later I learned that the money had been transferred, but my belongings had been stolen.

From the office, I was taken to an ordinary room, where I took off my camp uniform and began to put on brand new clothes. A suit, tie, and shoes – things I hadn't worn once since arriving at camp.

Behind the door I heard noise, conversation, a flurry of motion. I thought that all five members of our group might be about to be released.

While I got dressed, the guards were kind enough to pack my things into a little bundle. However, it turned out to contain nothing but my handkerchiefs and razor. The ball-point pens and fur pilot gloves – a memento from aviation – had been stolen, wrapped in a bit of old newspaper. These are all trifles, of course, nitpicking, when compared with how today's repatriates are being robbed – to make sure they don't forget about the organs. The organs are hard to forget.

After changing, I was led to the porch of the internal prison courtyard. A black Volga drove up. I sat on the back seat between two KGB agents in civilian clothes, both carrying "diplomat" briefcases. Two Volgas already stood at the prison gates. Through the rear windows of the cars, I could make out three passengers, one with a shaven head, but it was impossible to tell if he was one of our group or not. Once five Volgas had been loaded in this way, the gates opened, and our column of ten or twelve cars began to move. A police car drove ahead of us, clearing the road with its sirens. People on the street exchanged glances, evidently thinking we were some kind of foreign delegation. When I asked one of the agents where we were going, he answered, "We don't know ourselves. They told us to get ready quickly, nothing more."

I imagined we might be flying to Vienna, and from thence to Israel, but I didn't voice my suspicion. We drove up to the airport and headed immediately for the hardstand. The Volgas stopped one hundred yards from an IL-62, a plane which generally flew long distance flights. Could we really be flying straight to Israel? The thought that we might be flying to America didn't even occur to me.

Our cars were parked at such a distance from one another that it was impossible to tell who was inside. A group of KGB agents and flight crew had gathered by the gangway, talking animatedly. A few minutes later, the boarding ceremony commenced. At one-minute intervals, each Volga drove up to the gangway, such that we still had no chance of seeing each other. Only after boarding were we able to look around, and I saw Kuznetsov. The other three I didn't know. They sat us all separately from one another. Accompanied by twenty KGB agents, we occupied the central cabin of the aircraft. A short time later, general boarding concluded. Rather than crossing through our cabin, the ordinary passengers had been boarded on two different gangways into the neighboring cabins.

"Where are we going, to Israel or to Vienna?" I asked my escort.

"We don't know," they answered in perfect unison, anxious not to reveal any "state secrets."

A few minutes before the engines went on, a group of five people entered the cabin, two of whom introduced themselves as representatives of the American Embassy in Moscow. They offered to show us their identification. Then, one of them explained that according to an agreement concluded between the USA and the USSR, we were being taken to the USA.

"Does anyone have any questions or requests?"

All five of us requested that our families be informed of what was happening.

They wished us a good trip, and left the aircraft. We taxied to the runway. The engines began to whir. Takeoff. Though we were no longer on Soviet soil, we were still on a Soviet route – another form of Soviet territory. My neighbors and I embarked on a long, useless discussion of worn-out issues, which went from bad to worse. My interlocutors were intent on calling white black and vice versa, according to the Party line. One of them said, "I am certain that you will return to us some day."

"I would rather starve to death in a ditch," I said.

And I meant that. It was a testament to their ability to set nearly the whole world against them. You don't need much of a brain to make enemies. It is much harder to make friends of your enemies, but they never made the effort.

During the small breaks in our empty conversation, my thoughts revolved around the other guys: Mendelevich, Murzhenko, and Fyodorov. Where were they now? Had they been released before us, or were they still in the camps?

All five of us flew without handcuffs, although the instructions required them. The KGB was as free to break its own rules as it was to make them.

When lunch service began, the five of us were also attended to. When the stewardess placed a tray in front of me, I drew her attention to the fact that only I had been left without a knife. She grew embarrassed, blushed, and didn't know what to do. The KGB agent came to her rescue by offering me his own knife. He asked the stewardess to bring him another, which she did.

We were flying over the northern part of Canada: islands, ice, snow. We turned to the south: a mass of lakes, tundra, forest. When we landed in Canada for refueling, our group didn't leave the plane. An hour later, we were airborne again, and bound for New York. We landed at Kennedy airport.

The plane was emptied of passengers and the gangway removed, but we sat in the cabin, waiting. I began to make guesses about an imminent prisoner swap. The thought had occurred to me long ago, as my readers may remember, but faded with the years.

"What are we waiting for?" I asked my neighbor.

"I don't know," he answered with a knowing smirk.

"Are we being exchanged for someone?" I phrased the question more precisely.

Again, "I don't know."

We spent about an hour in the plane after the other passengers had left. Then, the plane was towed to the edge of the airfield. Through the window, I could make out a few cars and a crowd of people. My guess about the prisoner swap seemed justified. After a few moments, and a certain amount of confusion, we were told we might leave the plane.

As we walked down the gangway, a second gangway was approached by two Soviet spies. There was little joy on their faces. Downcast and apprehensive, they ascended into the plane. Now, the good life was over. They had failed at their jobs. Each had been sentenced to fifty years. Of course, they had been released now, and their heads weren't even shaved, but… You could understand them. These men may have been returning to their motherland, to their native birch trees, but who knows what the "evil empire" had in store for them?

After landing in the USA, we immediately became free men. We were approached by representatives of the State Department, the White House, the Secretary of State, and the Israeli Consulate in New York. They introduced themselves, congratulated us on our release, and asked each whether he wanted to remain in the USA. Kuznetsov and I expressed our wish to live in Israel. The representatives said that they would take care of us, but that right now we were going to a hotel in New York.

However they may have tried to keep our arrival a secret, the press managed to "smell us out" and had already gathered at the entrance to the hotel. A group of FBI agents fought them away, and we took an elevator to the thirty-sixth floor (perhaps in memory of camp No. 36?), which was closed to the public. We were given badges to pin on our lapels. I thought for years that the badges were meant to commemorate our release, and wore mine – even in Israel – until someone explained to me that the badges were given to people under FBI protection and were only valid for a short time.

We were accommodated in luxurious hotel rooms, the kind usually reserved for heads of state. An Arab sheik might not have felt out of place in

such rooms. The mini-fridge was full of snacks and every imaginable alcoholic beverage. On the table was an attractive basket of fruit, with strawberries in a separate little basket. But all this abundance wasn't for the likes of us,
who that very morning had breakfasted on wheat porridge made with water.
Out of caution, I had only a few sips of cognac to celebrate my release, after
treating myself to a banana and a few strawberries.

A short phone conversation took place with Israeli Prime Minister Begin.

On my first night of freedom, I barely slept two hours. I was alternately
watching some program or other on color television, or observing, from the
thirty-sixth floor, the flow of cars along the brightly lit streets of New York.
After the silence of the camps, and the habitual view of barbed wire and
soldiers in watch towers, I had suddenly landed in the largest city in the
USA. Skyscrapers, brightly lit streets, rivers of cars. Such a sharp contrast was
enough to make my ears ring.

The next morning, all five of us went for a walk, accompanied by police.
Next, there was a press conference, followed by meetings with television correspondents at the hotel. In the afternoon, I met with a correspondent from
the Israeli newspaper *Yedioth Ahronoth*, after which Kuznetsov and I were
transferred to the protection of the Israeli embassy in New York.

On the morning of the next day, April 29, we took part in a grandiose protest and rally for the rights of Soviet Jews, for their right to repatriate to Israel,
for the release of all Prisoners of Zion. Kuznetsov and I were among those
who spoke at the rally. We called our listeners to fight for the right of free
passage from the USSR to Israel, for the release of our fellow group members
who remained imprisoned in the USSR.

After lunch on April 29, we were already bound for the airport named for
John F. Kennedy.

On April 30, our Boeing 747, bearing the colors of the Israeli airline El Al,
touched down at the airport named for David Ben-Gurion. The weather was
hot, 32°C. We were met by family, friends, government officials, members of
the Jewish Agency, and representatives of social organizations. A rally took
place at the airport, at which we were welcomed by Prime Minister Begin,
Chairman Dulzin of the Jewish Agency, minister David Levy of the Ministry
of Absorption, and others.

After receiving my Israeli identity papers, I took my wife, daughters, and
son-in-law, and ran as far as I could from the mass of reporters. As a rule, I am

no lover of large gatherings, even of the festive kind with speeches, applause, shouts, and commotion. Though I had been a grandfather for more than a month, I still hadn't seen my grandson. After changing into summer clothes, I set off to meet my grandson Israel, before going home to Bat Yam.

I had achieved my goal, twelve years after it had first occurred to me to leave the Russian Empire for my historic motherland.

I had achieved my goal, nine years after our attempt to hijack an airplane.

Though the hijacking attempt failed, Operation Wedding succeeded. More than 170,000 Soviet Jews repatriated to Israel, and tens of thousands – sadly – became part of a wider diaspora.

All the defendants in the three airplane trials received different sentences. All of them served their sentences and left the USSR. There were no victims, and yet we all lost our health, and caused pain to our loved ones in varying degrees.

Twenty years later, some people praise our actions, others condemn them, and some know nothing about them, especially the young. There were Jews who condemned us, even in the USSR. We disturbed their "quiet," comfortable life as second-class citizens. They even condemned Israel for winning the Six-Day War.

There are all sorts of opinions, but I doubt that anyone would doubt the significance of our operation for the aliyah of the 1970s. I spoke with many different people in Israel about the significance of our operation, and never received a negative response. Here is one response: "You received a hero's welcome in Israel. That speaks for itself."

On April 30, 1979, as I stepped out of the plane onto Israeli land, I whispered to myself:

"Russia, goodbye forever!

Hello, Israel!"

11 Israel

1979–1990

After the meetings, banquets, speeches, and receptions – that is, after the fanfare was over – everyday life began. I began attending Hebrew language classes. After two weeks, I was sent on a fifteen-day tour of the USA: New York, Washington, Milwaukee, Los Angeles, Oakland, San Francisco, Denver, Chicago, Washington, New York. That was my route.

In all of those cities I spoke at rallies and met with local Jewish communities and Zionist leaders. There was a meeting with senators and congressmen as well as with National Security Advisor to President Carter, Zbigniew Brzezinski.

The main theme of all the speeches and meetings was the situation of Jews in the USSR (in particular, the situation of prisoners and refuseniks). And, of course, I never neglected my personal duty, calling everywhere for the release of my fellow operation participants: Yosef Mendelevich, Aleksey Murzhenko, and Yuriy Fyodorov.

In the case of Murzhenko and Fyodorov, I tried to underline the barbarity of the KGB's political game. On the one hand, they wanted to exhibit the dire consequences of association with Jews. On the other hand, it was as if they were saying, "Look, the Jews were only going to help their own people get an early release. They don't care about the others."

The Washington conference sent a telegram to President Carter, expressing confidence and hope for success, not only in the struggle for peace, but in the struggle for human rights – including the liberation of all Prisoners of Zion and the free passage of Jews to Israel without pressure or humiliation. The conference was convened by the All-American Organization for Soviet Jews.

My appearances were covered by the media, but only events in Russia could serve as a true indicator of their usefulness.

At that time, there was marked rise in the number of Soviet Jews emigrating to the USA on Israeli visas. An awkward detail, if ever there was one. I had to talk to these "short-cutters" as well. Many of them were embarrassed and, lowering their gaze or blushing, said things like, "We can't all be heroes and

243

go to Israel." Perhaps this was for the best. Natural selection. But sad, all the same. Life in the diaspora would prove ruinous to many.

After the meeting with Brzezinski at the White House, I was surrounded by a crowd of reporters, who asked me several questions about our conversation. One of them asked, "Mr Dymshits, would you like to live in the USA?" To which I answered, "No. I wouldn't have spent a single year in prison in order to live in the USA." The reporters, surprised by my reply, tried to get at the reason for my categorical decline.

I explained the USA was a wonderful, well-ordered, free, and wealthy country, but that it wasn't my country. I had lived more than forty years in Russia, and considered it my motherland. Then I was made to understand, to feel that it was not my motherland, not my home. I didn't want to be wrong a second time. Now I was fifty-two years old, and I wanted to feel myself at home in Israel. What is more, I hoped that I had already done something for Israel, that is, for the aliyah.

I had the opportunity to participate in a fundraiser for Israel, and it was there that I really felt the benefit of my American tour. There was a banquet in the evening, at which I was asked to make a speech, followed by a question and answer session. Towards the end of the evening, one of the directors of the Zionist Organization came up to me and, pointing to an imposing-looking gentleman across the room said, "You see that man over there? Before this evening, he had never donated more than $25,000. But after your story about life in prison camp, especially what you said about food in prison and how it compared to the abundance of our own tables, he donated ten times more. $250,000."

On my days off, I was able to visit a few museums. The National Air and Space Museum impressed me most of all. Due to the exhausting nature of the trip, I gained only a surface-level impression of the United States itself. In fact, I was so exhausted that I canceled my trip to Canada. One must take into account that I hadn't yet recovered from life in prison camp; add to that the frenzy of celebration in Israel.

When I returned home, I continued my Hebrew course, at the end of which I got a job in the aviation industry.

I had a few meetings with the Israeli secret service about Operation Wedding. I was informed that they had no evidence to justify my fears about Alya's cooperation with the KGB, and if I wanted any more clarity on the issue, I would have to conduct my own investigations.

There was no point putting off a difficult conversation just for the sake of it. I couldn't live with the suspicion of betrayal. The burden was too heavy.

One secret service agent suggested to me, "Maybe the KGB fabricated the whole issue with your wife in order to cover you?" What could I say to that? That the suspicion was entirely mine and had nothing to do with the KGB. Or tell him to mind his own business? It would have been awkward to begin my life in a new country with a stream of Russian obscenities.

And then, if I was able to suspect my wife, then he had the right, and maybe even the duty to suspect any Israeli citizen. In the end I said nothing, only laughed. I could have understood his suspicion in the days immediately following the operation, when everything was going the KGB's way, but after the trials and the beginning of aliyah, it seemed to me that the air would have been cleared. Had I really given up nine years of my life to fall under suspicion?!

A fellow inmate in transit prison once told me how a KGB or MVD agent had spent seven years in prison to uncover a network of counterfeiters.

Perhaps the Israeli secret service, just like the KGB, had a limited understanding of Operation Wedding and its consequences. They couldn't understand how we "Jews of silence," as Soviet Jews were then considered, could have planned an act of rebellion.

Now it seems to me that the reach of our operation in the Soviet Union extended beyond the "Jewish question." The operation and its aftermath mobilized other minority nations within the Russian Empire to solve their national problems. That the Jews had won their right to free passage showed other nations that they, too, could fight for their rights. But I digress.

To return to my own family drama. When I had asked Alya outright about her cooperation with the KGB, she had answered in the negative. That much was clear. But the KGB was known to use duress, hypnosis, and other forms of conditioning.

So, referring to information that I had supposedly been given by the Israeli secret service, I began yet another difficult conversation, which sent my wife into hysterics. I had great difficulty calming her down.

Alya told me that not only had she not cooperated with the KGB but that she had never even been called to KGB headquarters. I suggested that she take a lie detector test, and she agreed.

Then I admitted to her that I had not been given any information by the Israeli secret service and explained my suspicions to her. Indeed, Investigator

Ryabchuk had told her that I suspected her of betrayal while I was still in prison, but she had refused to believe him, imagining it was a KGB fabrication.

After our reconciliation, Alya told me about the trials she and our daughters had passed through after their release from prison. Some had suspected Alya of betraying our group and avoided her like the plague. Others deemed that she had betrayed her motherland and created unbearable conditions for her, both in the workplace and at home.

My relatives were afraid of helping her financially, or even showing an interest in her plight, due to the antisemitic and anti-Israel propaganda of the time. The only exception was my uncle Iosef, about whom I have already spoken. But he was already over seventy and needed help himself. This was the situation my wife and daughters had found themselves in.

A few more words about them. My younger daughter Yulia had to leave ordinary school. She transferred to an evening secondary school and worked at the post office during the day, distributing letters. My older daughter Liza worked at a factory in the company of old witches (witches, not women) who never said anything that wasn't obscene or offensive. Working conditions hadn't changed since the nineteenth century.

While holding my wife in suspicion, I had never considered my family's actual position and the horrors they had been subjected to. I had imagined that the KGB would protect them. In their letters, they never revealed the true difficulty of their situation. My insistence that they move to Israel was motivated not so much by a desire to improve their situation but to make Alya decide. I imagined that their situation was good enough.

But anyway, we had our difficult conversation, if you can call it a conversation, and were reconciled. However, the wounds will not heal to the end of our days.

It is hard to predict when the KGB will declassify our case materials, and indeed whether they will do this in the foreseeable future. For the time being I can only surmise what card they were trying to play as far as my relationship with Alya was concerned. Here is my best guess, judging from the events themselves:

On June 15, 1970, we set out for Smolny airport. The KGB searched Misha Korenblit's apartment and took him in for questioning. He was not allowed to answer the telephone. By six in the morning, Misha had already told the KGB a great deal, including information about the Zionist committee. After conducting multiple arrests, the KGB left Misha alone for a while, deciding to make a scapegoat of him. After all, he had seen me two days before the hijacking attempt, knew when it was going to happen, and ideally fit the role of traitor.

However, when I foolishly told my cellmate that I suspected Alya (although I managed to add an afterthought about Misha Korenblit), the KGB – who had heard the conversation – decided to change their plan. They arrested Misha and started putting increased pressure on me, intensifying my suspicions.

Time passed. The fight for aliyah intensified. Then Jews began to leave the USSR. The KGB saw that their plan of squashing the Jewish nationalist movement was unravelling. They understood that that no speech on my behalf to the Jewish community could stop Jews from leaving, but they could still play on my suspicions. Then, they slipped me the fabricated letter, imagining they would kill two birds with one stone. They considered, rightly, that a Russian, or at least a russified person, would almost certainly destroy his wife for betraying him. After that, they would be able to launch a propaganda campaign about the cruelty of Zionists and their racist crimes. "He even killed his wife because she was Russian!" They further considered that this would be a legally justified way to get rid of me, that is, by condemning me to death for killing my wife.

This plan crumbled when Alya submitted her application for an Israeli visa. They initially demanded that she divorce me, but then, seeing that her emigration would intensify my suspicions, they let her go. And this worked. I was troubled by my wife's emigration, in light of my suspicions.

After my wife left for Israel, the KGB decided to use Fyodorov as their next pawn. The reader may remember he had told me, "You won't get out of this camp alive! Don't even think of revealing the name of the person who denounced you. It will only make things worse." Back then, I took the KGB's threat for true currency and sent a message to Israel about the threat and my own suspicions. I hoped that my message would incite the West, that is, politicians and secret services, to action. In any case, I gave them some information about what was happening in the USSR, raising the curtain of secrecy and removing the weight of secrecy from myself.

But it was entirely possible that the KGB played out the scenario with Fyodorov after they already had known a prisoner exchange was in the offing.

Imagining that my suspicions of Alya would intensify, the KGB decided to carry out their plan in Israel, using me as a medium. I have already described what the two parts of this plan might have been. True, in Israel, the punishment for murder is not death, but life imprisonment. However, they would have been able to add anti-Israel propaganda to the anti-Zionist, antisemitic mix.

I have often been asked whether it was really worth taking such a risk. I think it was. Any serious "game" involves a great deal of risk. And the result is black and white, win or lose. We won. And that felt good. It always feels good to win.

I am not over-fond of myself, but I was not ashamed to hold my head up high. It sounds banal to say that "nothing in this world is free," but it's true. We paid the price, and now we're in Israel. About another 300,000 Jews have left the "evil empire."

I have often been asked whether I would still go through with Operation Wedding, if I had my time again. I answer that I would do it all again, if only because I could not and would not live in the USSR for reasons I have already explained.

But I would add that only other secret services should play "games" with the KGB. It is much easier for them to take on responsibility than it is for single people, or small groups with limited resources. Limited, when compared to the powerful crushing machine that is the KGB.

Afterword

Today, April 6, 1990, is a Friday. I have decided to write the final lines of my memoir. I will describe the historical circumstances surrounding their writing.

The aliyah of the 1970s came to an end, and no one knew when it would resume. People were expecting an aliyah from Russia three years ago, two years ago, without doing anything to receive it.

Now tens of thousands of Soviet Jews are leaving the Soviet Union – not so much leaving as fleeing. Antisemitism in the Russian Empire is reaching an apogee and has already attained pre-pogrom levels. Those who had never contemplated leaving are now arriving in Israel.

Recently, while I was out shopping, I met an elderly man – an economist – who had condemned Operation Wedding. Now, after making a forced emigration from Azerbaijan, he condemned his own lack of foresight. There are many such people.

Various "patriotic" organizations and groups, who blame the Jews for all of Russia's ills, are spurring them to leave. Jews are becoming refugees.

First to come were the Varangians. Then they brought in the Germans. Then the French were invited. Together with conquered Polish lands, Russia got Polish Jews. But now it's time to say goodbye. In his novel *The Enchanted Soul*, Romain Rolland writes that if France loses its Jews, the country will turn into a stagnant bog. I think he was exaggerating. Jews have always played a significant role in Russia, on all levels of national life. After the Second World War, their role in the country's development suddenly became less significant. Now they have been allotted the role of refugees.

Where are the Varangians now, or the russified French? Russia's Germans and Jews are leaving. The Russian Empire is "purifying" itself of landless peoples, while keeping a firm hold on those who want to break off from the last empire on earth, together with their historic territory.

Israel is now faced with a great challenge – to take in and find a place for the hundreds of thousands of Jews who are now making their way to us from several European countries. This must happen in a dramatic time of coalition talks within the national government; in a time of increased Arab pressure on the West, the Soviet Union, and Eastern European countries, to make reparations; in a time when greater attention must be paid to Israel's national security due to threats from abroad of chemical attacks, such as those that have already taken place in Yemen, Iran, and against the Kurds in Iraq.

I am a natural optimist. Years in prison have brought me closer to realism. But my sense of planet Earth's future is rather pessimistic.

I can only hope that the grandchildren of my generation will not be the last representatives of humanity on our fragile planet. Humanity is threatened not only by nuclear war and ecological catastrophe, but by exponential population growth, which cannot be supported by the Earth's fast-depleting natural resources.

Once upon a time we were taught that Malthus's theory was reactionary bourgeois nonsense. Now the truth of his predictions is becoming more and more obvious.

If we do not put a stop to unbridled population growth, especially in developing countries, nature herself will begin to regulate the human population with epidemics of new diseases, famine, and cataclysmic natural disasters.

In light of these dire premonitions, the "games" played by blocs of countries, governments, parties, and groups of people can seem trifling. We played our "game" to the end, and won. We were forced to play by the USSR's totalitarian regime. But I pray that others will not have to play similar "games" in order to win their freedom. I take this to include free passage to other countries. Freedom should be the natural state of all men.

Mark with his parents when he was nine years old, 1936.

Mark towards the end of his service in the air force, 1960.

Mark and his wife Alevtina, 1949.

Mark and Alevtina with their daughter Elizabeth, 1953.

Mark and Alevtina with their two daughters, Elizabeth and Juliya, 1959.

Mark (second from left) upon his arrival in Israel, 1979.
From left to right: Alevtina Dymshits, Mark Dymshits, David Levy,
Edward Kuznetzov, Prime Minister Menachem Begin, unknown, Aryeh
Dulzin, and Yigael Yadin.

Mark receiving a letter of appreciation from Major General Avihu
Ben-Nun on behalf of the Israeli Air Force, 1988.

Mark with his grandson, Israel – two majors, 2013.

The arrest of the main group at Smolny airport
(including Mark, on the ground) on June 15, 1970.

The arrest of the second group at Priozersk forest near
the airport on June 15, 1970.

After the arrest. The prison cell at Leningrad prison.

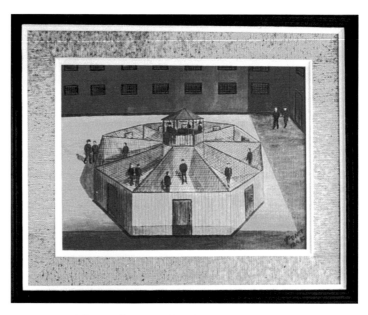

The walking yard at Leningrad prison.

The prison.

The search in prison. The Russian slang term is shmon, apparently from
the Hebrew word "shemoneh," meaning eight. The term originated
in Odessa, the Russian town on the Black Sea. At Odessa prison, the
searches were usually conducted at eight in the morning.

Death row, Leningrad prison, December 24, 1970.

Some of prison stages. Prisoners are loaded onto Stolypin carriages.
(Stolypin was the name of the prime minister under Emperor Nicholas II,
who advised the transportation of prisoners to Siberian labor camps
by train instead of by foot and horse carriages, which took many
months of travel.)

Prison stage. The inside of a Stolypin carriage.

Self-portrait of Mark Dymshits, second work group.
Perm lager (camp) in the Ural region.

The labor prison camp.

Cleaning up snow at the camp. The sign reads: "All roads lead to Communism."

Camp dining room.

Perm lager. The sign reads: "Labor is happiness."

Perm lager. Mark was allowed one family visit a year; it included two nights. This picture shows a visit of Alevtina with one of the daughters.

The dream and goal. After nine years of prison and camp, Mark was released and allowed to make aliyah in April 1979.